UB Law and Political Science Quarterly

University of Buea

UB Law and Political Science Quarterly

A publication of the Faculty of Laws and Political Science

Vol. 2, N° 1, October 2022

L'Harmattan
Cameroun

5-7, rue de l'Ecole-Polytechnique, 75005 Paris

http://www.editions-harmattan.fr

ISBN : 978-2-14-031406-3
EAN : 9782140314063

TABLE OF CONTENTS

SDG17: partnering to reduce inequalities, attain peace, justice and build strong institutions in Cameroon*

Atangcho N. Akonumbo

Professor of Laws and Dean, Faculty of Laws & Political Science, University of Buea, Cameroon
Email: atanjiak@gmail.com

Albert Mbiatem

Department of International Relations and Conflict Resolution, University of Buea, Cameroon
Email: albertmbiatem8@gmail.com

and

Emile Sunjo

Department of International Relations and Conflict Resolution, University of Buea
Email: emile.sunjo@ubuea.cm
ORCID ID: https://orcid.org/0000-0002-4545-0369

Abstract

This paper examines the role of Sustainable Development Goal 17 on partnerships in reducing inequalities, building strong institutions and attaining peace and Justice in Cameroon. Partnerships have been increasingly considered to be crucial in implementing Sustainable Development Goals (SDGs). Nineteen targets have been identified by the United Nations (UN) on goal 17. This study essentially relies on target 17.17 meant to encourage effective partnerships. Meeting this target can potentially contribute to reducing inequalities, build strong institutions and attain peace and justice in Cameroon. Local, regional, and international partnerships have been put in place to address questions of inequality, peace and justice and building strong institutions found respectively under goals 10 and 16. Cameroon, seven years into the SDGs agenda, is yet

* This paper was first prepared for the Why It Matters (WIM) Conference on the Sustainable Development Goals (SDGs) held at the Utah Valley University, USA from 5-7 October 2022. The authors are grateful to colleagues and anonymous reviewers for comments on an earlier draft of this manuscript. We are also grateful for the funding received from the Faculty of Laws and Political Science Research Grants Scheme, which enabled us to undertake this research.

to show a clear path to the realization of goals 10 and 16. These challenges can be attributed to the limited success in putting in place effective partnerships envisaged by target 17.17 of Goal 17. Peace, security and justice in particular have experienced significant challenges in recent years and inequalities have been on a rise. Using a qualitative case study research design, this study sought to examine the relevance of partnerships in the attainment of SDGs 10 and 16; understand the effectiveness/ineffectiveness of partnerships on the achievement of the Goals based; and explore the best strategies for the implementation of partnerships that may contribute to the attainment of SDGs 10 and 16 in Cameroon. It reveals that much still needs to be done for goals 10 and 16 to be satisfactorily realized in Cameroon. It also shows that partnerships are indispensable for the attainment of goals 10 and 16 in Cameroon and that to be effective, they must involve the active participation of beneficiaries. Finally, the study demonstrates that an advance in one of the three goals contributes to progress in the others.

Key Words: Partnerships, Sustainable Development Goals, Inequalities, Peace, Justice, Institutions, Cameroon

Introduction

Partnerships are vital in realizing the Sustainable Development Goals (SDGs).[1] Partnerships in the SDGs context are captured by goal 17 that recognizes multi-stakeholder partnerships as important vehicles for mobilizing and sharing knowledge, expertise, technologies, and financial resources to support the achievement of the sustainable development goals in all countries, particularly developing countries such as Cameroon. The SDGs were adopted in 2015 by the United Nations to address 17 most urgent challenges to sustainable development in the world. The SDGs are a collection of 17 global goals set by the United Nations (UN) to be implemented by the year 2030. The goals cover the following areas: Poverty, Hunger, Health, Education, Gender Equality, Energy, Economic Growth, Industry, Inequalities on all levels, Sustainable Communities, Responsible Consumption, Climate Change, Marine Life, Environment, Social Justice, and Partnership.

Among the SDGs are goal 10 to reduce inequalities; goal 16 to promote peace, justice and strong institutions and goal 17 to strengthen the means of implementation and build effective partnerships for sustainable development. Goal 17 can thus be considered a watershed goal since it is perceived to be necessary for the realization of others, including goals 10 and 16. In addressing the limitations of traditional state-led and top-down development approaches, partnerships have gained ground to become an indispensable paradigm in sustainable development[2] The scale and ambition of the new agenda requires a revitalized global partnership to ensure its implementation. Cameroon like many other African countries has been a party to the universal call to action to end poverty, protect the planet and to ensure that all people enjoy peace and prosperity by 2030.[3] In practice however, despite the

[1] MacDonald, A., Clarke, A., Huang, L., Roseland, M and Seitanidi, M.M., (2018). "Multi-stakeholder Partnerships (SDG #17) as a Means of Achieving Sustainable Communities and Cities; United Nations (2021). "Sustainable Development Goals Report 2021", United Nations, https://unstats.un.org/sdgs/report/2021/The-Sustainable-Development-Goals-Report-2021.pdf, accessed 14 February 2022.

[2] Stibbe, D., Reid, S. and Gilbert, J. (2018). "Maximising the Impact of Partnerships for the SDGs. A Practical Guide to Partnership Value Creation", The Partnering Initiative and United Nations Department of Economic and Social Affairs, Oxford.

[3] United Nations (2015), "Transforming our World: the 2030 Agenda for Sustainable Development", A/RES/70/1, sustainabledevelopment.un.org,

commitment to, and implementation of the SDGs agenda for almost seven years in Cameroon, sustainable development is yet to be a reality.

Cameroon is a country located in Central Africa and has an area of 475,440 km^2. It is a low-income country with a population of 26,545,864[4] inhabitants and has a moderate population density of 56 people per km^2. Cameroon is endowed with rich natural resources, including oil and gas, mineral ores, and high-value species of timber, and agricultural products, such as coffee, cotton, cocoa, maize, and cassava. Despite such natural resource endowments, poverty rate has been on an increase as shown by recent World Bank statistics: rate growing from 24.5% in 2019 to 25.3% in 2021.[5] Poor governance mainly characterized by corruption hinders the development of the country. The 2021 Transparency International Corruption Perceptions Index ranks Cameroon 144 out of 180 countries, with a score of 27/100.[6]

Cameroon remains lowly ranked on all development indices as it continues to encounter numerous challenges on the realization of the goals. It is ranked 150th out of 187 countries on Human Development Index (HDI) classification.[7] The 19 targets of goal 17 are broken into five categories: finance, technology, capacity building, trade, and science – have not considerably impacted in fostering equality, peace, justice, and strong institutions in Cameroon. After a low performance on the Millennium Development Goals (MDGs) – with only two targets (target 1.c and target 6.a) out of seventeen targets concretized, Cameroon is again encountering operational and functional challenges in attaining the SDGs agenda.

Cameroon has in the image of most Central African states, been facing wide-raging challenges relating to economic development, social

---

https://sustainabledevelopment.un.org/content/documents/21252030%20Agenda%20for%20Sustainable%20Development%20web.pdf, accessed 11 March 2022.

[4] This estimate is extrapolated from the last Population and Housing Census done in 2005.

[5] World Bank (2021), "The World Bank in Cameroon. The World Bank's Country Partnership Strategy in Cameroon focuses on increasing the country's competitiveness and improving service delivery". https://www.worldbank.org/en/country/cameroon/overview#1, accessed 1 March 2022.

[6] Transparency International (2021), "Corruption Perceptions Index 2021", https://www.transparency.org/en/cpi/2021, accessed 1 March 2022.

[7] World Population Review (2022), "Gini Coefficient by Country 2022", https://worldpopulationreview.com/country-rankings/gini-coefficient-by-country, accessed on 6 March 2022.

cohesion, administrative capacity and political governance.[8] The country which has for over five decades since independence been considered as the island of peace in the tumultuous Central Africa is currently affected by pockets of instability mainly in its regions of North West, South West, Far North, and East. The country is equally host to societal inequalities between citizens of varied social ranks and such have contributed to the lack of fair access to justice in a context where institutions need to be strengthened. The literature reveals that ineffective partnerships for goals in Africa has been characterised by poor collaboration across societal sectors. Kumar et al argue that the four major challenges that need to be addressed for achieving the SDGs across the African continent are financial, maintaining peace, measuring progress and accountability.[9] Vera Songwe discussed the implementation challenges as being linked to limited capacities on national planning agendas, evidence-based prioritisation and sequencing of policy interventions in a way that leverages intersectoral collaborations and minimizes policy trade-offs.[10] Another study deplored the lack of confidence in the ability of universities to contribute meaningfully to economic development, which was exacerbated by weak investments in research infrastructures and the pervasiveness of poor governance.[11] Gender disparity and gender based violence was identified among the most challenging forms of inequality with women encountering disadvantages in access to work, economic assets and participation in private and public decision-making.[12]

---

[8] Southern Voice (2019). "Global State of the SDGs. Three Layers of Critical Action", Report, http://southernvoice.org/wp-content/uploads/2020/08/State-of-the-SDGs-Global-Report-2019-Southern-Voice.pdf, accessed 2 March 2022.

[9] Kumar, S., Kumar, N., and Vivekadhish, S. (2016). "Millennium Development Goals (MDGs) to Sustainable Development Goals (SDGs): Addressing Unfinished Agenda and Strengthening Sustainable Development and Partnership". *Indian Journal of Community Medicine*, Vol. 4, No. 1, pp. 1-4.

[10] Songwe, V. (2018). "Implementing SDGs: Lessons from Africa", ECA, New York, https://sustainabledevelopment.un.org/content/documents/27415verasongwe.pdf, accessed 15 March 2022.

[11] Akpezi, O. (2018). "SDG 17 Partnerships for the Goals: A View from Inside Africa's Higher Education Institutions", in Josep, M.V., Alícia, B., Victoria, G., Marta, C. (eds), Approaches to SDG 17 Partnerships for the Sustainable Development Goals (SDGs), GUNi, Barcelona, pp. 28-36.

[12] Esuna, D. and Nergis, G. (2017). "Global Trends: Challenges and Opportunities in the Implementation of the Sustainable Development Goals", UNRISD, Palais des Nations 1211 Geneva 10, Switzerland, www.unrisd.org, accessed 5 March 2022.

Over half a decade following the adoption of the SDGs, their necessary interlinkages and interdependencies ascribed to goal 17 remain ineffective in Cameroon, thus the need to fill the gaps on partnership for goals strongly arises. This study examines the extent to which the partnership dimension drawn from goal 17 provides the required interlinkages and interdependencies among goals and specifically with respect to Goals 10 and goal 16. It is fundamentally an assessment on the aspects of inequalities, peace, justice and strong institutions in line with partnership prescriptions. This study seeks to answer the following three research questions: why are partnerships important for the attainment of SDGs 10 and 16? What makes partnerships to achieve the goals – effectiveness/ineffectiveness? What strategies for the implementation of partnerships can contribute to the attainment of SDGs 10 and 16 in Cameroon? The rest of this paper is structured into three main sections as follows: Methodology and Conceptual Framework, Results and Conclusion.

Methodology and conceptual framework

The approach adopted for this study was qualitative and inductive. Cameroon was used as a case study because of the rich experience of the country with both international and local partnerships for the SDGs. An interview guide was developed and pre-tested to generate initial data. Pre-testing the interview guide and carrying out a preliminary review of literature, helped in identifying patterns and relationships. This process was useful in developing a conceptual framework for the study as presented in Figure 1 below. The qualitative approach was useful in gaining an understanding of the views of stakeholders on the importance and motivations for engaging or supporting the use of partnerships in addressing goals 10 and 16. The case study design adopted for this study was particularly useful because the study sought to obtain an in-depth appreciation of the role of partnerships in the attainment of SDGs.

Field data were collected using key informant semi-structured interviews with local community leaders, government officials, senior staff of United Nations Agencies and academics in Buea, Douala and Yaoundé in Cameroon. Participants were recruited using the snowball sampling method. The researchers first carried out interviews with people they already knew. The initial contacts recommended other persons to the team based on their experience and knowledge of partnerships for the SDGs. To ensure that the right data was collected, open-ended questions were developed and pre-tested and reviewed before the effective commence of the interviews. The interviews lasted between 30 minutes and 1 hour. Data saturation was used as a criterion to determine the number of interviews to ensure that all shades of opinion on the subject were covered. This means that the interviews were conducted up to a point when no new information was being obtained.

Data collected were processed via thematic content analysis. The first step in the process was the transcription of the recorded interviews. The transcription process helped gain familiarity with the data to facilitate the identification of common themes. The transcripts were re-read and significant statements that directly addressed the research questions were underlined and extracted. The meaning of each significant statement was formulated and written down. These meanings were constantly compared with the original transcripts to ensure that they accurately reflected what the respondents had said. The formulated meanings were then organized into clusters and themes. Reliability was ensured by recording interviews and taking notes and reviewing each tape and all notes together with the transcripts to ensure they were accurate. Consistency was sought by ensuring that a guide was developed and pre-tested to ensure that the views of participants were solicited for the same questions.

Fig.1. Conceptual framework for the role of partnerships in the realization of goals 10 and 16

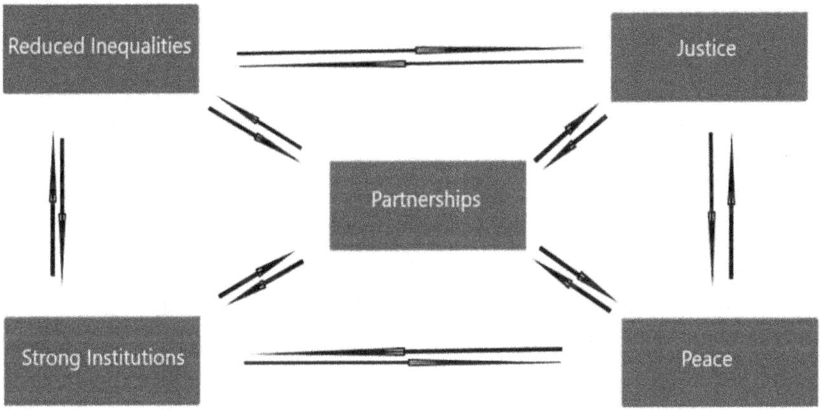

Source: Authors' conception

Figure 1 above conceptually visualizes the interactions among goals 10, 16 and 17, by illustrating the central role of partnerships to respond to issues of inequalities, peace justice and institutions. Partnerships are projected as key means to have the objectives attained. What is essentially drawn from the conceptual representation of figure 1, are the mutual interconnections among activities relating to reduced inequalities, peace, justice and strong institutions. This is to say that the building of strong institutions, the reduction of inequalities and the attainment of peace and justice are mutually supportive to one another and overall facilitated by effective partnerships. The various meanings given to the concepts – partnerships, reduced inequalities, peace, justice and strong institutions – in line with the three SDGs under study, strongly depict interconnections among the goals.

According to the UN system, partnerships for sustainable development as prescribed by goal 17, are multi-stakeholder initiatives freely undertaken by governments, intergovernmental organizations, major groups and other stakeholders, which efforts are useful to the implementation of inter-governmentally, agreed development goals and commitments. This partnership is mainly guided by three dimensions: exchange, integrate and transform.[13] Goal 10 on reduced inequalities, calls for efforts towards reducing disparities in income as well as those based on age, sex, disability, race, ethnicity, origin, religion or economic or other status within a country. Also, there are inequalities among countries, including those related to representation, migration and development assistance.[14]

Peace, as reflected in goal 16 is very much aligned with Johan Galtung's positive peace that refers to the integration of human society mainly guided by the following aspects: structural integration, optimism, prevention and peace by peaceful means.[15] The peace proposed by SDGs is development inclined with much attention given to human and structural development. Justice as captured in goal 16 specifically covers targets 16.3 and 16.C which are: "promote the rule of law at the national and international levels and ensure equal access to justice for all"; and "promote and enforce non-discriminatory laws and policies for sustainable development." The aspect of strong institutions by goal 16 is mainly captured in target 16.6 which refers to "developing effective, accountable and transparent institutions at all levels." Thus, the suppression of the over-personalization in policy making, decision making process and public service delivery will contribute to strengthening institutions.

---

13 Stibbe, D., Reid, S. and Gilbert, J. (2018). "Maximising the Impact of Partnerships for the SDGs"

14 United Nations (2022), "Sustainable Development Goal 10: Reduced Inequalities", United Nations Office for Outer Space Affairs, https://www.unoosa.org/oosa/en/ourwork/space4sdgs/sdg10.html, accessed 23 February 2022.

15 Galtung, J. (2011). Peace, positive and negative. *The encyclopedia of peace psychology.*

Discussion of findings

The objective of this qualitative study was to examine the role of partnerships in reducing inequalities, building strong institutions, and attaining peace and justice in Cameroon. As represented in Fig 1 above, we sought the views of stakeholders on the relationship between partnerships on attaining goals 10 and 16 of the SDGs in Cameroon. Cameroon ratified in September 2015, at the UN headquarters in New York, the 2030 Agenda for Sustainable Development. The country had previously joined another UN agenda on development known as MDGs.

Participants in the study came from diverse backgrounds. All participants had knowledge or experience of partnerships for the SDGs. Meanings were formulated from the interview transcripts and organized into themes. The analysis revealed main themes that were important in understanding the role of partnership in attaining goals 10 and 16 in Cameroon. These were: common goals are better achieved through collaboration, importance of partnerships, partnerships should include all stakeholders, their motivations for engaging in them, strategies for effective partnerships to attain the goals and factors that can undermine the success of partnerships. Thus, this section on results will cover the sub-sections: low scale of realization of goals 10 and 16 in Cameroon; reasons why Cameroon needs partnerships to attain goals 10 and 16; challenges to partnerships in achieving goals 10 and 16; strategies for the effective implementation of partnerships to attain the goals in Cameroon.

Low scale of realization of goals 10 and 16 in Cameroon

All participants were of the view that more needs to be done to attain peace, justice, reduce inequalities and build strong institutions in Cameroon[16]. Cameroon was also considered by most participants to have not met the targets set for the Millennium Development Goals (MDGs) agenda that preceded the SDGs[17]. The literature shows that this low level of realization of the goals is however not unique to Cameroon.[18] It has

[16] Interviews in Buea, Douala and Yaoundé, March 2022

[17] Interviews in Yaoundé and Douala, March 2022

[18] Crossette, B. (2019). "Big Holes in the UN Development Goals Are Exposed by New Studies", PassBlue, https://www.passblue.com/2019/03/18/big-holes-in-the-un-development-goals-are-exposed-by-new-

been observed that most countries, especially in the developing world are lagging in efforts to attain the goals.

Under the 2015 agenda for MDGs, Cameroon concretized only two targets out of the seventeen. Cameroon had pledged to specifically track 17 targets and ultimately only materialized two targets. This is target 1.c ("halve in 2015 the proportion of people suffering from hunger") and target 6.a ("by 2015, have ended the spread of HIV/AIDS and begin to reverse the current trend"). Indeed, the proportion of the population living below the poverty line effectively fell from 40.2% in 2001 to 37.5% in 2014, registering a drop of 2.7 points for this period.[19] While the HIV/AIDS prevalence rate has fallen from around 5.5% to 3.0% in 2014.[20] A participant from the National Institute for Statistics (INS) made the following observation of the country's performance: "Yes poverty has certainly declined on 2.7 rate but in terms of mass it has rather increased with the rise in the number of poor people. Models specific to the social context must be adopted."[21]

This low scale achievement led the country to renew the MDGs for the 2020 deadline.[22]. At the same time, the country embarked on the new 2030 agenda for SDGs. Cameroon joining the current development agenda without having considerably achieved the goals of the previous agenda, has logically raised many doubts on its readiness and capacity to perform efficiently on SDGs. Besides, Cameroon on its SDG journey has been seriously affected by the COVID-19 pandemic which has unprecedentedly affected the 2030 Agenda.[23]

Economic growth in Cameroon since 2010 has not met expectations as projected by the Growth and Employment Strategy Paper. The country has performed well below the 7%, the expected annual average

---

tudies/?gclid=EAIaIQobChMIjefNlPPd9gIVGKp3Ch1FEAzuEAMYASAAEgKfsfD_BwE, accessed 13 March 2022.

19 *Institut National de la Statistique* Cameroon (INS) (2015). "Rapport National sur les Objectifs du Millénaire pour le Développement, Septembre", Institut National de la Statistique du Cameroun.

20 Ibid

21 Interview with Officer in Charge of Studies at National Institute for Statistics in Yaounde, 16 March 2022.

22 Cameroon Policy Analysis and Research Centre (CAMERCAP-PARC) (2020). "Covid 19 et les Agendas de Développement au Cameroun, en Afrique et Dans le Monde. Sortie de Piste ?", No. www.camercap-parc.org. Accessed 5 March 2022.

23 Ibid

over the period of the strategy for growth and employment, supposed to mark the first phase towards the vision of being an emerging country in 2035.[24] The SDGs agenda in Cameroon is very much in line with Cameroon Vision 2035 initiated in 2009. The overall objective of the vision is to make Cameroon an emerging country over the next 25-30 years which is the period required to move from one generation to another. The vision also has medium-term objectives, notably: poverty alleviation; becoming a middle-income country; becoming a newly industrialized country and consolidating democracy and national unity while respecting the country's diversity. This vision in principles further matches the SDGs in the sense that it promotes the cooperation between the government, civil society, private sector and development partners.[25] But in practice, the collaboration between these key sectors is still to meet societal expectations in a context where the government remains every much dominant and as a result the civil society and private sector have limited margin for maneuver to influence the development goals.

The 2020 UNDP's Human Development report – a key benchmark in measuring sustainable development – describes the encouraging Human Development Index (HDI) trends in Cameroon from 1990-2019. During this period, Cameroon's HDI value increased from 0.448 to 0.563, an increase of 25.7 percent. Cameroon HDI's score according to the World Population Review is maintained to 0.563 in 2022. Table 1 below reviews Cameroon's progress in each of the HDI indicators. Between 1990 and 2019, Cameroon's life expectancy at birth increased by 5.9 years, mean years of schooling increased by 2.8 years and expected years of schooling increased by 4.1 years. Cameroon's GNI per capita increased by about 15.5 percent between 1990 and 2019. Cameroon's HDI of 0.563 however remained below the average of 0.631 for countries in the medium human development group.[26]

---

[24] Ibid

[25] Ministry of the Economy Planning and Regional Development (2009), "Cameroon Vision 2035", Working Paper, https://www.lse.ac.uk/GranthamInstitute/wp-content/uploads/laws/1816.pdf, accessed 6 March 2022

[26] UNDP (2020), "Cameroon" Human Development Report 2020

Table 1: Cameroon's HDI trends based on consistent time series data and new goalposts

Year	Life expectancy at birth	Expected years of schooling	Mean years of schooling	GNI per capita (2017 PPP$)	HDI value
1990	53.4	8.0	3.5	3,101	0.448
1995	51.6	7.5	4.2	2,400	0.432
2000	51.0	7.3	4.8	2,589	0.440
2005	52.8	8.4	5.1	2,902	0.470
2010	55.1	10.2	5.3	3,056	0.505
2015	57.6	12.2	6.0	3,410	0.549
2016	58.1	12.1	6.1	3,465	0.553
2017	58.5	12.1	6.2	3,487	0.557
2018	58.9	12.1	6.3	3,526	0.560
2019	59.3	12.1	6.3	3,581	0.563

Source UNDP, Human Development Report 2020

The increase in Human development measurement does not however imply Cameroon's realization on key constituents of sustainable development. For instance, the minimum wage in Cameroon is very low. That is 36,270 CFA (USD 61.73) francs per month, applicable to all employees in all sectors.[27]

The 2021 Sustainable Development Goals Report has raised serious concerns about the attainment of goals 10, 16 and 17 mostly in low- and middle-income countries. On goal 10, the report states that, "inequality persists, whether in income, wealth, opportunities or other dimensions…The pandemic is exacerbating existing inequalities within and among countries and hitting the most vulnerable people and the poorest countries hardest.[28] It states on goal 16 that, "The world is still a long way from achieving the goal of peaceful, just and inclusive societies… the average prevalence rate of bribery in low-income countries is 37.6 per cent, versus 7.2 per cent in high income countries." The report on goal 17 indicates: "The pandemic is further testing multilateral and global partnerships that were already shaky. Although Official Development Assistance (ODA) increased and remittance flows

[27] Federal Minimum Wage (2022), "Cameroon Minimum Wage, Labor Law, and Employment Data Sheet Cameroon Minimum Wage Rate 2022", Minimum-Wage.org. Accessed 10 March 2022.

[28] United Nations Department of Economic and Social Affairs (2021). "The Sustainable Development goals report 2021: Reducing inequalities" UN-iLibrary, DOI: https://doi.org/10.18356/9789210056083c014

declined less than expected in 2020, Foreign Direct Investment (FDI) dropped by 40 per cent."[29]

A recent report on countries' performance has captured the different levels of achievement of goals in Cameroon. Almost seven years down the line, only two out of the seventeen goals are on track. That is goal 12 (Responsible Consumption and Production) and goal 13 (Climate Change). For the goals under study, goals 16 and 17 are stagnating meanwhile goal 10 lacks enough statistics on its performance. Cameroon on attaining SDGs is ranked 134 out of 165 countries with a score of 53.5.[30]

The country on goal 10 is yet to be effective on income distribution as the Gini coefficient has only been adjusted for top income. It is important to note that the higher the Gini coefficient, the greater the gap between the incomes of a country's richest and poorest people. A country's Gini coefficient is important because it helps identify high levels of income inequality, which can have several undesirable political and economic impacts.[31] A respondent from a civil society organization gave a sad picture of the gaps on incomes:

> The incomes of many Cameroonians are close to the minimum wage. Those who do not occupy influential administrative positions only rely on their relatively low salaries while those in charge rely not only on their salaries but also on extravagant allowances. This has continued to widen the gap between the rich and the poor. Recently, the minister of Territorial Administration gave brand new cars to Divisional Officers while teachers on the other hand are unheard when requesting their incomes restored duly and on time.[32]

Another respondent explained the low level of realization in the following words when asked whether there were successful examples of partnerships to address goals 10 and 16 in Cameroon:

> Not sure there are successful examples which could be cited as we still have visible inequalities, and some parts of the country are still not that peaceful. However, we see trends towards public collaboration with civil society organizations. We also see a trend of civil society organizations working with one another. External partners

---

[29] Ibid

[30] Jeffrey, D. S., Christian, K.l., Guillaume, L., Grayson, F., and Finn, W. (2021) Sustainable Development Report 2021, The Decade of Action for the Sustainable Development Goals, Cambridge University Press, Cambridge.

[31] World Population Review (2022), "Human Development Index by Country 2022", https://worldpopulationreview.com/country-rankings/hdi-by-country, accessed on 14 February 2022.

[32] Interview with Chief Executive of People Earthwise in Buea, 2 March 2022.

often involved in the collaborative path include UN, AU institutions and other international development organizations.[33]

The trends in collaboration mentioned by this participant however show that there are efforts being made to attain goal 17 in Cameroon which can be helpful in effectively addressing goals 10 and 16. The difficulties in identifying successful partnerships to address 10 and 16 pointed to by the participant show that the level of realization cannot be considered significant or visible.

The UN's 2021 SDGs report on goal 16 has given a picture of not good performance relating to aspects of peace, justice and institutions. It mainly reveals the country's poor record on access to and affordability of justice, press freedom index, corruption perception index and penitentiary detention. Peace in Cameroon is seriously affected as the current situation contrasts with the rather positive feedback of the report on homicide. The Anglophone conflict in the North West and South West regions has led to the rising number of killings since October 2017. In the space of less than five years, the death toll has ranged between 4000-12000[34], hundreds of villages have been burnt and pillaged[35], over 750,000 people have been internally displaced, with a further 60,000 Cameroonian refugees in Nigeria.[36]) An estimated 2.2 million people in need of humanitarian assistance within Cameroon as a result of the conflict.[37] This conflict has affected the justice system and institutional mechanism with victims of violence not obtaining due reparations.

Reasons why Cameroon needs partnerships to attain goals 10 and 16

All the respondents said that partnerships were indispensable for Cameroon to achieve goals 10 and 16[38]. The literature reviewed also

---

[33] Interview with an Official of the United Nations Agency in Yaounde, 16 March 2022

[34] Centre for Human Rights and Democracy in Africa (CHRDA) (2021). "Anglophone crisis: the Cameroon government and separatist leaders should engage in a veritable and unconditional dialogue to seek a sustainable solution to the crisis to avoid further bloodshed" accessed on 17 October 2022.

[35] Ibid

[36] UN Office for the Coordination of Humanitarian Affairs (OCHA). (2022) "Global humanitarian overview - Cameroon: analysis of the context, crisis and needs", Cameroon | Global Humanitarian Overview (unocha.org), 17 October 2022.

[37] Ibid

[38] Interviews, Yaounde, Buea and Douala, March 2022

shows that partnerships are needed for the attainment of the SDGs. Three reasons were advanced for the need of partnerships by Cameroon. These were: to avoid duplication and waste of efforts, effectively and efficiently address common goals and sharing experiences on best practices[39]. According to all participants, partnerships are necessary because common goals are better fulfilled through collaboration. They explained that such goals as peace, justice, reducing inequalities and building strong institutions were of interest to both national and international actors who can best realize them by working together. One respondent in Douala for example said partnerships are needed because:

> SDGs 10 and 16 are common problems in many societies, especially in less developed ones such as Cameroon. As such, partnering with countries that have attained at least 70% of SDGs 10 and 16 will help Cameroon to accelerate their attainment by taking advantage of their experiences.[40]

Similarly, another respondent said partnerships are necessary to effectively carry out the volume of work that needs to be done to address these goals. According to this respondent:

> There is so much that needs to be done to address goals 10 and 16 that Cameroon cannot do working alone. In addition to working with international partners, stakeholders within Cameroon need to be involved to effectively tackle the problems addressed under goals 10 and 16. This need for broad-based collaboration is important because these issues affect not only people of Cameroon, but also other countries and those who are involved in different relations with the country.[41]

These findings are in line with those found in the literature. Stibbe et al for example see common goals as a reason why partnerships are needed.[42] They however caution that it is not in every case that stakeholders may engage in partnerships because there is a common challenge that should be addressed. According to them, some stakeholders are not natural collaborators that will instinctively act towards achieving common goals. For such actors they contend, "a

---

39 Interviews in Yaounde, Buea and Douala, March 2022

40 Interview with a Business owner in Douala, 12 March 2022

41 Interview with Official at the Ministry of External Relations in Yaounde, 16 March 2022.

42 Stibbe, D., Reid, S. and Gilbert, J. (2018). "Maximizing the Impact of Partnerships for the SDGs"

partnering mindset is something that may need to be actively cultivated".[43]

Challenges to partnerships in achieving goals 10 and 16

Partnership is designed to facilitate an intensive global engagement in support of implementation of all goals and targets bringing together government, private sector, civil society, UN system and other actors and mobilizing all available resources.[44] Partnering to achieve goals is a fundamental prescription of the 2030 agenda. In Cameroon, partnership to reduce inequalities, attain peace and justice, and build strong institutions has for the past seven years since SDGs adoption in 2015 encountered numerous challenges as collaborative efforts among stakeholders are yet to show a clear path in achieving goal 10, 16 and 17.

Participants for interviews largely raised the aspects of structural deficiencies affecting mostly vulnerable strata of the population in Cameroon. They are of the opinion that, amidst infrastructural and security deficiencies in Cameroon, inequalities have deepened for vulnerable populations having at their disposal weaker health systems and facing existing humanitarian crises. Refugees and migrants, as well as indigenous peoples, older persons, people with disabilities and children are particularly at risk of being left behind. And hate speech targeting vulnerable groups is rising.[45] Participants also described as difficult the journey to achieve peace given that Cameroon is currently affected by pockets of instability in four out of ten regions of the country.[46]

The inequalities were very striking on health aspects as a respondent from the Ministry of Health laid emphasis on the lack of access to health facilities: "Despite collaborating with good number of international partners, access to health facilities remains extremely difficult among low-income Cameroonians and those living in remote or rural areas. Urban areas equally encounter serious medical equipment challenges."[47] Recently in March 2022, a mainstream media in Cameroon revealed the reproachable medical care given to quarantined cholera patients in public medical centres. It reported on medical equipment shortage in terms of

---

43 Ibid

44 United Nations (2015), "Transforming our World: the 2030 Agenda for Sustainable Development"

45 Interviews in Douala, Buea, and Yaounde, March 2022.

46 Interviews in Douala, Buea, and Yaounde, March 2022.

47 Interview with a Field Agent at the Ministry of Health in Yaounde, 15 March 2022.

beds, drips, and other essential equipment to administer treatments to patients in Limbe Mile1 and Bota Hospitals[48]

The security crisis in the northern regions of the country with the Boko Haram phenomenon, the socio-political crisis in the North-West and South-West regions transformed into a secessionist crisis and the uncontrolled influx of Central African refugees, all constitute the pockets of instability in Cameroon.[49] For almost five years, the crisis in the two Anglophone regions, threats posed by Boko Haram in the northern regions, and conflicts in the CAR and the DRC have been creating and posing obstacles to peace and internal security. This situation greatly weighs on state budget and funding that can be allocated to development projects.

Implementation challenges are largely presented from governance and institutional capacity perspectives. The lack of clarity around ratification, reporting, accountability mechanisms, and roles and responsibilities is a result of poor governance and weak institutionalization. (Belay, 2019). In many countries, capacity needs, and gaps represent a critical obstruction to meaningful SDG 16 implementation and follow-up. These capacity issues are often, though not exclusively, felt in countries that are post-conflict, transitioning out of conflict, fragile, or least developed. Issues such as social cohesion, illicit financial flows, corruption and many forms of discrimination remain grave challenges.[50]

A civil society organization respondent described challenges ascribed to goals 10 and 16 as closely interrelated and linked to cause-effect analogy:

> The country is rife with inequalities between sexes & gender; exercise of authority between the arms of governance (Executive, Legislative, Judiciary); various professional corps, tribes, regions, people with disabilities or vulnerabilities and others as the case may be. The exercise of authority is not democratic, not transparent and often corrupt. These inequalities directly impact peace and the quality of institutions which has resulted in the national conflicts

---

48 Equinox TV news, 25 March 2022.

49 CAMERCAP-PARC (2020)

50 High-Level Political Forum on Sustainable Development (2019), "2019 HLPF review of SDG implementation", https://sustainabledevelopment.un.org/content/documents/23672BN_SDG16_LV.pdf, accessed 7 March 2022.

as with the Separatist movement, intertribal wars, injustice and abuse of human rights.[51]

Another respondent, from a civil society organization described the challenges pertaining to goal 16 from a peace, justice and institutional perspectives:

> In the Cameroonian context, SDG 16 is based on the understanding that conflicts, insecurity, weak institutions, and limited access to justice are threats to sustainable development. Crisis in 2016 in the CEMAC zone, leading all the countries to a program of economic reforms under supervision by the IMF and other partners. In addition to the so-called objective reasons, it is our duty to recognize the weaknesses of our essentially extroverted economic model, with a trade balance structurally in deficit for more than a decade, the weak competitiveness of the Cameroonian economy to which is added poor governance, in particular in the public sector with its corollary that is Corruption. All this environment was not already very conducive to a resumption of growth in the country and sub-region.[52]

Similarly, a respondent from the Ministry of Water Resources and Energy insisted on the so far poor performance of goal 16 in Cameroon amidst partnership:

> I strongly believe more has to be done to attain these goals and most especially goal 16. I say so because we are in constant quest for peace in our country, our judicial system is very corrupt, thus, the exacerbation of the unjust Cameroon in which we live. Our institutions are mere window dressing. A good goal 16 will solve goal[53]

According to a respondent in charge of cooperation at the ministry of Agriculture, the predominance of the government on partnering with local actors does not ease collaboration.[54]The required collaboration between the government, the civil society, the private sector and citizens has been described by most interviewees as lacking necessary mutuality. The government dominates the interactions with the other sectors thus leaving them limited margin for manoeuvre to influence SDGs and their implementation.

---

[51] Interview with the Chief Executive of People Earthwise, Buea, 17 March 2022.

[52] Interview with Officer of United Nations Office for Project Services (UNOPS) in Yaounde, 16 March 2022.

[53] Interview with an Engineer of the Ministry of Water Resources and Energy in Yaounde, 16 March 2022.

[54] Interview with an Officer in Charge of Cooperation Ministry of Agriculture in Buea, 7 March 2022.

The challenges as discussed above is an indication of the remaining long journey for Cameroon in using goal 17 to attain goals 10 and 16. Thus, strategies to respond to the challenges linked to inequalities, peace, justice, and institutions must be centered on effective implementation of partnerships

Strategies for the effective implementation of partnerships to attain the goals in Cameroon

The partnership journey starts with building an understanding of an overlap of alignment of interest among the partners which allows them to together build an overarching vision – the big picture change that the partnership wants to contribute to.[55] A successful sustainable development agenda entails partnerships between governments, the civil society and the private sector. These inclusive partnerships built upon principles and values, a shared vision, and shared goals that place people and the planet at the center, are needed at the global, regional, national and local level.[56] Participants were of the view that an inclusive and participatory strategy that ensures local ownership or leadership is necessary for the effective realization of goals 10, 16 and 17 in Cameroon.

The importance of an inclusive and participatory strategy to partnerships was emphasized by all participants. The participants believed that beneficiaries are seldom involved in the setting-up of partnerships, the definition of issues to be addressed by the partnerships and decisions regarding the resources required and how projects are to be implemented. Partnerships set-up this way according to most participants, tend to serve the interests of the donors or the government and as such, make it unlikely that problems such as inequalities and the near absence of peace that are felt more by communities will be effectively attended to.[57] One respondent from an international governmental organization in Yaoundé for example said:

> Partnerships need to be based on the needs expressed by the beneficiaries to succeed. The only way to ensure the needs of intended beneficiaries will be effectively expressed, is to involve the supposed beneficiaries in the partnership

---

[55] Stibbe, D., Reid, S. and Gilbert, J. (2018). "Maximising the Impact of Partnerships for the SDGs"

[56] SDG Tracker (2020), "Revitalize the Global Partnership for Sustainable Development" https://sdg-tracker.org/global-partnerships, accessed 1 March 2022.

[57] Interviews in Douala, Yaounde and Buea, March 2022

from the very beginning when the partnership is being set-up. To guarantee such active participation of beneficiaries, it is essential their needs are clearly expressed in policies designed to achieve goals 10, 16 and 17.[58]

The above statement is much line with the statement of a respondent at the Ministry of Economy, Planning and Regional development:

> The relative growth paths for each country should be implemented so that developed countries can assist less developed countries specifically with their shortcomings. Adopt a growth path specific to concerns of the countries in need. Adopt path which would guarantee a sustainable development in line with endogenous means.[59]

Still in the same vein, a participant of the Ministry of Secondary Education suggested inclusive education strategies to accommodate everyone in schools: "Creation and running of schools that take into account the needs of all including that of disabled persons in the construction of school infrastructure; provide persons with disabilities with appropriate materials for their education."[60]

The top-down approach to attaining the goals is therefore one of the main obstacles to their realization. The criticism of this approach in the literature shows that many authors such as Richard Manning[61] and Thomas Hák et al[62]. recommend the participatory strategy that participants believed will be more useful. Decisions regarding partnerships, the attainment of peace and justice, the reduction of inequalities and the development of strong institutions thus need to be made with adequate knowledge of the context so that grassroots support is obtained, and the right issues are addressed.

---

[58] Interview with Official of an International Non-governmental Organisation in Yaounde, 16 March 2022.

[59] Interview with Official of Ministry of Economy, Planning and Regional development in Yaounde, 17 March 2022.

[60] Interview with Director of Cooperation Ministry of Secondary Education in Yaounde, 17 March 2022.

[61] Manning, R. (2010). The impact and design of the MDGs: some reflections. *IDS bulletin*, *41*(1), 7-14; Manning, R. (2010). The impact and design of the MDGs: some reflections. *IDS bulletin*, *41*(1), 7-14.

[62] Hák, T., Moldan, B., & Dahl, A. L. (Eds.). (2012). *Sustainability indicators: a scientific assessment* (Vol. 67). Island Press.

Conclusion

The aim of this study was to examine the views of stakeholders in Cameroon on the role of partnerships in attaining goals 10 and 16. To achieve this aim, the research focused on understanding the reasons why different actors in Cameroon including the government prioritize partnerships, what motivates them, the challenges they face and the strategies that can be used to overcome them. The study reveals that partnerships are indispensable for the realisation of common goals such as peace, justice, reducing inequalities and building strong institutions. Without partnerships, participants believed it would be difficult to realise the goals. The reasons advanced as to why they are important or why Cameroon needs partnerships to attain goals 10 and 16 included increased agency to address these goals for the government and increased legitimacy for international partners to operate in or access some communities in Cameroon which would otherwise be inaccessible. The results also show that the attainment of goals 10 and 16 would create a space that is conducive for the initiation and development of effective partnerships. The relationships between goals 10, 16 and 17 is therefore one of complementarity.

Despite the importance of partnerships, the study shows that there are important challenges that need to be overcome for Cameroon to effectively benefit from the opportunities they offer in its bid to realise SDGs goals 10 and 16. The design of the partnerships has been a major challenge to ensuring success. Poignantly, participants believed that current partnership structures have failed to ensure participation of beneficiaries in decision making and that communication with beneficiaries in the conception and implementation processes was also limited. The contributions of this study notwithstanding, it has some methodological limitations. As with other case studies, the sample includes only participants from a very specific context. The generalization of conclusions from this study should thus be made with caution. It is necessary to undertake more research and extend the sample to other countries. The study has nonetheless answered some interesting questions. It has shown how differences in views have not undermined interest in and engagement in partnerships to achieve SDGs 10 and 16, although their achievement and sustainability were not investigated in this study.

Les singularités juridiques de la liquidation amiable de droit commun des sociétés commerciales en droit OHADA

Pierre Etienne Kenfack

Agrégé de droit privé et des sciences criminelles,
Enseignant à l'Université Yaoundé 2- Cameroun

Résumé

Non nommée expressément par les textes, peu signalée par la doctrine, la liquidation amiable des sociétés commerciales dans l'espace OHADA, composante de la liquidation « au sens du droit des sociétés » organisée par l'acte uniforme OHADA relatif au droit des sociétés commerciales et des groupements d'intérêt économique, mérite d'être présentée et évaluée dans ce qui l'identifie et la distingue des autres formes de liquidation. L'analyse de ce texte révèle que la liquidation amiable qui est celle au cours de laquelle n'interviennent ni juges, ni autorités, se singularise par un processus particulier dans son déclenchement et son déroulement et par une issue qui fait intervenir les associés dans sa clôture et ses suites.

Mots clés : Associés- Actif- Actif social- Amiable-Comblement- Dissolution-Liquidation- Passif- Réalisation- Société-Tiers –

Abstract

Although not widely discussed in existing literature and only cursorily mentioned in doctrinal sources, the non-judicial liquidation or voluntary liquidation of companies is a key aspect of the OHADA Uniform Act on Commercial Companies, which should be distinguished from other forms of liquidation. The analysis of this law reveals that the distinctive feature of voluntary liquidation, which occurs without a legal procedure, lies in the manner in which it is triggered and its outcome, which ensures the participation of all shareholders in the process.

Introduction

Liquider une société commerciale c'est mener des opérations juridiques et comptables destinées à réaliser son actif pour combler son passif [1] avec pour objectif ultime faire cesser sa personnalité juridique. Dans l'espace OHADA, le régime de droit commun de la liquidation des sociétés commerciales est fixé par deux textes principaux complétés sur certains points par la jurisprudence : L'Acte uniforme du 10 septembre 2015 portant organisation des procédures collectives d'apurement du passif et l'Acte uniforme du 30 janvier 2014 relatif au droit des sociétés commerciales et du groupement d'intérêt économique.

Le premier, ayant pour champ d'application les entreprises en difficultés, organise une liquidation, sous le contrôle de la justice, des entreprises déclarées par le juge en cessation des paiements. Cette liquidation échappe totalement au contrôle des associés. Dans ce régime, c'est la mise en liquidation qui entraine la fin de la société que les dirigeants maintenaient artificiellement en vie, alors qu'elle n'était plus capable de faire face à son passif exigible avec son actif disponible[2].

Le second texte ayant pour champ d'application les entreprises non déclarées en cessation des paiements[3], organise un régime de liquidation qui tire les conséquences de la dissolution de la société conformément à l'article 201 de l'Acte uniforme qui dispose que « la dissolution de la société pluripersonnelle entraine de plein droit sa mise en liquidation ». La dissolution est l'acte ou la décision ordonnant ou prenant acte de la cessation d'activité d'une entreprise qui est encore capable de faire face à

---

1 Ph. Merle, droit des sociétés commerciales, Dalloz, Paris, n° 116 et s. ; G. Ripert, R. Roblot et M. Germain, *Traité de droit commercial, tome 1 – Volume 2, Les sociétés commerciales*, Paris, LGDJ ;

2 G. Ripert, R. Roblot et M. Germain, *Traité de droit commercial, tome 1 – Volume 2, Les sociétés commerciales*, Paris, LGDJ ; F. ANOUKAHA et autres, OHADA. Sociétés commerciales et G.I.E., Bruylant, Bruxelles, 2002

3 D'après l'article 203 de ce texte, les dispositions de ce chapitre s'appliquent à toute liquidation de société commerciale qu'elle soit organisée à l'amiable ou conformément aux statuts ou à l'accord des associés ou ordonnée par décision de justice.... Toutefois, elles ne s'appliquent pas lorsque la liquidation intervient dans le cadre des dispositions de l'acte uniforme portant organisation des procédures collectives d'apurement du passif »

son passif exigible par son actif disponible[4]. Les causes de dissolution en droit OHADA sont énumérées par l'article 200 de l'Acte uniforme relatif au droit des sociétés commerciales et du groupement d'intérêt économique qui dispose que la société prend fin : par l'expiration du temps pour lequel elle a été constituée, par la réalisation ou l'extinction de son objet, par l'annulation du contrat de société, par décision des associés aux conditions prévues pour modifier les statuts, par la dissolution anticipé prononcée par la juridiction compétente, à la demande d'un associé pour juste motifs, notamment en cas d'inexécution de ses obligations par un associé ou de mésentente entre associés empêchant le fonctionnement normal de la société, par l'effet du jugement ordonnant la liquidation des biens de la société, par toute autres cause prévue par les statuts.

La dissolution, qui ne fait pas automatiquement disparaitre la société de la scène juridique, entraine la mise en liquidation des biens de celle-ci en vue de sa radiation du registre du commerce pour faire cesser sa personnalité juridique, sans compromettre les droits des associés et des tiers. Elle peut être organisée par la justice à la demande des représentants de la masse des obligataires dans les sociétés anonymes ou des créanciers sociaux dans toutes les autres formes de sociétés, ou par les statuts ou accords des associés. Dans le premier cas, la liquidation est judiciaire et dans le second elle est dite amiable.

« La liquidation amiable des sociétés commerciales », est un sujet qui passionne peu la doctrine juridique se préoccupant du droit applicable à l'espace OHADA. Malgré l'abondance et la variété de la littérature consacrée à la liquidation des sociétés commerciales, publiée par les lieux de diffusion du droit OHADA[5], rares sont les publications consacrées à cette question. Sans doute peut-on signaler des allusions au sujet, faites par quelques auteurs à l'occasion des annotations des actes uniformes OHADA traitant de la liquidation des sociétés[6], mais celles-ci ne

[4] Cf. *OHADA, Traité et actes uniformes commentés*, Poitiers, Juriscope 2016, pp. 454,

[5] Les principaux lieux de diffusion du droit OHADA sont, les sites OHADA.com et OHADA.org qui s'efforcent de rendre public tous les titres et parfois le contenu des travaux se rapportant au droit OHADA, et L'encyclopédie du droit OHADA qui s'est donné pour ambition une présentation exhaustive des questions traitées par les textes juridiques de l'OHADA.

[6] Sur ce point, cf. notamment, J. ISSAH-SAYEGH, « présentation des dispositions sur la dissolution et la liquidation des sociétés commerciales », www.OHADA.com,*Ohodata D-06-15* ; OHADA, *Traité et actes uniformes commentés et annotés*, Juriscope,

contribuent nullement à satisfaire la curiosité de celui qui recherche, ne serait-ce qu'une information exhaustive sur les liquidations amiables des sociétés commerciales dans l'espace juridique OHADA.

Ce peu d'engouement des auteurs quant à l'étude de la liquidation amiable des sociétés, peut avoir deux autres explications : le peu d'égard que les textes accordent à la question et l'absence d'accord de la doctrine sur l'expression « liquidation amiable ».

Relativement au peu d'égard que les textes accordent à la question, il faut faire observer que malgré son importance, seul l'article 223 de l'Acte uniforme relatif aux sociétés commerciales et groupements d'intérêts économique signale cette forme de liquidation, et, de manière tellement incidente que, dans un environnement essentiellement légicentriste, on pourrait se demander si c'est une catégorie juridique méritant une grande attention.

En ce qui concerne l'absence d'accord sur l'expression, on a fait observer que l'emploi du terme « amiable » pour désigner cette forme de liquidation n'est pas satisfaisant « car il suggère l'idée inexacte que cette liquidation serait nécessairement non contentieuse et non judiciaire. Or, il n'en est rien. La liquidation qui suit la dissolution d'une société peut évidemment être le théâtre d'un litige entre associés et n'avoir rien d'amiable. Ce sera particulièrement vrai lorsque lesdits associés ne parviendront pas à s'entendre pour en régler le cours et que le liquidateur sera nommé par décision de justice et la liquidation gouvernée par les dispositions légales »[7]. L'auteur suggère de remplacer liquidation amiable par « liquidation au sens du droit des sociétés »[8]. Cette contestation justifiée par la possible mutation d'une situation non conflictuelle en situation conflictuelle, met de côté l'idée que la mutation n'est qu'une éventualité et qu'il est possible qu'une liquidation organisée par les associés s'achève sans difficulté.

Faite dans un contexte purement français, cette critique ne tient pas compte de ce que dans certaines législations, le régime général des liquidations au sens du droit des sociétés, s'articule autour de deux pôles : celui où la liquidation ne rencontre aucune contestation qu'on qualifie d'amiable et celui où elle rencontre des contestations qu'on pourrait

[7] F.X Lucas, « Vade mecum de la liquidation dite « amiable » des sociétés », *Les petites affiches*, n°71, 9 avril 2009, p. 42

[8] F.X. « Vade mecum de la liquidation dite « amiable des sociétés », idem.

qualifier de contentieuse sans qu'elle ne bascule dans le régime de la liquidation des entreprises en difficultés. Il en est ainsi du droit OHADA qui au titre 2 du livre 7 de la première partie de l'acte uniforme relatif aux sociétés commerciales et aux groupements d'intérêt économique, intitulé « liquidation des sociétés », met en perspective deux formes de liquidation des sociétés au sens du droit des sociétés : la liquidation organisée de bout en bout par les associés, sans intervention du juge, qui est amiable et la liquidation qui fait intervenir le juge qui est contentieuse. Variante de la liquidation au sens du droit des sociétés, la liquidation amiable est finalement celle qui est organisée sans intervention du juge à quelque stade que ce soit de la procédure. Prolongement du contrat social conclu par les associés, la liquidation amiable des sociétés commerciales est une question juridique tellement importante qu'il serait injustifié de ne pas y accorder plus d'attention.

La liquidation amiable est celle par laquelle il est mis fin à la société sans porter atteinte aux droits des tiers et des associés. Contrairement à une liquidation judiciaire, procédure collective qui vise essentiellement à l'apurement du passif et à la satisfaction des créancier, qui vise à mettre un terme à l'activité de l'entreprise par une cession globale ou séparée de ses droits et de ses biens , la liquidation amiable consiste à désigner une personne qui va réaliser, avec le regard bienveillant des associés, une série d'opérations successives visant à apurer le passif social avec espoir de dégager un actif net qui va permettre de rembourser leurs apports aux associés et, le cas échéant de partager entre eux un boni de liquidation. On a fait observer avec justesse que ce partage est une modalité de la « vocation des associés aux bénéfices »[9]. La liquidation amiable vise la conciliation de deux impératifs majeurs : la préservation des droits des tiers en s'assurant que la société paie ses dettes et la préservation des droits des associés en organisant la répartition entre eux de l'actif net dans des conditions conformes aux prévisions contractuelles ou légales.

Comme toute liquidation de société, la liquidation amiable de la société entraine le dessaisissement des dirigeants au profit du liquidateur. La liquidation amiable partage également avec la liquidation contentieuse des entreprises qui ne sont pas en cessation des paiements, des dispositions communes qui se trouvent dans le titre 2 du livre 7 de la première partie de l'acte uniforme relatif aux sociétés commerciales et

---

[9] F.X Lucas, « Vade mecum de la liquidation dite « amiable » des sociétés », Les petites affiches, n°71, 9 avril 2009, p. 42.

aux groupements d'intérêt économique. Simplement chaque type de liquidation a ses singularités, plus exactement des éléments qui la distinguent des autres. Quelles sont celles de la liquidation amiable des sociétés commerciales dans l'espace OHADA ?

Rechercher des éléments de réponse à cette interrogation présente plusieurs intérêts, parmi lesquels celui de mettre en perspective et d'évaluer un régime juridique peu diffusé, mais également celui d'aider les praticiens et acteurs de la vie économique à faire des choix éclairés lors de la rédaction des textes des sociétés.

Pour répondre à cette interrogation aux confluents du contractuel et du légal, l'analyse des sources de droit dans cet espace met en lumière deux éléments majeurs qui permettent de singulariser la liquidation amiable des sociétés commerciales dans l'espace OHADA, de les distinguer des autres types ou formes de liquidation : la singularité du processus (I) et de l'issue (II) de la liquidation.

I. La singularité du processus de liquidation

Au sens juridique, un processus désigne, soit un enchainement des faits dans le temps aboutissant à un résultat lorsqu'il se rapporte à des faits juridiques, soit une suite élaborée d'opérations pour aboutir à un certain résultat lorsqu'il s'agit des actes juridiques[10]. La liquidation amiable d'une société relevant de la catégorie des actes juridiques, le processus permettant de la réaliser s'entend de l'enchainement des actes à poser. Ce processus est singulier par l'originalité de son déclenchement (A) et de son déroulement (B).

A. L'originalité du déclenchement du processus de liquidation

Déclencher le processus de liquidation c'est poser des actes permettant de la démarrer. Dans l'espace OHADA, toute liquidation d'entreprise non déclarée en cessation des paiements, qu'elle soit contentieuse ou amiable, commence par la désignation d'un liquidateur. C'est ce qui résulte des article 204 et 230 de l'Acte uniforme relatif au

[10] Sur la distinction entre actes juridiques et faits juridiques, lire notamment, J. Ghestin, G. Goubeaux, M. Fabre-Magnan, *Traité de droit civil, Introduction générale*, Paris, LGDJ ; H. Barbier, J.S Bergé, J. Ghestin, Traité de droit civil, *Introduction générale, t.1. Droit objectif, droits subjectifs et sources du droit*, Paris, LGDJ , F. Terré et N. Molfesis , *Introduction générale au droit, Paris*, Dalloz ; M. Fabre-Magnan, F. Brunet, *Introduction générale au droit*, Coll. thémis, Paris, PUF

droit des sociétés commerciales et du groupement d'intérêt économique. L'article 204 dispose : « la société est en liquidation dès l'instant de sa dissolution pour quelque cause que ce soit. La mention « société en liquidation » ainsi que le nom du ou des liquidateurs doivent figurer sur tous les actes et documents émanant de la société et destinés aux tiers ». L'article 230 alinéa 1er ajoute : « Le liquidateur représente la société qu'il engage pour tous les actes de la liquidation ».

Ces deux textes imposent, dès la dissolution d'une société sa mise en liquidation et la désignation d'un liquidateur qui devient seul apte à engager la société dont la personnalité morale est maintenue pour les besoins de la liquidation. Cette désignation dessaisit automatiquement les dirigeants sociaux.

La singularité de la liquidation amiable dans cette phase tient aux modalités de désignation du liquidateur dominées par l'idée que la société n'étant pas en cessation des paiements, les associés en gardent le contrôle. Ces modalités mettent en perspective les acteurs de la désignation et la matérialisation de la désignation.

A la question de savoir qui désigne le ou les liquidateurs, la réponse est singulière pour les liquidations amiables. Contrairement aux autres liquidations, ce n'est pas le juge qui désigne le liquidateur, mais plutôt les associés. D'après l'article 206 de l'Acte uniforme, lorsque la liquidation est décidée par les associés, un ou plusieurs liquidateurs sont nommés : « dans les sociétés en nom collectif à l'unanimité des associés ; dans les sociétés en commandite simple, à l'unanimité des commandités et à la majorité en capital des commanditaires ; dans les sociétés à responsabilité limitée, à la majorité en capital des associés ; dans les sociétés par actions, aux conditions de quorum et de majorité prévues par les assemblées générales extraordinaires ».

Ils peuvent en désigner un ou plusieurs pour une durée librement fixée par les statuts. Les associés ont le droit de choisir un ou plusieurs liquidateurs pour une durée fixée librement par les statuts ou une convention ultérieure. D'après l'article 207 de l'Acte uniforme, ils peuvent les choisir parmi les associés ou les tiers y compris les personnes morales.

Ayant le pouvoir de désigner le ou les liquidateurs, les associés peuvent également le révoquer ou le remplacer pour motifs légitimes. La possibilité de choisir le liquidateur parmi les associés se justifie par le fait que, la société n'étant pas en cessation des paiements, les associés continuent à en garder le contrôle.

Pour que la désignation des liquidateurs soit effective et opposable, elle doit être matérialisée selon des modalités précisées par l'acte uniforme. La désignation du liquidateur n'est considérée comme effectuée que lorsque des formalités de publicité sont accomplies. C'est ce qui ressort de l'article 212 de l'Acte uniforme qui dispose que « l'acte de nomination du liquidateur doit être publié dans les conditions fixées à l'article 266 de l'Acte uniforme ». L'article 266 impose que l'acte soit publié dans un délai d'un mois à compter de sa nomination dans un journal habilité à recevoir les annonces légales de l'Etat partie du siège social. L'acte de nomination publié doit contenir entre autres indications : la forme de la société suivie de la mention « société en liquidation », la cause de la liquidation etc. Cette formalité, tout en informant le public sur le nouvel interlocuteur de la société rappelle qu'elle est en liquidation et procède au dessaisissement des représentants légaux. Le non-respect de celle-ci rend la désignation du liquidateur inopposable aux tiers ; sur cette base les actes posés par le liquidateur engagent les représentants légaux de la société. C'est ce qui ressort de l'article 259 de l'acte uniforme qui dispose : « les formalités de publicité sont effectuées à la diligence et sous la responsabilité des représentants légaux ».

Tout au long de la liquidation, les tiers doivent être informés non seulement de ce que la société est en liquidation, mais également du nom du ou des liquidateurs. Cette formalité qui incombe au liquidateur est imposée par l'article 204 alinéa 2 de l'Acte uniforme qui dispose : « la mention société en liquidation » ainsi que le nom du ou des liquidateurs doivent figurer sur tous les actes et documents émanant de la société et destinés aux tiers, notamment sur les annonces et publications diverses ». Elle est destinée à renseigner les tiers sur la fin prochaine de la personnalité morale de la société et surtout à éviter que sous le couvert d'une subsistance de la personnalité morale, le liquidateur ne prenne des engagements vis-à-vis des tiers qui ne pourront être tenus par la société qui disparaitra à la fin de la liquidation. Le non-respect de cette formalité engage la responsabilité du liquidateur conformément à l'article 267 de l'acte uniforme qui dispose : « au cours de la liquidation de la société, le liquidateur accomplit sous sa responsabilité les formalités incombant aux représentants légaux ». Sur la base de ce texte, le liquidateur est responsable vis-à-vis des tiers des dommages qu'ils auraient subis en concluant avec la société dans l'ignorance de sa liquidation en cours.

Par les acteurs de la désignation du ou des liquidateurs, par la technique de matérialisation de la désignation, la liquidation amiable se singularise des autres formes de liquidation des sociétés. Mais elle se singularise davantage par l'originalité du déroulement du processus de liquidation.

B. L'originalité du déroulement du processus de liquidation

L'acte uniforme relatif au droit des sociétés et des groupements d'intérêt économique a organisé le déroulement du processus de liquidation en tenant compte de ce que tout en étant en liquidation, la société n'est pas en cessation des paiements. Partant de cette contrainte, il accorde d'importants pouvoirs au liquidateur mais organise un contrôle des opérations de liquidation.

La première originalité du déroulement du processus de liquidation amiable est l'octroi des pouvoirs au liquidateur. En effet, la publication de la désignation du liquidateur entraine automatiquement le dessaisissement des dirigeants de la société au profit du liquidateur qui a désormais la charge de la gestion de la société. Simplement, ce dessaisissement n'a pas pour effet de transférer au liquidateur les prérogatives des dirigeants sociaux, mais de déclencher ses propres prérogatives de liquidateur[11] qui se déclinent en actes qu'il a le droit de poser et les actes qu'il ne peut poser.

L'Acte uniforme relatif au droit des sociétés commerciales et au groupement d'intérêt économique donne au liquidateur le pouvoir de poser seul l'essentiel des actes se rapportant aux opérations de liquidation, c'est-à-dire de réalisation de l'actif et de comblement du passif.

Réaliser l'actif d'une personne physique ou morale c'est recouvrer ses créances, recenser et récupérer tous ses biens et éventuellement les convertir en somme d'argent. Le pouvoir de réaliser l'actif est reconnu au liquidateur par l'article 230 alinéa 2 de l'acte uniforme qui dispose que le liquidateur « est investi des pouvoirs les plus étendus pour réaliser l'actif, même à l'amiable ». D'après ce texte, le liquidateur est investi du pouvoir de poser tous les actes permettant de récupérer en quelques mains qu'ils se trouvent tout bien de la société, de recouvrer toutes les créances de l'entreprise. Il peut à cet effet mobiliser les voies de recours classiques ou recourir à des techniques amiables de recouvrement. Le texte lui donne

---

[11] Ch. Lebel, « Le liquidateur amiable : représentant légal, mais pas dirigeant de la société dissoute », *Lexbase Hebdo- Edition affaires*,14 juillet 2016.

également le pouvoir de transformer les biens de l'entreprise en somme d'argent dans la perspective du règlement des dettes de celle-ci.

Combler le passif c'est payer les dettes de l'entreprise. D'après l'article 231 de l'acte uniforme: « le liquidateur est habilité à payer les créanciers et à répartir entre les associés le solde disponible ». Ce texte autorise le liquidateur à utiliser les revenus de la société en liquidation pour payer les créanciers de celle-ci, sans solliciter l'autorisation de qui que ce soit. La question qui se pose est celle de savoir quelles sont les modalités de règlement des créances ? Le liquidateur a-t-il un ordre de distribution à respecter ? Elle se pose parce que l'acte uniforme portant procédures collectives d'apurement du passif détermine un ordre de distribution des deniers provenant de la réalisation de l'actif de la société en liquidation sur la base d'une distinction entre créanciers privilégiés et créanciers chirographaires. Mais un tel ordre n'est pas imposé au liquidateur dans le règlement amiable parce que, la société n'étant pas en cessation de paiement, chaque créancier doit pouvoir être payé et, dans ce cas l'instauration d'un ordre de règlement n'est pas nécessaire.

En ce qui concerne les actes que le liquidateur ne peut poser, l'article 214 dispose que « la cession de tout ou partie de l'actif de la société au liquidateur, à ses employés ou à leurs conjoints, ascendant ou descendant est interdite ». Ce texte vise à éviter que le liquidateur ne brade les biens de l'entreprise ou n'en minimise la valeur pour les vendre à ses proches. A côté de cette disposition générale, l'analyse de l'esprit de l'Acte uniforme permet de faire apparaître d'autres actes que le liquidateur ne peut poser. N'étant pas gestionnaire, mais plutôt accompagnateur de la société vers sa fin, il lui est interdit de poser des actes qui sortent du cadre de la liquidation et engagent la société. Ainsi, même avec l'accord du juge ou l'autorisation des associés, il n'a pas le droit de poser des actes de réalisation de l'actif qui engagent la société au-delà de la durée de la liquidation. Il est ainsi de la cession à crédit pour une durée dépassant la période de liquidation des biens de la société.

L'interdiction la plus évidente concerne les actes qui alourdissent le passif de la société. Le liquidateur n'a pas le droit de poser un acte qui, au lieu de combler le passif de la société l'alourdit. Il en est ainsi des conventions de prêt engageant la société, de l'engagement de la société comme caution d'une autre personne etc. Quelles seraient les conséquences du non- respect de cette interdiction ?

La réponse varie selon que l'acte de nomination du liquidateur a été publié ou non. S'il n'a pas été publié dans un journal habilité à recevoir les annonces légales de l'Etat partie du siège social de la société, il engage la société qui n'est pas considérée comme en liquidation. C'est ce qui ressort de l'article 212 alinéa 2 qui dispose que « la nomination et la révocation du liquidateur ne sont opposables aux tiers qu'à compter de cette publication ». S'il a été publié, les actes accomplis par le liquidateur dépassant le cadre de son mandat l'engagent personnellement, car ils sont constitutifs de fautes, de manquement à ses obligations. C'est ce qui résulte de l'article 221 de l'acte uniforme qui dispose que « le liquidateur est responsable à l'égard tant de la société que des tiers, des conséquences dommageables des fautes par lui commises dans l'exercice de ses fonctions ». La liquidation amiable atténuant la personnalité de la société sans la faire disparaître, le législateur OHADA a maintenu aux associés un pouvoir de contrôle sur le déroulement de la liquidation.

La seconde originalité du déroulement du processus de liquidation amiable réside dans la particularité du contrôle des opérations de liquidation placé à la fois sous l'autorité des associés et du juge. Relativement au contrôle exercé par les associés, contrairement à la liquidation judiciaire qui a pour effet la mise à l'écart total des associés de la gestion de la société, la liquidation amiable maintien d'importants pouvoirs de contrôle aux associés qui démontrent que c'est leur volonté qui a mis fin aux activités de l'entreprise et non une éventuelle faute ou une cessation des paiements. Ils contrôlent les opérations de liquidation et la gestion financière du liquidateur.

Relativement aux opérations de liquidation, malgré l'étendue des pouvoirs qui lui sont reconnus, le liquidateur doit solliciter l'accord des associés, pour certains actes se rapportant aux cessions d'actifs. Ainsi, d'après l'article 231 de l'acte uniforme : « sauf consentement unanime des associés, la cession de tout ou partie de l'actif de la société en liquidation à une personne ayant eu dans cette société la qualité d'associé en nom , de commandité, de gérant , d'administrateur , d'administrateur général, de directeur général ou autre dirigeant social ou commissaire aux comptes, ne peut avoir lieu qu'avec l'autorisation de la juridiction compétente, le liquidateur et le commissaire aux comptes entendus ». Cette mesure vise à éviter que des personnes ayant des liens étroits avec la société, anticipant sur la liquidation ne déprécient certains biens pour les racheter à vil prix[12].

Le liquidateur a un large pouvoir dans la gestion de la liquidation, mais sa gestion financière est soumise à un contrôle strict des associés.

D'après l'article 232, dans les trois mois de la clôture de chaque exercice, le liquidateur établit les états financiers de synthèse annuels au vu de l'inventaire qu'il dresse des divers éléments de l'actif et du passif existant à cette date et un rapport écrit par lequel il rend compte des opérations de liquidation au cours de l'exercice passé. Les associés ont le droit de prendre connaissance de ces documents dans les mêmes conditions d'accès que lorsque la société était gérée par les dirigeants sociaux. C'est ce qui résulte de l'article 234 de l'acte uniforme qui dispose que les associés peuvent prendre communication des documents sociaux dans les mêmes conditions qu'antérieurement, c'est-à-dire dans les mêmes conditions que lorsque la société n'était pas en liquidation et sa gestion assurée par des dirigeants sociaux. Ce pouvoir permet d'évaluer la gestion financière du liquidateur et éventuellement de demander sa révocation en cas de gestion non conforme à sa mission.

D'après l'article 233, sauf dispense accordée par la juridiction compétente statuant à bref délai, le liquidateur convoque, selon les modalités prévues par les statuts, au moins une fois par an et dans les six mois de la clôture de l'exercice, l'assemblée des associés qui statue sur les états financiers de synthèse annuels, donne des autorisations nécessaires et renouvelle le mandat du commissaire aux comptes.

Le contrôle du juge porte sur les affaires en cours. Bien que le liquidateur soit autorisé à poser tout acte concourant à la liquidation, il ne peut continuer les affaires en cours ou en engager de nouvelles dans cette perspective qu'avec l'autorisation du juge. C'est ce qui ressort de l'alinéa 2 de l'article 231 qui dispose que le liquidateur « ne peut continuer les affaires en cours ou engager de nouvelles pour les besoins de la liquidation que s'il y a été autorisé par décision de justice ».

La question est de savoir ce qu'il faut entendre par affaires en cours ou nouvelles pour des besoins de liquidation. En l'absence de réponse législative et jurisprudentielle, il faut recourir à la théorie des affaires pour

---

12 Cf. P.G. Pougoue et autres, annotation de l'acte uniforme du 30 janvier 2014 relatif au droit des sociétés commerciales et du groupement d'intérêt économique ; in ; *OHADA, Traité et actes uniformes commentés et annotés,* p. 459.

rechercher des éléments de réponse. Pour y apporter des éléments de réponse, il faut partir non pas de la notion d'affaire qui conformément à la définition de la société donnée par l'article 4 de l'acte uniforme, s'entend de toute opération d'affectation des biens en numéraire ou en nature dans le but de partager le bénéfice ou de profiter de l'économie qui peut en résulter, mais de celle de liquidation.

La liquidation consistant en la réalisation de l'actif pour combler le passif, l'affaire en cours ou nouvelle pour des besoins de liquidation est celle qui permet de collecter des ressources pour combler le passif. Cette considération exclut de fait les actes par lesquels le liquidateur engage la société, en vue de son développement, alors que celle-ci est destinée à disparaitre à la fin de la liquidation. Il en est ainsi du financement des opérations pour des durées supérieures à celle de la liquidation. Il en est de même de l'engagement de la société dans des dettes futures. Par contre, rentrent dans la catégorie toutes les opérations susceptibles de faire rentrer des revenus dans l'entreprise, sans en faire perdre pendant la durée de la liquidation. Il peut continuer les baux en cours ou en conclure de nouveaux pour une durée qui n'excède pas celle de la liquidation. Il peut mettre en location des machines ou des meubles de l'entreprise. Ces opérations doivent dans tous les cas être autorisées par le juge, à défaut, elles n'engagent pas la société, mais le liquidateur.

Par l'originalité de son déclenchement et de son déroulement, le processus de liquidation amiable permet de la distinguer des autres formes de liquidation. Cette singularité s'observe également au niveau de l'issue de la liquidation.

II. La singularité de l'issue de la liquidation

L'issue de toute liquidation est l'accomplissement des formalités de fin de la personnalité juridique et la gestion des suites éventuelles. Cette issue peut être consensuelle ou conflictuelle. L'une des singularités de la liquidation amiable est que l'issue ne peut être que consensuelle, puisque, si les associés ne s'entendaient pas, il y aurait eu mutation de la nature de la liquidation qui serait devenu judiciaire. Mais la singularité la plus remarquable de cette issue c'est l'intervention des associés dans l'accomplissement des formalités de fin de la personnalité juridique (A) et dans la gestion des suites de la fin de la personnalité juridique (B).

A. L'intervention des associés dans l'accomplissement des formalités de fin de la personnalité juridique

Dans l'espace OHADA, la fin de la personnalité juridique d'une société commerciale résulte de sa radiation du registre de commerce et du crédit immobilier. Dans les liquidations régies par l'acte uniforme relatif au droit des sociétés commerciales et du groupement d'intérêt économique, dont font parties les liquidations amiables, la demande de radiation est formulée par le liquidateur. C'est ce qui résulte de l'article 220 du texte qui dispose : « sur justification de l'accomplissement des formalités prévues à l'article précédent, le liquidateur demande la radiation de la société au registre du commerce et du crédit immobilier dans le délai d'un mois à compter de la publication de la clôture de la liquidation ». Simplement, le liquidateur ne peut faire la demande qu'après avoir déposé au registre de commerce et de crédit mobilier de l'Etat partie du siège social, conformément à l'article 219 de l'acte uniforme, les comptes définitifs qu'il a établis, accompagnés de la décision de l'assemblée des associés statuant sur ces comptes, du quitus de sa gestion et de la décharge de son mandat. Cela signifie que préalablement à la demande, le liquidateur doit être muni de tous ces documents qui sont établis lors de la clôture de la liquidation.

Clôturer la liquidation d'une société, c'est mettre fin aux différentes opérations de réalisation de l'actif et de comblement du passif et constater formellement la fin de l'activité du mandataire. Dans les liquidations amiables des sociétés commerciales en OHADA, cette activité est, conformément à l'article 217 de l'acte uniforme relatif aux sociétés commerciales et au groupement d'intérêt économique, l'œuvre du liquidateur et des associés. D'après ce texte « les associés sont convoqués en fin de liquidation pour statuer sur les comptes définitifs, sur le quitus de la gestion du liquidateur, sur la décharge de son mandat et pour constater la clôture de la liquidation ». Malgré les termes de l'article 231 de l'acte uniforme qui habilitent le liquidateur à payer les créanciers et à « répartir entre les associés le solde disponible », c'est à cette occasion que sont réglées les questions de reprise des apports et de partage de bénéfices. En effet, comme on l'a dit avec justesse, « le partage des actifs sociaux entre les associés doit normalement intervenir après règlement de l'intégralité des dettes sociales. L'apurement du passif est en effet un préalable qui va permettre de déterminer si la société dispose d'un actif net que ses associés vont avoir vocation à se partager »[13].

Sur cette base, un partage d'actif fait par le liquidateur en cours de liquidation, ne peut être que prévisionnel s'il s'avère qu'ils ont été fait alors que toutes les dettes n'avaient pas été prises en compte. La jurisprudence l'a clairement rappelé dans un vieil arrêt rendu par la Cour de cassation française le 2 décembre 1885, qui conserve toute sa pertinence dans la plupart des Etats OHADA grâce à la règle de succession d'Etat. La Cour affirme que « les partages qui peuvent intervenir entre les associés ne sont, jusqu'à la clôture des opérations de liquidation, que des actes anticipés qui ne produisent que des droits éventuels et ne peuvent porter atteinte au gage des créanciers sociaux ni à leur droit de préférence sur l'actif social à l'encontre des créanciers personnels des associés »[14].

Relativement à la reprise d'apport, elle est inévitable dès lors que la société n'était pas en cessation de paiement. Après le règlement de toutes les dettes sociales, en dehors des apports en industrie qui ne sont ni repris, ni remboursés[15], les associés reçoivent le nominal de leurs actions ou parts sociales selon les stipulations des statuts.

Pour ce qui est du partage des bénéfices, d'après l'article 237 de l'acte uniforme, « sauf clause contraire des statuts, le partage des capitaux propres subsistant après remboursement du nominal des actions ou des parts sociales est effectué entre les associés dans les mêmes proportions que leur participation au capital social ».

La dernière préoccupation concerne le délai de clôture de la liquidation amiable. D'après l'article 216 de l'acte uniforme, la clôture de la liquidation doit intervenir dans un délai de trois ans à partir de la dissolution de la société. Mais ce délai peut être prorogé à la demande du liquidateur. Dans sa demande de renouvellement, le liquidateur doit indiquer les raisons pour lesquelles la liquidation n'a pu être clôturée, les mesures qu'il envisage de prendre et les délais que nécessite l'achèvement de la liquidation. En application de ce texte, la Cour commune de justice

---

[13] F.X. Lucas, « Vade mecum de la liquidation dite « amiable » des sociétés, op. cit. p. 4.

[14] Cass. civ., 2 décembre 1885, DP 1886. 1, p. 35

[15] G. Jiogue, « La liquidation de la société coopérative », in, *Droit des coopératives OHADA* (Dir.) D. Hiez et A. Kenmogne Simo, Aix, Marseille, PU. Aix Marseille, Vol. 10, pp. 257 et s.

et d'arbitrage a, par ordonnance, prorogé de trois mois, à sa demande, le mandat du liquidateur d'une société[16].

L'intervention des associés se poursuit dans la gestion des suites de la fin de la personnalité juridique de la société liquidée.

B. L'intervention des associés dans la gestion des suites de la fin de la personnalité juridique de la société

Intervenant dans la désignation du liquidateur et dans le contrôle des activités de liquidation les associés d'une société liquidée de manière amiable ne devraient normalement rien à voir avec la société dès qu'elle a été radiée du registre de commerce avec pour conséquences la fin de la personnalité juridique. Mais justement parce qu'ils sont acteurs, ils peuvent être tenus de subir une action en responsabilité, ou une action en paiement d'une dette oubliée.

Relativement à l'action en responsabilité, la forte implication des associés dans le contrôle des activités de liquidation pourrait gêner l'activité du liquidateur. Ils peuvent en effet refuser au liquidateur une autorisation nécessaire pour accomplir certains actes de réalisation de l'actif, ils peuvent répondre au liquidateur avec du retard compromettant son activité, ils peuvent refuser, à tort de valider ses comptes et de le décharger alors qu'il a terminé son activité etc. Dans chacun de ces cas, si le liquidateur estime avoir subi un préjudice, il peut en demander réparation auprès de la juridiction compétente en mobilisant le régime de la responsabilité pour faute de l'article 1382 du Code civil.

En ce qui concerne l'action en paiement d'une dette oubliée, il peut arriver qu'après la clôture de la liquidation et la radiation de la société du registre de commerce et du crédit mobilier, un créancier oublié fasse valoir ses droits. La société n'existant plus la question s'est posée de savoir si une telle dette doit être payée et qui la prend en charge. La doctrine met en perspective deux voies explorées pour résoudre la difficulté[17]. D'après la première, la personnalité morale de la société subsiste aussi longtemps que les droits et obligations à caractère social ne sont pas liquidés. Cette voie qui invite à la réouverture d'une phase de liquidation avec la nomination d'un liquidateur ad hoc est l'objet de vives

---

[16] CCJA, Ordonnance 006/2015 du 29 octobre 2019, Ohadata J-16-204.

[17] M. Cozian, A. Viandier et Fl. Deboissy, Droit des sociétés, Litec, LexisNexis, 24e ed., n° 486

critiques de la doctrine[18]. Elle est d'ailleurs incompatible avec le caractère amiable de la liquidation et son utilisation transformerait la nature de la liquidation, puisqu'elle impliquerait l'intervention du juge.

D'après la seconde, le créancier peut agir contre les anciens associés de la société dissoute. Cette voie en phase avec la nature amiable de la liquidation est sans doute utile, mais l'efficacité de son utilisation dépend du type de société. Dans les sociétés à risque illimitée, elle permet le paiement de la dette puisque les associés sont tenus personnellement et indéfiniment des dettes sociales. Par contre, dans les sociétés à risque limité, les associés n'étant responsables que dans la limite de leurs apports, le recours n'est efficace que s'ils ont obtenu la restitution de leurs apports, *a fortiori* s'ils se sont partagé un boni de liquidation.

Que ce soit pour répondre de l'action en responsabilité intentée par le liquidateur, ou pour prendre en charge les dettes oubliées, les associés d'une société en liquidation amiable sont acteurs dans la gestion des suites de la perte de la personnalité juridique de celle-ci.

Conclusion

La liquidation amiable des sociétés commerciale est une opération singulière parce qu'elle est dominée par deux impératifs contradictoires. Le respect de la nature juridique de l'activité de liquidation d'une part et l'obligation de tenir compte de ce que la société n'était pas en cessation de paiement d'autre part.

L'impératif de liquidation impose le dessaisissement des associés pour permettre la réalisation de l'actif et le comblement du passif, avec obligation de laisser le liquidateur travailler. L'obligation de tenir compte de ce que la société n'était pas en cessation de paiement oblige à ne pas écarter les associés comme dans les autres cas de liquidation où leur mise à l'écart apparaît comme une sorte de sanction, mais de leur donner des moyens de contrôle de l'activité du liquidateur pour qu'elle ne reste conforme à ses missions.

C'est autour de l'articulation de ces deux impératifs qu'est construit le régime juridique de la liquidation amiable des sociétés commerciales dans l'espace OHADA.

[18] G.Jiogue, « La liquidation amiable des sociétés coopératives « , op. cit.

Political Economy of Regional Security in Central Africa

Kiven James Kewir

Department of Political Science and Comparative Politics, University of Buea, Guest Lecturer, Department of Political Science, University of Bamenda
Email: jameskewir@yahoo.com

and

Ekang Adventus Nzikie

Department of Political Science, University of Douala

Abstract

Interest in regional security cooperation has been growing in Africa since the late 1990s. Despite the declared interest and the setting up of several regional security institutions on the continent, little progress has been made in rolling back or preventing the conflicts they are meant to address. Using dependency theory as a framework for analysis, this paper examines the performance of regional security integration in Central Africa. Regional security missions in the sub-region have been heavily dependent on financial and technical support from donors. This dependence continues to deepen as more countries in the region descend into conflict and see their financial and technical capacities restricted. Using a qualitative research strategy, this paper explains the weak performance of the Economic Community of Central African States (ECCAS) on security. Data for the study is collected using extensive literature searches. The study reveals that the nature of the post-colonial state in Central Africa explains why ECCAS continues to depend on foreign donors for its security efforts. It also shows that this dependence makes it difficult for the organisation to prioritise and effectively plan its activities.

Key words: Regional security, Central Africa, Post-colonial state, Dependence

Introduction

Since 1990, Central African states like their counterparts in other sub-regions on the continent have increasingly shown interest in security integration. In spite of the growing interest and actions taken, regional security remains a major challenge. In 2019 for example, 25 state-based conflicts were recorded[1]. Security can be defined as the sum of measures taken to shield a state from threats to its survival. It comprises such elements as protecting states borders, and the choice to decide the desired political system and adequate conditions for the development of members of society. Regional security can hence be considered as structured efforts by states to create, maintain or modify the provision of security in each region. The Central African region is one of the most turbulent parts of the contemporary world. Security in the region is threatened both by political instability and rising international terrorism among other factors. It is increasingly recognized that most of the threats to security including political instability and terrorism cannot be addressed by states working independently. To address the growing security threats in the sub-region, Central African states have thus adopted security integration as a tool for action. At the time ECCAS was created in 1983 by the Treaty of Libreville, following the adoption of the Lagos Plan of Action by the then Organisation of African Unity (OAU), security was not a priority for the founding members.[2]

The first major step towards security integration was made when members of the more restricted Economic and Monetary Community of Central African States (CEMAC), Chad, Cameroon, Gabon, Equatorial Guinea, and the Republic of Congo took a decision in October 2002 to deploy a security force in the Central African Republic.[3] In July 2008, the mission was transferred to the Economic Community of Central African States (ECCAS) that can be considered to be more representative of the

---

[1] Palik, Júlia; Siri Aas Rustad & Fredrik Methi ,2020, "Conflict Trends in Africa, 1989–2019", Oslo, PRIO. Accessed on 21 May 2022 at: https://www.prio.org/projects/1894

[2] ECCAS currently has 11 members (Angola, Burundi, Cameroon, Central African Republic, Chad, Democratic Republic of the Congo, Equatorial Guinea, Gabon, Republic of Congo, Rwanda, Sao Tome and Principe) from the initial 10 in 1983 when it was founded.

[3] Mayer, A., 2009, 'Regional Conflict Management in Central Africa: From FOMUC to MICOPAX', *African Security, 2:158–174,* DOI: 10.1080/19362200903362075

sub-region and became the Mission for Peacebuilding in the Central African Republic (CAR) known by its French acronym MICOPAX (Mission de Consolidation de la Paix en République Centrafricaine). Despite the long presence of sub-regional security efforts in the CAR, armed violence remains a major preoccupation which has attracted the engagement of African Union and other international actors including the United Nations, France and Russia.

Using dependency theory as a framework for analysis, this paper examines the factors that explain the failure of sub-regional security efforts in Central Africa. The study is qualitative, drawing extensively from secondary sources of data. Following this introduction, the theoretical framework for the study is presented. The third section discusses the security structures of CEMAC and ECCAS. Section four examines the challenges to regional security in the sub-region while the last section is the conclusion.

Theoretical framework

Several theories of political economy can be used to examine the phenomenon of regional security in Central Africa. The main theories that can be employed include hegemonic stability theory, dependency theory, geopolitical analysis theory, constructivism, world systems theory, pluralism and realism. This review is based on dependency theory which was introduced by Raúl Prebisch (1963).[4] The theory emphasizes the factors that explain the dependence of states and institutions in the worlds' periphery. The periphery which consists of former colonies is now locked in a neo-colonial capitalist system which maintains its social structures under the influence from the industrialized Centre.[5] The state of regional security structures like other features of underdevelopment from this perspective can thus be seen as a consequence rather than a condition.

Although conceived to explain political development, dependency theory can thus be used to understand regional security. Regarding regional security, dependency is the reliance of peripheral states on

---

[4] Raul Prebisch, 1963, "Towards a Dynamic Development Policy for Latin America", New York.

[5] Isbister, John., 2006, Promises Not Kept. Poverty and the Betrayal of Third World Development , 7th edn., Bloomfield, CT: Kumarian Press, Inc, p. 43

developments and expansion of security interests of industrialized countries for the initiation and sustenance of security cooperation.

Dependency theorists argue that there exists a 'core' of rich states that actively dominates a 'periphery' of poor/less developed states[6]. The system of interaction between rich and poor states therefore stands as an obstacle to meaningful progress in the developing/poor states including in the field of security. Dependency is thus seen as a function of a historical pattern of interaction between the two. Dos Santos contends that dependency is 'an historical condition which shapes a certain structure of the world economy such that it favours some countries to the detriment of others, and it limits the development possibilities of subordinate economies.'[7]

Other scholars such as Karl Popper in his book *The Open Society and Its Enemies* contend that dependency is explained by the closed nature of developing countries. Unlike open societies which according to Popper accept change an easily adapt to new situations developing countries resist change and face difficulties in responding to new challenges. Although relevant, it can be noted that this view fails to consider the historical explanation of these differences. Both views are relevant in understanding the problem of dependency. It appears to be as much a question of the domestic factors and rigidities as it is a problem of influence from the Centre.

Regional security structures of CEMAC and ECCAS

Since its creation in 1983, it was at the Libreville Summit of 1998 in Gabon when ECCAS activities were re-launched after over 10 years of dormancy that member states identified security as a priority for the organization. This change led to the establishment of the ECCAS Peace and Security Council (COPAX) at the Malabo Summit of 1999 in Equatorial Guinea. It is regulated by the Protocol on the Peace and Security Council of the 24 March 2000. The structure of COPAX comprises three main decision making bodies: the Conference of Heads of State and Government, the Council of Ministers and the General Secretariat.

---

6 Wallerstein, Immanuel, 2004, World – Systems Analysis. An Introduction, Durham and London: Duke University Press

7 Theotonio Dos Santos, "The Structure of Dependence," in K.T. Fann and Donald C. Hodges, eds., Readings in U.S. Imperialism. Boston: Porter Sargent, 1971, p. 226

The Conference of Heads of State and Government is the highest decision-making body of the Council on questions of security. The Conference decides on the appropriate measures to be taken for the prevention, management and settlement of conflicts especially the use of military intervention; the setting up of a peace-keeping force (FOMAC); ensures that the early warning mechanism functions well; appoints a Special Representative for each operation and determines its mandate; appoint the Force Commander, the Deputy Force Commander and the Joint Chief of Staff for a specified period of time; takes all initiatives relating to the missions of COPAX and decides on measures of humanitarian assistance in the event of crisis or open conflict.

The Council of Ministers (mostly of Foreign Affairs, Defense and Security) is led by the minister representing the member state whose President is the Chairman of the Conference. Its main mission is to follow up and implement the decisions of the Conference.

The General Secretariat of the ECCAS is responsible for the day-to-day management of COPAX. The secretariat services of COPAX are provided by the office of the Deputy Secretary General for Peace and Security of ECCAS.

The other institutions are of operational nature and are discussed below. These are the Defence and Security Commission (DSC), Central African Early Warning Mechanism (MARAC) and the Multinational Force of Central Africa (FOMAC).

The (CDS) brings together chiefs of staff, their representatives or their members. According to Article 14 of the COPAX Protocol it is responsible for examining all administrative, technical, and logistic problems and assessing the needs of peace-keeping operations. The meetings of the DSC are convened by the serving Chairman of the Conference of Heads of States and Governments or depending on the circumstances, the serving Chairman of the Council of Ministers. The Commission meets twice a year in ordinary sessions and in extraordinary sessions where the need arises. Article 15 of the COPAX Protocol states that the coordination and follow-up of peacekeeping and peacebuilding by the DSC are placed under the authority of the serving Chairman of the Conference of Heads of States and Governments of ECCAS.

MARAC is responsible for informing and alerting the decision-making bodies on the risk. It collects and analyses information to facilitate decision making for the purpose of preventing crisis and conflicts. MARAC is part of CEWS with which it interacts.[8] Through a network of correspondents in the Member States MARAC is expected to ensure a daily monitoring of political, social and security situation in the sub-region.

FOMAC is non-permanent force of military contingents, police and civilians from member states. It is responsible for setting up and managing peace, security and humanitarian missions.

It is one of five regional brigades within the African Union Peace and Security Architecture (APSA). The decision to set up FOMAC can be taken by the Conference at the request of a member, the AU or the UN. According to Article 27 of the Protocol, activities of COPAX are financed by a special ECCAS fund, provisioned by contributions of members and external donors. FOMAC is mainly responsible for peacekeeping, peacemaking and delivering humanitarian assistance to address conflicts.[9]

FOMAC organises joint military exercises and cartographic exercises (MAPEX) with the support of its external partners. It should be noted that although most of the member states take part in these exercises, they are dominated by French-speaking member states of CEMAC.

Regarding field operations, they have all been deployed in CAR, albeit in different contexts and with different mandates and objectives. It is in 2008 that the MICOPAX passed under the responsibility of ECCAS to replace the Multinational Force in Central Africa (FOMUC) which was created by CEMAC in 2002. The initial aim of FOMUC was to ensure the safety of President Ange-Félix Patassé, the restructuring of the armed forces of the CAR (FACA) and carry out surveillance along the border with Chad.[10] Following the coup d'état of François Bozizé in 2003, the mandate of FOMUC was changed to a stabilization mission.

The contribution of FOMAC to the stabilisation of the political and security situation in the CAR, though relatively important, did not however prevent the escalation of violence in the country. As the

---

[8] Réseau de Recherche sur les Opérations de Paix , «Fiche d'information de l'organisation : CEEAC », available at ; http://www.operationspaix.net/3-fiche-d-information-de-l-organisation-ceeac.html

[9] Réseau de Recherche sur les Opérations de Paix, op. cit.

[10] Réseau de Recherche sur les Opérations de Paix, « Historique de l'opération FOMUC, » available at ; http://www.operationspaix.net/42-historique-fomuc.html

security situation evolved, so also did FOMAC's role. FOMAC moved from being a neutral third party attempting to mitigate tensions, to being a "passive" actor, overwhelmed by events in the wake of the Seleka rebellion in 2013 before the Seleka leader, Djotodia, was forced to resign by ECCAS.[11]

The above shows that ECCAS has security mandate. CEMAC on the other hand lacks a mandate and although it initiated the first peacekeeping mission in the sub-region it withdrew from the security domain in favour of the more representative grouping, ECCAS. As discussed, the result is however unsatisfactory. Despite the poor performance of ECCAS in its lone security mission since the creation of FOMAC, the security effort in the CAR has at least provided the institution with an opportunity to test its security management system.

Choice and capacity for regional security in Central Africa

Unlike regional economic integration, domestic groups have played a limited role in promoting regional security integration in Central Africa. The development of regional security in Central Africa has largely been influenced by External Actors especially France and western governments. The security efforts of ECCAS like individual government projects of member states have depended on external financial support and guidance.

The most prominent domestic group that has visibly promoted regional security has been the academia. Governments stood as the main obstacle to regional security before 2002 because of the mutual suspicion that characterized relations between the ten states in the sub-region. Interest in security integration by governments developed as the regional character of the conflicts that member states faced became increasingly evident. Continental and international influence has however played a major role in the promotion of regional security among ECCAS states.

ECCAS is part of the African Peace and Security Architecture (APSA). The implementation of its policies on peace and security are thus influenced by the African Union (AU). The influence of the AU on

[11] BBC, 10 January 2014, « RCA: démission de Djotodia et Tiangaye », accessed on 27 December 2018 at ;
https://www.bbc.com/afrique/region/2014/01/140110_rca_demssion_djotodia_ndjamena.shtml

questions of security is exercised through the African Union Commission and the Peace and Security Council. Within the framework of the APSA, there are also meetings between the Central African Early Warning System (MARAC) with the Continental Early Warning System (CEWS). Although the crisis in the CAR is the only instance where ECCAS has deployed a mission, the poor resource capacity organisation quickly became apparent, and it turned to the AU and the UN for assistance. The AU led International Mission for the Support of the Central African Republic, known by its French acronym (MISCA, Mission Internationale de Soutien à la Centrafrique sous Conduite Africaine) that was deployed on 19 December 2013, did not also have adequate resources to end the violence that erupted since 2012. The weak capacity of MISCA in turn necessitated the deployment of a UN mission, the United Nations Multidimensional Integrated Stabilization Mission in the Central African Republic (MINUSCA) in 2014.[12]

Support from the European Union (EU) has also played a major role in promoting regional security integration in Central Africa. Through the European Development Fund, the EU has played a determining role in the advancement of ECCAS peace and security efforts. Since 2007 the EU has supported ECCAS with over 5 759 571[13] Euros. Capacity building for MARAC was largely supported through the EU facilities for ECCAS peace and security, PAS I and PAPS II. According to Guicherd the EU approach does not match financial conditionality with absence of institutional and political support thus limiting the impact of her support in a context characterized by a lack of mutual trust among sub-regional actors and a strong resistance to change by national institutions and political elites.[14]

In addition to EU influence, it is important to also mention interest from France and the United States of America (US) and the United Nations (UN). French influence is exercised both through the EU and through direct and active engagement in peace operations. France has provided operational support for the structuring of the Central African Multinational Force (FOMAC), primarily through the joint BOALI

---

[12] Security Council, 10 April 2014, Resolution 2149

[13] European Court of Auditors based on contracts audited.

[14] CEEAC-BAD: lancement du projet PARCI-CEEAC, octobre 2013.

training from October 2002[15] and more recently Operation Sangaris in CAR since December 2013.[16] The US has also shown interest in regional security efforts of Central Africa states. The visit of Commander of United States Africa Command (AFRICOM) to the General Secretariat of ECCAS in May 2012[17] is evidence of growing influence in the sub-region's security management structure. During this visit, the two parties committed to strengthen cooperation which covers joint maritime security activities in the Gulf of Guinea such as "Cutlass express"[18] or more generally those organized within the context of the African crisis response initiative (ACRI).

The UN has carried security interventions of different types and in different countries in the Central African Sub-region. These have also influenced the nature and scope of ECCAS security efforts. In addition to political cooperation and joint diplomatic efforts, the UN has fielded the largest peacekeeping mission in the DRC (MONUSCO, United Nations Organization Stabilization Mission in the Democratic Republic of the Congo) with over 18000 troops and police.[19] In the CAR, the UN mission has over 12000 troops. ECCAS member states contribute very little in personnel to its operations in relation to other actors. Compared to the UN and France, the ECCAS mission has not only relied mainly on external support, but deployed the smallest number of troops, over 3000 in 2013.[20] The low resource potential of ECCAS could thus partly explain its heavy reliance on international partners for its security efforts.

Challenges to regional security

The evaluation of the institutions put in place and the field efforts of COPAX in the CAR confirms that apart from the commendable effort of fielding a peacekeeping mission, very limited results have been

[15] Ministère de la Défense, 2013, « L'opération Boali » accessed on 19 November 2018 at https://www.defense.gouv.fr/operations/terminees/operation-boali-2002-2013/l-operation-boali

[16] Ministère de la Défense, 2013, « Opération Sangaris », accessed on 13 October 2018 at; https://www.defense.gouv.fr/operations/terminees/sangaris/dossier-de-presentation-de-l-operation-sangaris/operation-sangaris

[17] Moussavounick , 2012, « Le Commandant d'AFRICOM en visite au Gabon », accessed on 3 October 2018 at ; http://moussavounick.unblog.fr/2012/05/

[18] https://www.africom.mil/what-we-do/exercises/cutlass-express

[19] https://thisisafrica.me/peacekeeping-missions-africa/

[20] http://cmi.fi/wp-content/uploads/2017/03/Principle_of_Subsidiarity_ECCAS_CMI_French.pdf

achieved. It is therefore important to consider the challenges facing sub-regional security by ECCAS. The main problems faced by ECCAS in its security efforts are: the nature of the post-colonial state in Central Africa, inadequate financial resources and dependency, political commitment, the intergovernmental character of ECCAS, multiple and overlapping memberships and the existence of rivalries between members.

Nature of the post-colonial state in Central Africa

The post-colonial African state suffers from a crisis of legitimacy which manifests itself in real difficulties in ensuring cohesion and stability and satisfying the basic needs of the populations. The result is a search for legitimacy and support mostly from former colonial masters. According to dependency theory, this reliance on former colonial masters is explained by the position of ECCAS states in the world capitalist system.

The expanding security interests of France and Europe among other countries in the world's centre can only be met via influence on security governance in peripheral states of which ECCAS states are part. Several studies have demonstrated that Central Africa is of significant geostrategic importance to key states in the Centre, especially France and the United States of America. In addition to the deliberate interest in influencing security cooperation by countries in the world's Centre, several other reasons can be advanced to explain the dependence of ECCAS on Europe and the USA.

The post-colonial state is a combination of the 'colonial state' and the Westphalian state. The result of this survival of the colonial system in what is considered as post-independence period is a state that is like the colonial state before it, disconnected from the population. While the state in other parts of the world includes a population as a key component, the post-colonial state was handed to an elite that has perpetrated itself with the support of former colonial masters from which it derives its legitimacy. Regional security like national security is first and foremost about the security of people within a given region. The character of the state has thus made it difficult for regional institutions to effective play a security role as it is as expected a reflection of its members. The mandate of the very first regional security mission in Central Africa, FOMUC is very illustrative of this. To the decision makers of the CEMAC, the security of President Patasse was synonymous to the security of the CAR. Except for the Djotodia government, the situation has not changed significantly under FOMAC as security efforts have largely focused on the survival of the regime in Bangui.

The post-colonial state has become ideologically dependent and a tenacious and pernicious dependence on external actors, especially former colonial powers. As with the colonial state, the resulting artificial states in the sub-region rely only on coercion and violence as a means of action when responding to demands of their populations. Without a people centred security approach within states, it is unlikely that regional security efforts will address the current weakness that stem from the heavy reliance on former colonial masters and other organisations in the Western World for the direction and sustenance of regional security.

Inadequate political commitment

This is a major constraint to regional integration in Central Africa. Although concealed, the interests in regional integration have been predominantly political in the sub-region. Economic development has constantly been professed as the rationale for integration but it is very unlikely that it constitutes a real motive for integration in the sub-region. This is also the case with security that is yet to be given serious attention. In such a situation, it is not the number and content of sub-regional protocols that is lacking. Rather, member states take no serious interest in their implementation. The choice of projects that are taken seriously appears to be linked to external support especially by France. All security missions undertaken by ECCAS have been with the support of France and the EU.

It can be surprising that inadequate political commitment should constitute a challenge especially after heads of state took a decision to put in place a mechanism for peace and security (COPAX) in 1999 and later signed a protocol that gave the community a clear legal mandate on security. However, it can be argued that for it to take close to a decade before the ECCAS fielded a mission despite the recurrence of armed conflict in the CAR and the DRC shows that there is at best some reluctance to intervene and at worst the near absence of political commitment to addressing conflicts. This problem is pertinent even at the level of CEMAC although it took the first step in sending a peacekeeping mission to the CAR not all its members contributed troops.

Another factor that shows that the level of commitment is low is the repeated delay to pay financial contributions and sometimes the refusal to contribute by members. The ECCAS Secretariat is for example not just poorly staffed but dysfunctional because workers are not regularly paid. It is in this light that Narcise Mouelle Kombi argued that the weaknesses and insolvency regarding contributions to community budgets are among the main causes of the failure of integration in Central Africa[21]. The near absence of political commitment is thus important in understanding the poor participation in financing the activities of an organisation that is expected to satisfy the common interests of members.

Inadequate financial resources and dependency

Poor financial resources and dependency adversely affect regional integration. For a sub-regional integration scheme to be effective, it needs a self-financing mechanism. ECCAS notwithstanding relies heavily on external partners to finance its security activities. The institutions of ECCAS depend on contributions from member states but these have proven difficult to collect. Efforts to put in place autonomous sources of funding have been ineffective as mentioned above. In a paper presented at the ERD workshop in Florence from the 16-17 April 2009, Emmanuel Fanta observes that grave financial limitations have led to the virtual paralysis of the early warning mechanisms of ECCAS.[22]

The Contribution Communautaire d'Intégration (CCI) was only put in place in 1999, almost two decades after the creation of ECCAS in 1983. It took another two years before it was instituted by decision No. 05/CEEAC/CCEG/X/02 of 17 June 2002 that was expected to take effect in 2004. Despite the institution of the CCI, members continue to default without being sanctioned. With the institution of the CCI, member states are expected to collect 0.4% of import taxes on goods from outside ECCAS for the organisation following allocations agreed on by consensus. Angola, Cameroon, Gabon, Congo Brazzaville, and Equatorial Guinea have to contribute 13% of the community budget each. The DRC and Chad are to contribute 10% while Burundi and Sao Tome and Principe are to contribute 5%. The first CCI contributions

[21] Kombi, N., l'Integration Regionale en Afrique Centrale. Entre Interetatisme et Supranationalisme, in Hammouda, H., Bekolo-Ebe, B, Mama, T., 1999, l'Integration Regionale en Afrique Centrale. Bilan et Perpectives, Kartala, Paris, p. 214

[22] Fanta, E., 2009, 'The Capacity of African Regional Organisation in Peace and Security' paper presented at ERD Workshop: Transforming Political Structures: Security, Institutions and Regional Mechanisms, Florence, 16-17 April 2009

were paid in 2005. However, in 2007, Angola expressed discontent at having to pay more than other members she considered as having the same resource potential with her. Equatorial Guinea similarly argued that she ought to pay 10% given that the DRC with more resources than her was only paying 10%. Angola also argued that where the 0.4% tax share was above the expected national contribution, the surplus should remain with the country of origin. This ceiling on the amount of money that could be paid to the community budget by a member state was consequently adopted. A major problem with this is that it did not only limit the amount of money the organisation could generate but prevents any member from assuming some 'financial hegemony' that could help glue the organisation together by encouraging more contribution to supporting community activities.

The unpredictable nature of member contributions makes the respect of budgetary allocations difficult and obviously frustrates most activities. This situation has rendered very heavy the contributions of foreign partners. Such contributions have accounted for more than half of the budget required to sustain the activities of COPAX. With most of its finances coming from foreign partners, there is not just a limit to the level of assistance these can provide but to what the organisation can achieve under such dependence. In addition, changes in donor policies can have devastating consequences on the organisation activities where such change is on the downside or where there is a complete loss of interest by the donor in the activities being funded. It is in this light that Cederic de Coning has observed that countries and regional organisation schemes that rely substantially on external support must comply with the demands and choices of the creditors. In the same light, Mayer observes that "Donors can determine the duration of a mission and can influence a mission's mandate by placing terms and conditions on continued funding or by withdrawing funding".[23] Over dependence on foreign support is definitely linked to the political nature of interests in security integration in the sub-region. Countries that assume or that are not fully aware of the conditions for funding regional security activities have most often taken a passive approach to conflict situations.

---

[23] Mayer, A, 2011,' Peace and Security Cooperation in Central Africa: Developments challenges and prospects', Nordiska Afrikainstitutet, UPPSALA

Intergovernmental character of ECCAS

ECCAS is essentially an intergovernmental organisation. Those organs of intergovernmental character play a decisive role in its activities. This primacy of the role of governments is apparent in the ECCAS treaty, the COPAX protocol and other important documents. In practical terms, this means that decision making is given to those bodies made up of government representatives. Member states have not transferred responsibilities for decision making to a supranational body acting on their behalf.

The Conference of Heads of State and Government is thus at the centre of all decision making in the ECCAS. This is clear from Article 8 (2) of the ECCAS treaty, which states that 'the Conference of Heads of States and Governments shall be the supreme organ of the community,' and Article 9 on the powers of the Conference that include among others, the power to define the policy and major guidelines of the community and overseeing the functioning of its institutions.[24]

It may be argued that the vertical flow of authority and the concentration of powers in the Conference can facilitate decision making and increase the confidence and interest of members in the activities of the community. This will, however, be misleading. The intergovernmental character of the structure can rather be perceived as a challenge for several reasons.

Decision making is slow since according to Article 10 of the ECCAS Treaty, the Conference meets only once a year and requests for a special session and require the support of two thirds of the members.[25] The situation is made worse by the irregular nature of the meetings that do not follow the calendar set by the Treaty. All major decisions are taken by the Conference. The Conference also directly oversees the activities of its operational organs. Under such tight control from the states and with very limited and often unavailable resources, it is difficult to expect much in terms of results. Steering a security operation successfully requires sustained action which is impossible when decisions are taken by an institution that only meets once a year and is disconnected from the realities on the ground.

---

24 ECCAS, 18 October 1983, Treaty Establishing the Economic Community of Central African States, Libreville,

25 ECCAS, 1983, Treaty Establishing the Economic Community of Central African States, Libreville, 18 October

Multiple and overlapping memberships

It is common to find countries belonging to several regional or international organisations without any apparent problems associated. Most members of the European Union belong to the North Atlantic Treaty Organisation and several other international governmental organisations. Overlapping membership of large groups and the existence of smaller groups within the large groups sometimes referred to as 'variable geometry approach,' is nonetheless viewed in contrasting ways by different scholars.

According to Lyakurwa and others, for example, in Africa, variable geometry can mean making progress at the ECCAS level for example while still benefiting from the achievements of CEMAC like the shared currency.[26] Other scholars like Aryeetey and Uduro, however, contend that overlap among other things, can only lead to a duplication of effort. The latter view is taken in the 2011-2015 Regional Integration Strategy Paper for Central Africa, published by the African Development Bank. The paper concludes on this problem of multiple memberships that 'for the moment, (...), membership in several RECs creates constraints for countries concerned, notably in terms of difficulties in honouring their financial obligations to the various RECs ...'[27] Similarly, Drapper, Hallesson and Alves have concluded that:

> problems of multiple and overlapping memberships constitute a 'spaghetti bowl' that hinders regional integration by creating a complex entanglement of political commitments and institutional requirements adding significantly to the costs of conducting intra-regional business.[28]

The Minister of the Economy and Planning of Cameroon, Louis Paul Motaze took this position in an interview with *Réperes* in July 2010 arguing that multiple memberships, the duplication of programmes and the resulting dispersal of resources are difficulties that need to be overcome for integration projects in the sub-region to succeed.[29]

---

[26] Viewed on 30 May 2011 at *vi.unctad.org/digital-library////?act*

[27] African Development Bank (ADB), 2007, Central Africa Regional Integration Strategy Paper, African Development Bank

[28] Draper, P., Halleson, D. and Alves, P., January 2007, SACU, Regional Integration and the Overlap Issue in Southern Africa: from Spaghetti to Canelloni?, Trade Policy Report No. 15, South African Institute of International Affairs (SAIIA), p. 7

[29] Andzongo, R., 2010, ' Intégration: Fusion envisagée de la CEMAC et de la CEEAC', Réperes No. 180, Wednesday 07 July 2010

ECCAS was formed by the coming together of states that formed the then UDEAC and those that constituted the CEPGL. The birth of ECCAS did not, however, mean that these organisations ceased to exist. While CEPGL project, that came into existence in 1976 with the objective of fostering political, economic and social cooperation between the DRC, Rwanda and Burundi never actually materialised, the ECCAS remained dormant and was revived as CEMAC in 1994. A United States Institute for Peace briefing in August 2009 titled 'Beyond Emergency Responses in the Democratic Republic of Congo: Regional Solutions for a Regional Conflict' contemplated a revitalisation of CEPGL.[30] What is important is to note here that two projects have never really been abandoned (ECCAS and CEMAC) although it is only UDEAC, turned into CEMAC that is significantly active today. The situation is worsened by the fact that some members of the ECCAS belong to other sub-regional groupings completely outside Central Africa.

Although the debate over actual impact of variable geometry is far from settled, it can be convincingly argued in the light of the above that multiple memberships can be a disincentive for regional integration where the states involved have resource problems. In such a situation, integration schemes with overlapping memberships are perceived as wasting effort and resources.[31] This argument can be used to explain in part some of the difficulties experienced with sub-regional security integration in Central Africa.

Rivalry between member states

It is difficult for states to commit effectively to security where their relations are characterised by rivalry and suspicion. This is a real problem in Central Africa. ECCAS suffers from internal rivalries. Thomas Stevens, Hans Hoebeke and Koen Vlassenroot, for example have observed that "one of the factors that explains the lethargy of the Central African region is the (geo) politics of antagonism..."[32] There exist rivalries between Equatorial Guinea and Cameroon as well as between

[30]Gilpin, R., Morris, C., and Funai, G., United States Institute of Peace (USIP), August 2009, Beyond Emergency Responses in the Democratic Republic of Congo: Regional Solutions for a Regional Conflict, USIP, Washington D.C.

[31] FONDAD, December 2005, Africa in the World Economy- The National, Regional and International Challenges, FONDAD, the Hague

[32] Stevens, T., Hoebeke, H., Vlassenroot, K.., (c) 2008, Political Economy of Regionalisation in Africa, Institute for Security Studies (ISS), Pretoria, South Africa

the former and Gabon mainly over disputed borders. There are also rivalries between Cameroon and Gabon, between the DRC and Angola and in the case of Chad and the CAR, relations appear to depend on how close the authorities in Bangui are to the Derby Government.

In addition to border and political disputes there are leadership quarrels. Cameroon and Gabon have been in a constant struggle for influence and leadership and with the recently discovered oil wealth of Equatorial Guinea, tensions have risen between her and the two as well. In spite of this struggle for leadership it is striking that none of these countries can be seen to have the confidence of really taking a leadership role within ECCAS. Their competition is thus mostly manifest over competition for control of projects within the less representative CEMAC as was the case for example with the location of the regional stock exchange. This geopolitics of distrust has not only hampered the realisation of integration objectives like freedom of movement which is one of the core principles of ECCAS. Some states enforce tough border controls as they believe uncontrolled immigration from neighbouring states will have a destabilising effect. Equatorial Guinea treats Cameroonian citizens on its soil with suspicion. In 2011, Gabon used brute military force to expel 3500 Cameroonians from its soil on the pretext that they were gold prospectors.[33] Angola equally exercises tight and often violent controls on its border with the DRC. Cases of rape and death have been reported in the aftermath of these expulsions by the UN Officer for Humanitarian Affairs (OCHA).[34] In October 2018, 330,000 Congolese migrants, including about 80,000 children were deported from Angola.[35]

The impact of this atmosphere of distrust and suspicion needs not be overemphasized. Countries are unlikely to accept peacekeeping missions with contingents from dreaded member states. It is, for example, impractical to envision deploying an ECCAS mission to the DRC with a Contingent from Burundi. The presence of Chadian forces in the FOMUC mission is believed to have favoured the overthrow of the President Patasse who did not have the support of Chad.

---

[33] 'violente expulaion de 3500 orpailleurs étrangers par des militaires gabonais', Radio France Internationale, 12 June 2011

[34] 'Angola accused of border terror', *mail & Guardian*, 22 July 2011

[35] https://news.un.org/en/story/2018/10/1024212

Conclusion

Promoting regional security integration will require strong political commitment and a change in the nature of the post-colonial state in Central Africa. Along with these efforts there is a need to ensure financial and political ownership of the security institutions in the sub-region. There is also a strong need to improve the state of relations between ECCAS members and to review commitments with similar organizations on the continent. Finally, more autonomy should be given to regional intuitions especially with regard to taking initiative of and the day to day management of security operations. The most critical element of the security integration process is dependency on external actors, especially France and the EU. With increased political will and commitment toward security integration, greater efforts will also have to be made to build confidence and fill the huge trust deficit between the countries. These should pave the way for greater participation in the financing of security activities and enhance efficiency.

Protection of refugees in Cameroon: legal and human rights challenges

Patience Sone

Associate Professor of Law, Department of English Law, University of Buea
Emial: pattysonem@gmail.com

and

Mbianyor Arrey J.

Department of English Law, University of Buea, Cameroon.
Email: arreymbianyor@gmail.com

Abstract

In fleeing either persecution or situations of violence, people are forced to cross international boundaries and seek protection as refugees. Cameroon playing host to a huge refugee population, has ratified and enacted laws geared at protecting the rights of refugees. Such an effort is however falling short in the protection of refugees. This has spurred the researchers to investigate the protection accorded to refugees in Cameroon. Relying on primary and secondary information through interviews and content analysis of relevant documents, findings revealed though some strides have been made in protecting refugees, there are some challenges towards their effective protection. Based on the findings, this paper highlights some relevant recommendations that may improve the protection accorded to refugees found in Cameroon.

Introduction

The primary aspiration of a person fleeing from danger to another country as a refugee is to meet an improved situation in the host country from that which he/she fled. Unfortunately, this is not the case as it was observed by the League of Nations Advisory Commission for Refugees that, 'the characteristic and essential feature of the problem was that persons classed as 'refugees' have no regular nationality and are therefore deprived of the normal protection accorded to the regular citizens of a state'.[1] This is because there existed no universally applicable legal text, or in a situation where such exists, the interpretation is open to the whims and caprices of the host country. Such restrictive interpretation raises a problem as to who qualifies as a refugee and the standard criteria to be used in determining their status. This thus affects the rights which refugees are supposed to enjoy in the host country.

The displacement of persons arising from especially conflict situations generally poses a problem to the receiving or host countries[2] and Cameroon is not immune. Being a country wherein most of its own citizens do not enjoy some basic rights like health and shelter, the problem then lies on how to protect the rights of refugees who are considered as outsiders. This resulting conflict between her humanitarian obligation and national needs is further compounded by the fact that despite the numerous instruments on refugee protection, only the duties of non-refoulement, non-penalisation and non-expulsion have received some form of attention[3] unlike some rights like the freedom of movement, the right to work and education. Though there exists in principle conducive laws aimed at ameliorating the conditions of refugees in Cameroon, preliminary findings reveal that in practice, the state is failing to live up to its minimum treaty obligation. It is against

[1] James C. Hathaway, *The Rights of Refugees under International Law*. Cambridge: Cambridge University Press, 2005, p84.

[2] Volker Turk et al, "Refugee Protection in International Law: An Overall Perspective" in Erica Feller, et al (ed), Refugee Protection in International Law: UNHCR's Global Consultations on International Protection. Cambridge: Cambridge University Press, 2003, p4.

[3] James C. Hathaway, supra, p2. See generally Erica Feller et al, Refugee Protection in International Law: UNHCR's Global Consultations on International Protection (supra) pp87-179, 185-258 and 555-608.

this backdrop that this study seeks to examine the policies put in place to protect the rights of refugees and to bring out their legal and human rights challenges.

The development of the concept of refugee under international instruments

Relying on the Latin verse *tum tua res agitur parties cum proximus ardet*,[4] countries over the world have welcomed persons fleeing from danger in their own country to seek protection in such host countries as refugees. The fleeing from danger or persecution by people resulting in mass refugee exodus is however not a new phenomenon nor is it restricted to specific regions of the world especially as such movement of persons has been recorded as an enduring and global issue in the twentieth century.[5]

The world experienced a great influx of refugee during the period of the Great Wars when several violent conflicts and political problems especially in Europe, led to the displacement of large number of people. This mass exodus clashed with the wish of sovereign states to control immigration and led the international community to respond to the refugee issue.[6] The League of Nations did so by formulating agreements to provide for refugee protection. Such agreements related to specific refugee situations as it concerned refugees from a particular country and were thus ad hoc in nature. Moreover, they contained a group or category approach, where the sufficient and necessary conditions to achieve refugee status were that someone was outside his or her country of origin and, without the protection of the government of that state.[7] There was neither a general definition of refugee status, nor any standardized measure of international protection for refugees during this period.[8]

---

[4] Which means your interest is at stake when your neighbour's house is burning. Gerrit. J van Heuven Goedhart, *The Problem of Refugees*. Brill Nijhoff, 1953, Volume 82, p 6.
[5]Claudena M. Skran, *Refugees in Inter-War Europe: The Emergence of a Regime*. Oxford: Oxford University Press, 1995, p 4.
[6] John Vrachnas et al, *Migration and Refugee Law: Principles and Practices in Australia*. Cambridge: Cambridge University Press, 2005, p 17.
[7] Guy. S. Goodwin-Gill, *The Refugee in International Law*. Oxford: Clarendon Press, 1996, p 4.
[8] Tony Musgrave, 'Refugees' in Samuel K. N. Blay et al (ed), *Public International Law: An Australian Perspective* Melbourne: Oxford University Press, 1997, p 302.

Responding to an appeal made by the International Committee of the Red Cross to address the needs of Russian refugees, the League of Nations appointed in 1921 Fridtjof Nansen as the high Commissioner of the newly created office of the High Commissioner for Russian Refugees.[9] Nansen's mandate was extended in 1924 to accommodate Armenian and in 1928 Assyrian and Christian refugees from Turkey. The efforts of Fridtjof Nansen especially his creation of the first refugee travel documents (Nansen Passport) has been considered by some scholars as the birth of international refugee law.[10]

In responding to such case-by-case protection of persons considered as refugees, international legal instruments like the 1951 Refugee Convention; the 1967 Protocol to the Refugee Convention and the 1969 OAU Refugee Convention where put in place to address this address the shortcomings of the League of Nation. In considering who a refugee is, the 1951 Convection and its 1967 Protocol relied on the criterion of persecution as the hallmark of recognizing a refugee. They considered a refugee as anyone forced to flee his or her country and seek protection in another country due to a well-founded fear of being persecuted for political, social or religious reasons. Thus, if such a person flees his or her country on any other reason than persecution, he or she does not qualify for protection as a refugee under these instruments.

The African continent was not immune to the concept of refugee which was common because of struggles for independence from colonial rule. The prevalent notion which was geared towards pan-Africanism and anti-colonialism, proved to be a fertile ground for persons fleeing from the struggles against colonialism and apartheid.[11] This was an openness era in refugee protection considered as the golden age of African asylum consideration[12] which prompted the organization of African Unity (OAU) to adopt the Convention Governing the Specific Aspects of Refugee Problems in Africa (1969).[13] While adopting the

[9] Claudena M. Skran, 'Profiles of the First Two high commissioners' *Journal of Refugee Studies*, (1988) Vol.1, Issue 3-4, pp277-296:277.
[10] Claudena M. Skran, *Refugees in Inter-War Europe: The Emergence of a Regime.* Oxford: Oxford University Press, 1995, p 105.
[11] Jeff Crisp, 'Africa's Refugees: Patterns, Problems and Policy Challenges', *New Issues in Refugee Research.* Working paper No. 28 UNHCR (2000) pp 1-23:5.
[12] Bonaventure Rutinwa, 'The End of Asylum? The Changing Nature of Refugee Policies in Africa', *Refugee Survey Quarterly,* (2002) Vol 21, No. 1&2, pp12-41.
[13] 10011 UNTS 14691, done in September 10, 1969 (entered into force June 20, 1974).

definition of the 1951 Convention of a refugee, it added in Article 1(2) that a refugee is someone who is forced to leave his or her country due to external aggression, occupation, foreign domination or any event which has serious disturbing effects on the public life in whole or part of his or her country of origin. This definition goes beyond the notion of a refugee as a victim of persecution to incorporate victims of new types of conflicts and violence which are prevalent in Africa.[14]

Cameroon's compliance with international refugee instruments

Cameroon, through its open-door policy and coupled with its relative peaceful and conducive nature, has been a choice environment for refugees in Africa. Since 1972, Cameroon has hosted hundreds of thousands of refugees originating from neighbouring Nigeria, Chad, Rwanda, Equatorial Guinea, Democratic Republic of Congo and Central African Republic. Cameroon is a key player in the international refugee protection especially as she is a party to salient human rights protection instruments in general and refugee protection in particular. Such international instruments like the 1951 Refugee Convention; the 1967 Protocol to the Refugee Convention and the 1969 OAU Refugee Convention are supplemented by national Law No. 2005/006 of 27 July 2005 relating to the protection of refugees. These instruments consider anyone who is forced to flee his country due to persecution or insecurity because of his or her race, religion, nationality, membership in a particular social group or political opinion or due to situations of violence such as wars and seek protection in another country as a refugee.

Through such instruments, Cameroon commits itself to protecting the refugees within its territory. Cameroon plays host to over four hundred thousand refugees predominately from the Central African Republic (CAR) and Nigeria.[15] These refugees are located either in the refugee camps like Minawao in the Northern part of Cameroon which

[14] Erica Feller, 'International Refugee Protection 50 Years On: The Protection Challenges of the Past, Present and Future', IRRC September (2001) Vol 83. No 843, pp581-606 at p586.

[15] UNCHR Cameroon Factsheet January 2020 available at https://data2.unhcr.org/en/documents/details/74135 (accessed on 23 February 2021)

hosts largely refugees of Nigerian origin, the Gado refugee site[16] located in the Eastern part of the country that caters for CAR refuges or in cities like Douala and Yaoundé. Though these instruments do exist, the mechanisms instituted in protecting their rights are not hitch free. The difficulties or challenges faced in implementing the promotion and protection of refugee rights, affect the effective enjoyment of these rights.

The Protection accorded to Refugee rights in Cameroon

Cameroon has generally maintained an open border approach in welcoming refugees. Such refugees most especially the registered ones, have a right to movement which is protected both by the 1951 Refugee Convention and the 2005 Cameroon Law on refugee protection. The benefit of the right to movement is an avenue for the refugee to enjoy other rights like to choose a residence (right to housing), go to school (right to education), go in search of a job (right to employment) or go to the hospital (right to health).

In practice, restrictions are placed on this right which deeply affect the ability of refugees to access or implement many other rights which are vital to their functional integration and capacity to become independent. Given that the right to movement is mostly enjoyed by refugees who have registered their presence; deposited applications for recognition of status determination as refugees or those whose status has been successfully determined, there are still instances of harassment in the exercising of this right. Some elements of the Gendarmerie and Police corps extort money from the refugees they meet especially those that possess no documents.[17] It is not uncommon for some Police officers sometimes to feign not to recognize the document or suggest that they are bogus.[18] The result is that these restrictions augment the vulnerability and dependence of refugees, making refugees more open to

[16] The difference between a camp and site is that a refugee camp is temporal while a refugee site is more permanent with the refugee population easily interacting or integrating with the local population.

[17] This is the case especially with refugee recognized prima facie whose sole document in meant for the rationing of commodities of basic necessity and thus has no strength as a valid document to use for identification when moving around especially when outside refugee camps or designated settlement area.

[18] This is common in the rural; unlike urban, areas were some elements of law and order do not recognize at first instance identification documents concerning refugees.

corruption (e.g. paying bribes), abuse and exploitation especially on women and children who are the most vulnerable among the refugee population.[19]

Security for refugees is still an issue to be dealt with, be it in the rural or urban areas. Generally, in urban areas, the right to personal security is borne by the refugees. This is not the case when it comes to rural refugees especially those found in authorized settlements or refugee camps like those in Gado in the East Region of Cameroon or Minawao in the Far North Region. The personal security of refugees in the Eastern and Northern parts of Cameroon is not the best. Despite the deployment and stationing of the elite Rapid Intervention Battalion (better known by its French acronym BIR) in these regions, it has not assuaged attacks on this right to security. Armed groups and rebels are known to have crossed from neighbouring Chad and Central African Republic to attack, kidnap and steal from some refugees living at the outskirts the of town.[20] Additionally, the Minawao refugee camp has about two security posts; one for the police and one for the gendarmerie, to offer security for over about fifty thousand refugees. This is overwhelming and near impossible to offer protection in the refugee camp. On the other hand, the refugee camp at Gado has no security post to monitor security activities within the refugee camp.

A common avenue for discussing common issues affecting refugees can be met in their forming associations. This right to form or join an existing association is guaranteed by most human rights instruments. Of paramount concern or importance to the protection of refugees in Cameroon are the 1951 Refugee Convention, the 1969 OAU Refugee Convention and Law No. 2005/006 of 27 July 2005. The issue to note is that as concern the right to association, most of these instruments relating to refugee protection are bias as they require such associations to be socially, economically, or culturally inclined. Political associations, however peaceful or non-violent, are not recommended. The OAU Refugee Convention provides in *Article III* that refugees should refrain from carrying out subversive activities against any member state of the OAU (now the AU) and that states should ensure this by prohibiting

---

[19] Rosa da Costa, *Rights of Refugees in the Context of Integration: Legal Standards and Recommendations*. Geneva: UNHCR, 2006, p 162.

[20] United States Committee for Refugees and Immigrants, *World Survey 2008-Cameroon,* (2008) available at https://www.refworld.org/docid/485f50c66c.html (accessed on 11 February 2021).

refugees found in their territory from attacking member states. It is important to state that the OAU Refugee Convention however does not define what constitutes subversive acts from which the refugee is to abstain.

This provision has been used or broadly interpreted to clamp down on political opponents in exile especially in the host country.[21] Upholding of restrictions on political associations and by extension political rights, is balanced by promoting and preserving economic, social and cultural related associations. This defies the interrelated character of human rights of which the promotion of one right improves the other. The stifling of political rights can be used as a tool to silence dissidents from criticizing the affairs of their country of origin and thus promoting democracy. It is important to state that some former refugees usually emerge as political leaders in their countries. They can equally play crucial roles in the reform process in their country of origin. By this logic, the availability of political rights can be necessary to develop their skills for the achievement of durable solutions especially if their countries have experienced wars. Being able to undertake peaceful political activity and having a political forum in exile is often indispensable to have effective and representative interlocutors for future peace and reconciliation processes in their country of origin when they return.[22]

A permanent solution to the refugee problem is the ability for them to return to their home country if the situation has returned to normal. The refugee is generally considered to fall out of the ambit of the protection of his country of nationality that is why he sought protection in the host state. Once he is accorded protection as a refugee, his link with his country ceases and he is protected under rules of international law as well as the rules of the host state. The act of a refugee going back to his country of origin should be a voluntary and intentional act otherwise, it will not amount to a voluntary act and therefore cannot cause him to lose his protection as a refugee. If such movement is caused by duress with the complicity of the forces of law and order of the host state, it can amount to violating the principle of non-refoulement. As concerns voluntary repatriation of refugees, Cameroon signed a tripartite agreement with the Federal Republic of Nigeria and the UNHCR on

[21] Rosa da Costa, *supra*, p 170.
[22] Rosa da Costa, *supra*, p 166.

March 2, 2017, and another agreement involving the Central African Republic was signed on June 29, 2019. Though there have been instances of group repatriation of both Nigerian and CAR refugees, the most common form of repatriation practiced is of a spontaneous nature; individual and clandestine. Such a repatriation is without the knowledge or control of the Cameroonian as well as the home state authority. Due to it not being under the control and vigilance of the authorities of both the host and home state, the refugee may return to Cameroon at any time. This is most especially where the situation in the home state is still not favourable due to the existence of factors that initiated the flight into Cameroon. The volatile situation in the Central African Republic or Northern part of Nigeria is still enough to scare some refugees from opting to go home under the voluntary repatriation scheme organized by the host country Cameroon and the home states of Nigeria and CAR.[23]

The education of a refugee in particular hinges on the concepts of access, quality and protection. Access entails a completion of the educational process from the moment of enrolling to graduating at a particular stage of education. Quality on its part emphasizes on the services available in the educational process. Regarding protection the right to education, the refugee has to feel secure and safe from violence or any form of discrimination in relation to race, gender or nationality.[24] Most refugee children have not been in a school environment for usually a long period of time or have never been to school in the first place, and as such affects right to education. As regards Nigerian refugees in the Northern part of the country, there is the language problem in understanding the French language in the first place[25] or the children are above the age required at that particular stage of education; especially at

---

[23] Moki E. Kindzeka, "Hundreds of Cameroon's Central African Republic Refugees Voluntarily Repatriate" available at https://reliefweb.int/report/cameroon/hundreds-cameroons-central-african-republic-refugees-voluntarily-repatriate (accessed on 2 February 2021).

[24] See generally Sarah Dryden-Peterson, *Refugee Education: A Global Review.* Geneva: UNHCR, 2011.

[25] The official languages of Cameroon are English and French. However, French is the language of instruction in the Eastern and Northern regions of Cameroon. Host communities equally communicate in their vernacular. Most of the refugees from Central Africa speak their vernacular and understand little or no French. The Nigerian refugees understand nothing in the French language which is mostly used in the Northern part of Cameroon.

the primary level.[26] Such conditions make it difficult in facilitating integration with other classmates or for the pupil to focus. The resulting outcome is a very high rate of drop out which affects the right to education.

The quality criterion for proper effectiveness of the right to education is equally an issue for concern. This is evident with respect to infrastructure for use since schools are mostly makeshift and therefore not durable. Facilities like class benches are inadequate and it is common to see pupils - nationals and refugees inclusive, sitting on the floor to get their lessons. In situations like the Minawao camp, the existence of six primary schools and a secondary school does not foster education adequately.[27] Being one of the largest refugee camps in the country, a single school cannot satisfy the multitude of refugee children. The availability of teachers, be it in the refugee camps or rural communities hosting refugees is equally an issue for concern. The reason is that most teachers deployed to such areas, refuse to resume service in such areas and this fact affects the implementation of the right to education.

Implementing many other rights, including rights which are basic to the functional integration of refugees and their capacity to become self-reliant, such as the right to employment is very important. The right to employment is one of the rights which refugees are expected to benefit on the same par with nationals as well as other foreigners.[28]

In practice however, this is not the case due to several factors ranging from the applicable national laws, economic difficulties and even the behavior of nationals engaged in the economic sector which seriously limit refugee employment rights. Generally, foreigners (refugee inclusive) are not employed in the Cameroonian public service. Furthermore, Law No 92 -007 of 14th August 1992 on the Labour Code makes provision in *Article 27 (2)* for the Minister of Labour to endorse any contract of employment if one of the parties is a foreigner (refugee inclusive). Such provision is a drawback to Cameroon's commitment in enforcing the

---

[26]http://www.rescpectcameroun.org/index.php/projetc-2/school-return-for-2500-idps-refugees-in-cameroon/ (accessed on 5 February 2021).

[27] More information about Minawao are available at https://reliefweb.int/sites/reliefweb.int/files/resources/71301.pdf (accessed on 2 February 2021).

[28] *Articles 9* and *10* of Law No.2005/006 of 27 July 2005 relating to the status of refugees in Cameroon.

refugees' right to employment, thus making refugees reluctant to apply for better earning formal sector jobs.[29]

The guarantee of equality with nationals or foreigners in relation to the benefits accruing from gainful employment is far-fetched. This is so because some employers shy away from employing refugees out of the suspicion that they are criminals and some refugees, especially in the informal sector, receive little pay or even go for months without pay.[30] The result is that such restrictions and difficulties augment the vulnerability and dependence of refugees by creating and increasing poverty and violence. This has a particularly dire effect on women who are forced to engage in prostitution or resort to street begging to make money.[31]

The 2005 Law relating to the status of refugees in Cameroon, like the 1951 Refugee Convention which in its *Article 23*, did not expressly provide or define the right of health in its *Article 9*. These provisions simply provide as entitlement to refugees the right to benefit equally from the national welfare or public relief schemes available in the host country. These provisions can be widely interpreted to include the right to health especially if and when the health care service by the state is a public welfare.

To limit the deficiencies of the government who has the primary responsibility of developing and implementing health policies, non-governmental organisations engage in the domain of refugee healthcare. Though a commendable effort, most of their activities are limited predominately to urban cities like Yaoundé and Douala which have seen actors like the Catholic Relief Service have partnered with public hospitals. In the event where the health coverage accorded to refugees is exhausted or non-existent for certain types of treatment, the refugee's only recourse is private hospitals where access is usually beyond the purchasing power of most refugees.[32]

---

29 Emmanuel E. Mbua, "Law No. 2005/006 of 27 July 2005 Relating to the Status of Refugees in Cameroon: An Additional Hurdle or a Major Step Forward to Refugee Protection?", *Journal of Law, Policy and Globalization*, (2015), Vol.38, pp 63-77: 73.

30 Emily Mattheisen, "'Because I am a stranger' Urban Refugees in Yaoundé, Cameroon", *New Issues in Refugee Research.* (2012), Working Paper No. 244, p 4.

31 Emmanuel E. Mbua, *ibid,* Emily Mattheisen, *ibid.*

32 Morgan Walbert, ""Nous Souffrons" Examining the Problems Facing Urban Refugees in Yaoundé, Cameroon", *Independent Study Project (ISP) Collection*, (2014), Paper 1868, pp 1-40: 23.

Challenges faced in the protection of refugee in Cameroon

1. Silence of the law

The municipal legal framework is vague and ambiguous in providing for protecting certain rights of refugees. The Law No. 2005/006 of 27 July 2005 relating to the status of refugees in Cameroon, is not explicit for instance in protecting the right to health of refugees. The silence of the law on this right is a negative indicator and impediment to this right in relation to refugees of whom the old and young constitute a considerable number. This makes it a fertile ground for Cameroon to refute or downgrade its obligation with respect to the right of health of refugees. The obvious consequence is that it becomes difficult in enforcing or implementing this right in public hospitals. Besides, hospital infrastructure and personnel are in themselves not adequate. This is a phenomenon common in the North and East Regions of Cameroon where before the arrival of refugees, healthcare infrastructure and facilities were already insufficient due to many under-development issues that plague such region.[33] The seeming refurbishing or overhaul of this service, predominantly in the rural areas, has not done much effectively as problems such as overcrowding, running out of drugs and even the absence of adequate qualified personnel in the domain of mental health and psychological problems still persists.[34]

2. Financial constraints

The African Union which is the most prominent regional institution in the African continent, has a key role to play in the protection of refugees in Africa in general, especially through its office of the Special Rapporteur on Refugees, Asylum Seekers and Internally Displaced Persons. Coupled with the fact that the African Union does not have representation in all member states,[35] the result is a weak link when it comes to monitoring and enforcing the 1969 OAU

33 Veronique Barbelet, *Supporting Central African Refugees in Cameroon: Policy and Practice in Response to Protracted Displacement* (HPG Working Paper) 2017, p 7.

34 Justine G. Nzweundji *et al*, "Refugee Health Problems in the Central African Sub-Region: The Role of Traditional Medicine", *Journal of the Cameroon Academy Of Sciences,* (2019), Vol. 14 No. 3, pp 189-201: 194-196.

35 It should be stated here that the regional office of the AU located in Yaoundé (Cameroon) does not have the mandate to deal specifically with refugee matters. Its mandate is more of an agricultural nature in the prevention and control of pest See generally https://au.in/en/AUC/BCP/offices and https://www.ippc.int/en/external-cooperation/regional-plant-protection-organizations/interafricanphytosanitarycouncil/ (accessed on 10 February 2021).

Convention. Such a setback which can be attributed to absence of adequate financing, makes the load of catering for refugees in a region that produces most of the refugees in the world, overwhelming for a single Special Rapporteur located as far as in The Gambia.[36]

The Cameroon Human Rights Commission (CHRC) which replaced the National Commission on Human Rights and Freedom (NCHRF)[37] as a municipal institution is located in nine out of the ten regions in Cameroon: Far North, North, Adamawa, Littoral, Center, North West, West and South West.[38] It should be stated that the Eastern region which plays host to a huge number of refugees has no representative from the CHRC. This in itself does not advance the protection effort towards refugees especially in the Eastern region of the country. When it concerns the promotion and protection of the rights of refugees, the NCHRF usually organized workshops and seminars to sensitize especially members of the forces of law and order. It should be emphasized that, most of such seminars are organized in Yaoundé which is far from the hot zones of refugees-hosting communities of the country found mainly in towns like Bertoua or Maroua. The obvious reason for all these is the inadequate financial strength of both the state and non-state stakeholders. The protection and promotion of the rights of refugees entail huge financial wherewithal. A great source of such finances come from funding from the foreign governments or private donors. Such donors are enthusiastic to render financial assistance in order to provide tangible and lasting solutions to the problems facing refugees as well as producing them. If solutions take long to be materialized or a silver lining of hope of success shows, the donor bank begins to shrink up. This is the case with the protection of refugee rights in Cameroon especially as the situation of Boko Haram in Nigeria has not subsided for years now or in the Central African Republic where some level of calm is still not being registered.

3. Lack of political will

Though the Cameroonian state has shown some form of commitment in protecting some of the civil rights of Nigerian and Central African Republic refugees, the existence of laxity in instituting a strong political will challenges the protection of refugees in Cameroon. This laxity is a stark shift from the earlier welcoming spirit she had had towards refugees. This is evidenced in her shutting down its border with Nigeria on numerous occasions and even subjecting refugees to refoulement as was the case with some Nigerian refugees

[36] Malcolm D. Evans *et al, The African Charter on Human and Peoples' Right: The System in Practice 1986 – 2006*. Cambridge University Press, 2008, p 365.

[37] As of writing, the Cameroon Human Rights Commission is a very new institution which has officials who have been appointed to steer it.

[38] https://www.cndhl.cm//?q=fr/content/siege (last accessed 10 February 2021).

in the Northern part of the country in January 2019.[39] Not including state reporting on its refugee protection action in important national reports like the National Plan of Action for the Promotion and Protection of Human Rights is an indication of lack of political will for refugee protection. As at the time of writing, the National Plan of Action report which covered the years 2015-2019, had no mention concerning the protection of refugees. Even though Cameroon has been playing host to refugees. The lack of political will on the part of the government is evident in refugees not having a direct and free access to all levels of education. This is because the cost of education especially at the secondary and tertiary level has not been made more accessible for refugees. This makes it difficult for refugee especially in the urban centers to access such rights without scholarships to accommodate the high costs involved. Furthermore, the apparent laxity of the state that has the primary responsibility of protecting refugees, effectively implementing municipal laws, has transferred the total weight of protection to the UNHCR thereby exacerbating the logistic problem.

4. Limited mandate of protection institutions

It should be stated that the protection of the rights of refugees in Cameroon consist of actors that have a limited mandate in the promotion of human rights in general and refugee rights. Institutions like the Refugee Eligibility and Appeals Commissions are basically concerned with determining whether a person qualifies for protection as a refugee within the ambits of the applicable laws. They have little or nothing to say on the efforts made by the state in promoting the rights of such refugees whose status have been determined or those still to be determined. Additionally, the CHRC which is a very important actor in the promotion of human rights has the problem of a limited mandate. Even though this institution promotes the protection of rights or persons (refugees inclusive), this institution lacks a humanitarian mandate. This is the reason why it is not principally involved in the protection of refugees *per se* due to the reason of their falling outside the ambits of humanitarian law.

5. Suspicion of Legal Authorities

Equally there exists a *prima facie* bias or suspicion towards refugees from some elements of forces of law and order. Due to the volatile and strenuous atmosphere of insecurity especially in the Northern part of Cameroon, refugees are suspected by some elements of the forces of law and order as either being Boko Haram terrorists or their sympathizers.

---

[39] UNHCR, *Cameroon Factsheet January 2019* available at http://relief web.int/report/cameroon/unhcr-cameroon-factsheet-january-2019 (accessed on 10 February 2021).

Coupled with the fact that some of the members of the forces of law and order cannot easily identify and recognize refugee identification papers due to their unfamiliar nature, refugees are subjected to negative attitudes by those who are primarily to protect them.[40]

6. Dislike of foreigners

Even though a relatively hospitable country as seen in the number of refugees found in the rural and urban centers of the territory, there are still instances of xenophobia. This fright and in certain instances a strong dislike for foreigners has been registered in some communities hosting refugees in the Northern and Eastern parts of the country. Although most of the refugees in the rural communities of the Northern and Eastern regions of Cameroon share a common cultural identity with their host communities, xenophobia tendencies still exist. This may be due to a feeling that refugees have either overstayed in the host community or pose a risk to the community's security.[41] This raises serious challenges or setbacks to the protection of refugees in Cameroon especially as the host community cannot be left out in such a crucial humanitarian endeavor.

7. Ignorance of the refugee population

The refugee population or community does not equally pave the way for a proper protection of their rights. This is due to the fact that most of them do not even know the rights they have and as such cannot take action for enforcing it against defaulters. Some refugees equally do not understand the concept of human rights and these are the majority who see no good in sending their children to attain some level of education be it in the schools at the camps or those around the host community. Most of the refugees are not educated, some cannot speak either English or French, and as such find it difficult to integrate in the society. This results in some of them resorting to crime when the going gets tough. Such ignorance and illiteracy, make it difficult and challenging for especially non-state actors like the UNHCR to sensitize and educate them on their rights and the measures open to them to benefit and even report in situation of violation.

---

[40] Emmanuel E. Mbua, "Law No. 2005/006 of 27 July 2005 Relating to the Status of Refugees in Cameroon: An Additional Hurdle or a Major Step Forward to Refugee Protection?" *Journal of Law, Policy and Globalization*, (2015), Vol.38, pp 63-77: 74.

[41] Emmanuel E. Mbua, *ibid* and Veronique Barbelet, *supra*, p 6.

Recommendations

Article 9; which deals with the rights refugees enjoy in Cameroon, of Law No. 2005/006 of 27 July 2005 relating to the status of refugees in Cameroon, should be revised to explicitly provide for the promotion and protection of certain rights like that of health and nutrition. This will enable a rounded and holistic approach in the legal rights provided and protected by the municipal law.

There is need to recruit more personnel in the domain of refugee protection as well as expand the mandate of some institutions. In this regard, the protection mandate of municipal institution like Cameroon Human Rights Commission, should be expanded to cover the promotion and protection of the humanitarian concerns of refugees who first and foremost are human beings before becoming refugees.

An effective education in emergency program should be implemented in order to cater for refugee education. This is so because most of the refugee children do not go to school especially (but not limited) in the rural hosting communities due to financial inadequacies or even parental reluctance. Those who attend are above the class required age, understand little or no lessons taught in the French or English languages. More especially teaching is done in usually over-crowded and less equipped classrooms.[42]

The Cameroonian government should adopt a hands-on approach in the promotion of refugee rights. This can be by way of preventing and punishing perpetrators of violence or refoulement against refugees or engaging in state reporting of efforts taken in the protection of their rights in key reports like the National Plan of Action for the Promotion and Protection of Human Rights to create awareness.

Adequate sensitization of both members of refugee hosting communities and forces of law and order should be undertaken. Such host communities will be able to understand that being a refugee is not a choice but a misfortune of circumstances. The forces of law and order on their part will be able to recognize and identify refugee documents and as such enable refugees exercise the right to freely move and reside in Cameroon in their quest for a safe haven. The sensitization should equally be geared at the refugees themselves. Targeting them will enable them to know their rights and the approaches to use in the face of violations.

[42] In primary and early secondary schools.

Conclusion

To protect the rights of refugees, Cameroon has ratified international refugee protection instruments. She has equally enacted municipal legislation to address the situation of refugees in her country. This has seen refugees benefitting some form of protection of their rights. However, some basic rights of which refugees are entitled to enjoy and benefit, such as health and freedom of movements, are not fully realized. The perceived reason for such ineffectiveness is either total silence in the laws protecting these rights, financial constraints of institutions concerned with the protection of human rights in general or refugee rights in particular, the lack of political will and xenophobia. It is therefore important for the government institute measures that will render the effective protection of the rights of refugees in Cameroon.

La différence juridique entre réfugiés et déplacés internes sous le prisme du droit international en situation de conflit armé

Thomas Ojong

Lecturer of Law
Faculty of Laws and Political Science
University of Buea, Cameroon

Résumé

Cette étude porte sur les mouvements et déplacements de population massifs, contraints et collectifs qui marquent l'histoire récente des migrations de proximité qui surviennent à l'intérieur des territoires comme vers des pays voisins; Il s'agit des *déplacés* et *réfugiés* dont la présente étude considère comme deux statuts distincts des victimes d'exode en situation de conflit armé, deux sujets du droit international humanitaire qui obéissent, certes, à des régimes d'encadrement non identiques, mais convergent du point de vu de leurs objectifs.

Abstract

This paper focuses on the massive, forced and collective movements and displacements of populations that mark the recent history of local migrations occurring within territories as well as to neighboring countries. These are internally displaced persons (IDPs) and refugees whom this study considers as two distinct categories of victims of displacement in a situation of armed conflict. They equeally constitute two subjects of international humanitarian law with different framework regimes, nonetheless, converging from the point of view of their objectives.

Introduction

Bien que les débats sur les catégorisations demeurent ouverts et prêtent de plus en plus à controverses, la littérature pertinente sur les phénomènes migratoires classe souvent les migrants en deux grandes catégories : d'un côté, les migrants « volontaires » ou « spontanés », de l'autre, les migrants « involontaires » ou « forcés »[1]. Il s'agit d'un classement qui se fonde sur le pouvoir de décision des acteurs[2]. Comme le souligne R. Bocco, « le migrant "volontaire" serait essentiellement un migrant "économique " qui opère rationnellement et librement des choix de départ et de retour, alors que le migrant "involontaire" agirait dans un contexte contraignant qui empêche ou réduit fortement toute possibilité de choix »[3].

Cette étude porte sur les mouvements et déplacements de population massifs, contraints et collectifs qui marquent l'histoire récente des migrations de proximité qui surviennent à l'intérieur des territoires comme vers des pays voisins. En effet, de nombreux pays connaissent des troubles d'origines diverses, telles les guerres civiles, les conflits à caractère sécessionniste, irrédentiste ou interethnique, toutes ces violences étant génératrices d'exodes. Il s'agit des mobilités sous contrainte ou migration forcées de grande ampleur survenant en réponse

---

[1] R. Bocco, « Migrations, démocratisation, médiations : enjeux locaux et internationaux au Moyen-Orient » *in* R. Bocco et M. Djalili (eds) : *Moyen-Orient : migrations, démocratisation, médiations. Presses Universitaires de France*, 1993, pp. 9-29.

[2] D'emblée, il faut reconnaître que cette distinction fondée sur le libre-arbitre prête de plus en plus à controverses. À partir de quel seuil de contrainte, une migration volontaire devient-elle involontaire ? Les mobiles de l'exode se sont tellement complexifiés qu'ils ne permettent plus de dissocier facilement les deux groupes et la migration dite « volontaire » comporte de plus en plus un certain niveau de contrainte. Sur cette question, lire V. Lassailly-Jacob, « Migrants malgré eux. Une proposition de typologie », *in* V. Lassailly-Jacob, J-Y. Marchal et A. Quesnel (dir.), *Déplacés et réfugiés : la mobilité sous contrainte*, Paris, *Editions de l'Institut de Recherche pour le Développement* (IRD), collection Colloques et Séminaires, 1999, pp. 27- 48.

[3] R. Bocco, op. *cit.*, p. 13. Pour compléter cette distinction, Sauvain-Dugerdil et Preiswerk, ajoutent que dans le premier cas, « on part pour essayer de mieux vivre » alors que, dans le second, « on part pour fuir l'insupportable ». (« Vers un ailleurs prometteur ... », in *Vers un ailleurs prometteur. L'émigration, une réponse universelle a une situation de crise ?*), Cahiers de l'Institut universitaire d'études du développement, Genève et *Presses Universitaires de France*, Paris, 1993, pp. 15-26 (spéc. p. 24).

à des contextes de crises aiguës, violence politique, catastrophe ou destruction environnementale ou des situations de violence issues de conflits armés. Toutefois, cette entité fait référence à de multiples mouvements. Les termes de « réfugiés », « déplacés », « expulsés », « refoulés », « dispersés », « évacués », « chassés », « regroupés », « sinistrés » ou « victimes » s'appliquent aux individus ou aux groupes qui, tous, quittent leur lieu de résidence sous une contrainte externe impérative. Cette diversité de dénominations atteste de la multiplicité des mouvements et nous impose de préciser que cette contribution se limite à exposer les éléments d'une différence juridique entre réfugiés et déplacés internes pris sous le prisme du droit international. Les termes de *déplacés* et *réfugiés* sont utilisés, ici, à la fois dans le sens de leur définition première et dans celui, juridique, beaucoup plus restrictif, des organismes onusiens. Il en ressort que ces catégories constituent, d'une part, deux statuts distincts des victimes d'exode en situation de conflit armé **(I),** et d'autre part deux sujets du droit international humanitaire qui obéissent, certes, à des régimes d'encadrement non identiques, mais convergent du point de vue de leurs objectifs **(II).**

I. Refugiés et déplacés internes: deux statuts distincts des victimes d'exode en situation de conflit armé

Au 31 décembre 2021, le Haut Commissariat pour les réfugiés (HCR) recensait à l'échelle mondiale plus de 84 millions de personnes forcées de fuir leur foyer; Près de 26.6 millions étaient considérées comme « réfugiés » relevant de la compétence du HCR et près de 50.9 millions, comme « déplacés internes »[4]. Ces populations, qui fuient collectivement des situations de violence issues de conflits armés, appartiennent à la catégorie des réfugiés dans le sens où elles cherchent refuge dans un autre lieu pour échapper à un danger, se mettre en sécurité. Toutefois, la

[4]https://www.unhcr.org/statistics/unhcrstats/618ae4694/mid-year-trends-2021.html. (Consulté le 31/01/2022). Pour ce qui est de l'Afrique, les tendances globales indiquent 12.031.815 personnes relevant de la compétence du HCR, 1.572.780 réfugiés et demandeurs d'asile, 7.310.834 déplacés internes. Relativement au Cameroun, les tendances nationales globales indiquent au 31/12/2021 que les personnes concernées représentent 1.926.285. Soit une population réfugiée équivalente à 466.263; 575.507 déplacés internes dans les régions du nord-ouest/sud-ouest; 357.631 déplacés internes dans la région de l'Extrême Nord et 8.031 demandeurs d'asile. Voir Situation Bureau régional pour l'Afrique de l'Ouest et du Centre. http://data2.unhcr.org/fr/situations/rbwca.

législation internationale a créé trois groupes de réfugiés en fonction du statut qu'elle leur a reconnu : les « réfugiés statutaires » et les « réfugiés clandestins » qui sont des déplacés vers des pays voisins **(A)** et les « déplacés internes » qui trouvent refuge à l'intérieur du territoire national **(B)**.

A. Réfugiés : des déplacés vers les pays voisins

Relativement au statut de réfugiés, la législation internationale fait une claire distinction entre ceux qui sont enregistrés, réfugiés conventionnels ou statutaires **(1)** et ceux qui ne le sont pas, réfugiés clandestins **(2)**.

1. Les réfugiés conventionnels

Les « réfugiés statutaires ou conventionnels » sont enregistrés comme tels, car ils franchissent une frontière et répondent aux critères de la Convention de Genève de 1951, complétée par le Protocole de New York de 1967. En Afrique, ces instruments législatifs furent amendés par la Convention de l'OUA (Organisation de l'unité africaine), convention régionale relative aux problèmes spécifiques des réfugiés en Afrique. Le HCR s'est vu reconnaître par la communauté internationale une triple compétence à l'égard de ces réfugiés, en leur apportant une protection juridique internationale, une assistance matérielle et en recherchant des solutions durables à leur situation. Les réfugiés, au sens juridique du terme, sont assistés dans des camps ou bien sont aidés à s'installer dans un pays tiers. Notons que, dans les pays du Sud, le statut de réfugié est concédé en bloc à tous ceux qui franchissent en masse une frontière, tant que le pays qu'ils fuient est reconnu comme étant en guerre.

2. Les réfugiés clandestins

Il s'agit des « réfugiés de fait », c'est-à-dire ceux qui vivent une situation de réfugiés sans être reconnus comme tels par le droit international. En effet, ils franchissent une frontière et se fondent dans le milieu rural ou dans les villes, vivant en clandestins dans le pays d'accueil. Dans les pays du Sud, cette forme d'exode est la plus fréquemment adoptée par des populations frontalières qui ont des affinités ethniques de l'autre côté de la frontière. Très souvent, on donne le nom de « dispersés » à ces réfugiés qui ne sont ni enregistrés, ni assistés. Les « *boat people* » fuyant aujourd'hui le Vietnam, Cuba ou Haïti, appelés aussi « réfugiés de la mer », sont considérés comme réfugiés clandestins et traités comme tels.

B. Déplacés internes : des réfugiés de l'intérieur du territoire national

A la réalité, Il n'existe pas de définition juridique de qui constitue une « personne déplacée interne (PDI) » en droit international. La notion de personnes déplacées internes que la communauté internationale utilise le plus couramment est celle qui se trouve dans les « Principes directeurs relatifs au déplacement de personnes à l'intérieur de leur propre pays »[5]. Aux fins de ces Principes directeurs, le terme « déplacement interne » décrit des situations dans lesquelles des personnes ou des groupes de personnes sont forcés ou contraints à fuir ou à quitter leur foyer ou leur lieu de résidence habituel, mais qui restent à l'intérieur des frontières de leur pays[6].

Deux éléments sont décisifs dans l'identification des PDI : (1) le caractère coercitif ou involontaire du mouvement, et (2) le fait qu'un tel mouvement a lieu à l'intérieur des frontières nationales. Ce second élément permet de les distinguer des réfugiés, qui sont aussi des déplacés involontaires, mais qui franchissent des frontières étatiques internationalement reconnues. Cette deuxième condition doit être comprise au sens large. Il est significatif que les Principes directeurs ne se réfèrent pas à la notion de citoyenneté, indiquant ainsi que les étrangers peuvent également être qualifiés de PDI. En revanche, la référence au « foyer ou lieu de résidence habituel » indique que leur présence dans le pays concerné ne peut pas être de nature temporaire, mais doit avoir atteint un degré de permanence. D'où les catégories suivantes de personnes pouvant être qualifiées de PDI[7] :

• Les citoyens déplacés à l'intérieur du pays concerné ;

• Les anciens réfugiés qui sont revenus dans leur pays d'origine, mais qui sont dans l'incapacité de retourner dans leur ancien foyer ou de trouver une autre solution durable par le biais de l'intégration socio-économique dans une autre partie du pays ;

---

[5] Doc. ONU E/CN.4/1998/53/Add. 2 du 11 février 1998).

[6] Principes directeurs relatifs au déplacement de personnes à l'intérieur de leur propre pays, Introduction, paragraphe 2.

[7] Voir: La protection des personnes déplacées à l'intérieur de leur propre pays: Manuel à l'intention des législateurs et des responsables politiques préparé par Rhodri C. Williams, Institut Brookings, Université de Berne : projet sur les déplacements internes, 2008, p.12.

• Les personnes apatrides qui ont leur résidence habituelle dans le pays concerné ;

• Les citoyens d'un autre pays qui vivent là depuis longtemps (voire même depuis des générations) et qui ont largement perdu contact avec leur pays d'origine ;

• Les citoyens d'un autre pays qui ont leur résidence habituelle dans le pays concerné parce qu'ils ont été acceptés de façon permanente ou pour une période prolongée.

II. Refugiés et déplacés internes : deux sujets du droit international humanitaire à régime d'encadrement non identique mais convergeant

Malgré l'existence d'un dispositif juridique d'encadrement distinct entre réfugiés et déplacés internes **(A),** on note une convergence dans les réponses apportées en guise de traitement **(B).**

A. Des dispositifs juridiques d'encadrement distincts entre réfugiés et déplacés internes

Alors que le statut de réfugiés est encadré par un dispositif juridique international varié voire universel **(1),** le déplacement interne n'est pas un statut légal et par voie de conséquence de simples principes directeurs sont prévus au plan international bien qu'un pas géant soit accompli en Afrique avec la Convention de Kampala **(2).**

1. Le dispositif juridique varié d'encadrement du statut légal de réfugiés

La Convention des Nations Unies de 1951 relative au statut des réfugiés et le Protocole relatif au statut des réfugiés de 1967, la Convention de l'OUA de 1969 régissant les aspects propres aux problèmes des réfugiés en Afrique, la Convention de 1979 sur l'élimination de toutes les formes de discrimination à l'égard des femmes, la Charte africaine des droits de l'homme et des peuples de 1981 et le Protocole de 2003 à la Charte africaine des droits de l'homme et des peuples relatif aux droits des femmes en Afrique, la Charte africaine de 1990 des droits et du bien-être de l'enfant, le Document de 1994 d'Addis-Abeba sur les réfugiés et le déplacement forcé des populations en Afrique, et autres instruments pertinents de l'Union africaine et des Nations Unies sur les droits de l'homme, ainsi que les résolutions pertinentes du Conseil de Sécurité[8] constituent le vaste arsenal législatif encadrant le statut de réfugiés.

2. Des principes directeurs relatifs au déplacement de personnes à l'intérieur de leur pays et la Convention de l'Union Africaine sur la protection et l'assistance aux personnes déplacées en Afrique (Convention de Kampala)

Contrairement aux cas des réfugiés, les déplacements internes de population ne concernent qu'un seul État : celui dans lequel les personnes se déplacent. Théoriquement, dans l'ordre international où se juxtaposent des souverainetés étatiques, ce déplacement n'appelle pas une attention particulière de la part du droit international, car il n'y a pas de franchissement de frontières. Il n'a d'ailleurs pas donné lieu à la mise au point d'un statut conventionnel de personne déplacée, comme il y a un statut de réfugié. Cependant, la question des déplacements internes fait l'objet de textes au niveau régional et d'activités de la part de la communauté internationale depuis quelques années.

En effet, depuis leur adoption le 11 février 1998, les Principes directeurs ont été reconnus quasi unanimement comme étant le point de départ juridique pour traiter les cas de déplacement interne. Les chefs d'Etat et de gouvernement, réunis en septembre 2005 à New York à l'occasion du Sommet mondial, ont considéré que les Principes directeurs constituent un « cadre international important pour la protection des personnes déplacées », une adhésion réitérée à maintes reprises par l'Assemblée générale. Au niveau régional, des organisations régionales telles que l'Union africaine, l'Organisation des Etats américains et le Conseil de l'Europe ont enjoint leurs Etats membres à utiliser les Principes directeurs et à les incorporer dans leurs normes juridiques internes. C'est donc en reconnaissance de ces principes que le 22 Octobre 2009, les États africains ont adopté la Convention de l'Union africaine sur la protection et l'assistance des personnes déplacées en Afrique, connue sous le nom de Convention de Kampala. Il s'agit du tout premier et le seul instrument régional juridiquement contraignant au monde pour la protection et l'assistance des personnes déplacées de tout un continent. Y sont identifiés les droits et les garanties concernant la protection des personnes contre les déplacements forcés et la protection et l'aide qu'il convient de leur apporter au cours du processus de

[8] A l'instar de la Résolution N° 2198 (xxI) adoptée par l'Assemblée générale des Nations Unies.

déplacement, et les droits applicables dans la phase qui suit le déplacement, quand le retour ou d'autres solutions durables deviennent possibles. Il est important de souligner que c'est aux autorités nationales qu'incombent en premier lieu le devoir et la responsabilité de fournir une protection et une aide humanitaire sans discrimination aux personnes déplacées à l'intérieur de leur propre pays qui relèvent de leur juridiction. Toutefois, à leur demande ou sur proposition de leurs services, les organisations humanitaires internationales et d'autres parties concernées peuvent venir en aide aux personnes déplacées dans le respect des normes et codes de conduite internationaux sans pour autant que cela soit considéré comme un acte d'ingérence dans les affaires intérieures de l'Etat.

B. La convergence des objectifs humanitaires de traitement de réfugiés et déplacés internes : assister, protéger et réduire la vulnérabilité

Les personnes réfugiées ou déplacées sont, au même titre que les autres hommes et femmes, titulaires de droits de l'homme et de libertés en vertu du droit international. C'est une population qui a besoin d'assistance et de protection. Le droit humanitaire et les interventions de la communauté internationale vont dans ces deux directions. L'humanitaire comprend les normes traditionnelles du droit humanitaire mais également des droits sociaux, économiques et culturels, traduits sous forme de besoins essentiels, plutôt que sous la forme de droits. La communauté internationale fait écho à ces besoins dans ses documents de travail, rapports et résolutions. Ces besoins rassemblent tout ce qui est utile à une population en exode forcé. Les plus urgents concernent l'eau, le matériel de chauffage, le matériel pour construire des abris, les vêtements, la nourriture et les soins médicaux. S'ajoute à cela l'assistance pour les victimes de traumatisme. Et enfin, le déplacement ayant globalement tendance à s'allonger dans la durée, la population a besoin de mener des activités dans la région d'accueil dont l'équilibre économique, social et écologique peut être complètement dévasté. Cela passe également par l'éducation des enfants et leur prise en mains s'ils sont orphelins.

Certes, le droit international ne traite pas de manière spécifique du sort des déplacés internes, mais cela ne signifie pas qu'ils ne sont pas protégés par le droit. En fait, les trois corpus juridiques constitués du droit international des droits de l'homme[9], le droit international humanitaire[10] et le droit pénal international fournissent un cadre juridique global pour la protection dans toutes les situations de déplacement forcé hors des frontières nationales ou à l'intérieur, y compris pendant un conflit armé.

---

[9] Voir les Principaux instruments des droits de l'homme que sont la *Déclaration universelle des droits de l'homme (DUDH)* de 1948, le *Pacte international relatif aux droits civils et politiques (PIDCP)*, le *Pacte international relatif aux droits économiques, sociaux et culturels (PIDESC)* renforcés par un certain nombre d'instruments régionaux des droits de l'homme.

[10] Voir Règles 129-133 du *Droit international humanitaire coutumier : Volume I : Règles*, CICR, 2005. Voir aussi Art. 49 de la Quatrième Convention de Genève et Art. 17 du Protocole additionnel II.

Land scarcity, ethnic rivalry and conflict between the Wimbum and Mbororo of Donga-Mantung, Cameroon

Emile Sunjo

Department of International Relations and Conflict Resolution,
University of Buea, Cameroon
Email: emile.sunjo@ubuea.cm

and

Nyadi Francios Ndzi

PhD Conflict Resolution Student,
University of Buea Cameroon.
Email: francoisnyadi@yahoo.com

Abstract

This paper explores the reasons for the persistence of inter-ethnic conflict between the Mbororo and the Wimbum people of Donga Mantung Division, Cameroon. It also identifies what accounts for the recurrence of conflict between the two communities and examines the manifestations and the consequences. The paper is based on in-depth Key Informant Interviews (KIIs), Focus Group Discussions (FGD) and documentary analysis. The findings reveal that competition over scarce land, lack of conflict-sensitive development programming, politicization of ethnicity, ethnic rivalry, elite mobilization, and proximity to Nigeria make it easy for cross-border illegal trade in arms to flourish. These are the key issues that influence the persistence of the conflict despite the effort of stakeholders in managing the conflict and building sustainable peace. For the two ethnic groups to peacefully co-exist, the paper recommends a more inclusive approach to peacebuilding which tries to depoliticise ethnic differences. It also implores government agencies and other stakeholders to strengthen cooperation between the main development associations of the rival groups and promote conflict-sensitive development in the area as a peacebuilding strategy.

Key Words: Land, ethnic conflict, Wimbum, Mbororo, Donga-Mantung, Cameroon.

Introduction

Christopher Allan Miller and Mary King contend that conflict is a disagreement or a clash of views between two or more parties/groups aspiring towards incompatible/competitive means or ends.[1] Similarly, Stephan Wolf argues that conflict as a situation in which two or more actors pursue incompatible goals, whereby one of the actors experiences damage and the other actor causes this damage intentionally or ignores it.[2] He further posits that inter-ethnic conflict is a type of conflict in which the goals of at least one conflict party are defined in ethnic terms, and in which the primary fault line of confrontation is one of the ethnic distinctions.

Inter-ethnic conflicts involve distinct plural societies living in a certain geographical area while intra-ethnic conflicts involve internal feuds within a singular ethnic identity. The typical reasons that lie at the heart of inter-ethnic conflicts across the board have been the fear of their physical safety and survival especially when ethnic groups are evenly matched and neither can absorb the other politically, economically, or culturally; the spread of hate speech; competition over scarce resources and the collective fear of the future. Anders Wivel argues that with these common reasons in place, the security dilemma takes hold, with groups acting to ensure their safety and security against the other party in the conflict.[3] This makes groups fearful, and conflict becomes more likely to occur. According to Ishwari Bhattarai, ethnic activists and political entrepreneurs, operating within groups reinforce these fears of physical insecurity and polarize the society and drive ethnic groups further apart. In the same light, these between-group and within-group strategic interactions produce a toxic brew of distrust and suspicion that can explode into murderous violence up to and including the systematic slaughter of one people by another.[4]

---

[1] Miller, C. A., & King, M. E. (2005). A glossary of terms and concepts in peace and conflict studies.

[2] Wolf, S. (2006). *Ethnic Conflict: A Global Perspective.* Oxford University Press. Oxford, New York.

[3] Wivel, A. (2011). Security dilemma. *International Encyclopedia of political science*, *7*, 2389-91

[4] Bhattarai, I. (2015). Ethnic Entrepreneurs and Political Mobilization: Exploring a Case of Tharu-Pahadi Conflict. *Dhaulagiri Journal of Sociology and Anthropology*, *9*, 191-208.

In the early 1990s, a wave of ethnic conflict swept across parts of Eastern Europe, the former Soviet Union, and Africa. This is clearly demonstrated by David Lake and Donald Rothchild, who posit that localities, states, and sometimes whole regions have been engulfed in convulsive fits of ethnic insecurity, violence and, occasionally, genocide.[5] For Bjorn Hettne, ethnicity has been moulded by heterogeneous historical experiences and divergent contextual specificities, to become an inevitable concept as ethnic identities can be manipulated for political purposes and thereby transformed.[6] Inter-ethnic conflict is understood here as organized violent conflict between two or more ethnic groups especially when they are unable to manage their cultural diversity. In the same vein, Dhananjayan Sriskandarajah maintains that diverse developing countries feature prominently on the list of countries that have suffered from civil war and insurgency in recent decades.[7] Donald Horowitz considers tensions arising from ethnic diversity to have been the principal trigger of genocide in Rwanda, violent riots in the Democratic Republic of Congo, civilian mass killings in Burundi, army killings in Uganda and repeated hostilities in Chad that have occurred since the 1990s.[8]

John Mbaku argues that this has been a common occurrence not just at the global stage but equally in Cameroon where there exist over 250 ethnic groups with five of those ethnic groups in Donga Mantung Division.[9] Though the roots of some of these inter-ethnic conflicts predate the colonial era, most arose from increased identity consciousness among and between ethnic groups during the colonial period, caused by undue advantages given to particular chiefdoms and the redrawing of ethnic borders by the successive German and British colonial administrations.[10] Most inter-ethnic conflicts are anchored on

---

[5] Lake, D. A., & Rothchild, D. (1996). Containing fear: The origins and management of ethnic conflict. *International security*, *21*(2), 41-75.

[6] Hettne, B. (1993). The dynamics of ethnic conflicts. *Ethnicity and Nationalism: Formation of Identity and Dynamics of Conflict in the 1990s. Goteborg, Nordnes Padrigu Peace & Development Research Institute, Gothenburg University.*

[7] Sriskandarajah, D. (2005). Towards a political economy of Sri Lanka's 'ethnic' conflict.

[8] Horowitz, D. L. (2000). *Ethnic groups in conflict, updated edition with a new preface.* Univ of California Press.

[9] Mbaku, J. M. (2005). *Culture and customs of Cameroon.* Greenwood Publishing Group.

[10] Mbah, E. M. (2009). Disruptive colonial boundaries and attempts to resolve land/boundary disputes in the Grasslands of Bamenda, Cameroon. *African Journal on Conflict Resolution*, *9*(3).

land, with ethnic communities expressing opposing land ownership claims and differences over boundaries.[11] Besides, there is the issue of a hierarchical classification of Fondoms which gives room for some of the Fons to lord over those who rank below them.[12] Lang argues that this sort of power display makes an already bad situation worse and tends to threaten peace, induce population displacement, cause property destruction, and slow local development.[13]

The Mbororo came to the Grassfields as cattle pastoralists. They met the local Grassfields population who made a living from farming and hunting. In the initial phase of their coexistence, the two ethnic groups occupied distinct economic niches. At a later stage, members of both groups began to diversify their economic activities, a process encouraged by the colonial and post-colonial administration. Most Mbororos have become agro-pastoralists. They combine transhumance with limited subsistence agriculture in which they partially rely on the assistance of their Grassfields neighbours[14] Conversely, many enterprising Grassfielders decided to invest in cattle husbandry. While for some it was only a temporary venture, others succeeded in building up considerable herds which they tend to entrust to salaried herdsmen.

Despite these processes of economic diversification, the two groups are still associated with distinct economic activities; Grassfielders count as farmers and Mbororo as cattle herders. These identifications reflect individuals' self-understanding as well as their perception by others, including neighbouring groups and state agents. These are complex ethnic-occupational identities that are rooted in the groups' economic practices at the time of their establishment in the Grassfields, but no longer correspond to current economic practices.[15] Many Grassfields and Mbororo interlocutors described the relationship between their two groups as generally amicable, though overshadowed by frequent farmer-herder disputes which result from incidents of crop damage and mutual

---

[11] Lang, M. K. (2019). Inter-Ethnic Conflict Management and Prevention in Cameroons Northwest: Assessing the Role of the Justice and Peace Commission of the Catholic Archdiocese of Bamenda. *Asian Journal of Peacebuilding, 7.*

[12] See decree No. 77/245 of 15 July 1977 governing the organization of traditional chiefdoms in Cameroon.

[13] Lang, M. K. (2019). Inter-Ethnic Conflict Management and Prevention in Cameroons Northwest

[14] Pelican, M. (2006). Getting along in the Grassfields-interethnic relations and identity politics in Northwest Cameroon.

[15] Ibid

encroachment. The quest for grazing land in an environment of an increasing population of farmers puts the Mbororos in daily conflicts with their neighbouring farmers. The Mbororos became regarded as "undesirable aliens" and the local farming population clamoured for their expulsion.[16]

The paper is based on fieldwork undertaken in September 2020 in Donga Mantung Division. During which twenty-three interviews and six focus group discussions were conducted (undertaken in English, Pidgin or Limbum) with men, women, and youths from Wimbum and Mbororo communities, state bureaucrats and traditional authorities. Materials from the Cameroonian press and archival documents from the Buea National Archives Annex supplement our primary data.

After this introduction there is an analysis of the drivers of the conflict, which is followed by a discussion on the major actors involved in the conflict. The next two sections focus on the impact of the conflict and the peacebuilding measures that have been employed so far to manage it.

Drivers of conflict between the Wimbum and Mbororo

The causes of conflict between the Wimbum and Mbororo in the Donga Mantung are both multidimensional and complex. According to Sisay Gebre-Egziabher, to include historical, political, economic, social, and cultural factors.[17] Similarly, as the results from key informants and Focus Group Discussion (FGD) participants indicated a blend of factors causes the inter-ethnic conflict between the Wimbum and the Mbororo.

Scarcity and competition over land

In Cameroon like elsewhere across the global south, land is the most vital basis for the livelihood of the people. Almost all Cameroonians depend on the utilization of land for their daily survival. Because of population growth and environmental degradation, land becoming increasingly scarce. As Sunjo and Page have argued, the possession of land means access to many other resources and therefore land often

---

[16] Amadou, J. M. (2017). The Mbororo problem in North West Cameroon a historical investigation. *American Academic Scientific Research Journal for Engineering, Technology, and Sciences, 33*(1), 37-48.

[17] Gebre-Egziabher, S. (2007). What Role Should Civil Society Organizations Play to Address Ethnic Conflicts in Ethiopia?

holds a high economic value. In addition, communities often have a strong emotional and symbolic attachment to the land and the resources on it. Thus, competition for control of valuable land can cause or sustain conflict.[18] The Wimbum and the Mbororo inter-ethnic conflict has in many ways been driven by and sustained by competition over land resources. As one government informant declared, "the Wimbum-Mbororo inter-ethnic conflict is partly caused by competition over land resources (forest, grazing fields and farmland)."[19] As different studies and surveys have contended, the Wimbum and Mbororo communities are vulnerable to infertility of land and climate change which has increasing caused limited rainfall over the years. In the area, land per capita productivity is declining in from overuse. As a result, due to such decrease in arable and pastoral land, the Wimbum and the Mbororo compete over control of the available land (grazing fields, forests and farmlands). This was the principal cause of the violent clashes between the two communities in 1996, which have since become a regular occurrence.

Moreover, population pressure has heightened the competition over the land and produced conflict between the opposing communities. An average Wimbum nuclear family size has about four members. The increase in the population of the Wimbum led to a corresponding increase in the quest for farmland meanwhile the Mbororo occupied large portions for grazing as they no longer practice transhumance. Therefore, there is a dense population settlement on a very limited surface area made up mostly of the Wimbum. This dense population settlement and scarcity of arable land with other factors, in turn, produce a tense relationship between the Wimbum with the neighbouring ethnic groups like the Mbororo. This often then escalates to violent clashes with the least trigger.

In his work titled "Environment, Scarcity, and Violence" Thomas Homer-Dixon[20] states five general types of violent conflicts caused by environmental/resource scarcity. Among the types of conflicts he identifies, the first two seem to be relevant in understanding the

---

[18] Sunjo, E. and Page, B. (2022). Land restitution and conflict in Cameroon: the case of the Bakweri. African Affairs (forthcoming)

[19] Interview with George Ncham, Delegate of Agriculture for Donga Mantung Division, Nkambe, 13 September 2020.

[20] Homer-Dixon Thomas F. (1999). *Environment, Scarcity, and Violence.* Princeton: Princeton University Press

Wimbum-Mbororo inter-ethnic conflict. These include (1) disputes arising directly from local environmental degradation and (2) ethnic clashes arising from population migration and deepened social cleavages due to environmental scarcity.

In general, the inter-ethnic conflict between the Wimbum and the Mbororo is caused by competition over scarce land resources. The scarcity of land stems from environmental degradation and population pressure, particularly of Wimbum. A government official narrates that "competition over scarce resources has been one key cause of the repeated clashes between the Wimbum and Mbororo inter-ethnic groups.

The politicization of ethnicity and ethnic mobilization

In the inter-ethnic conflict between the Wimbum and the Mbororo, ethnicity is the most potent tool for group mobilization, and it gives enough grounds for local elites to compete along ethnic lines. Instrumentalist scholars, Raymond Taras and Rajat Ganguly state that politicized ethnicity is the construction of elites to gain political as well as an economic advantage for their groups as well as for themselves.[21] As a most government official interviewed for this paper stressed, in the Wimbum-Mbororo inter-ethnic conflict, ethnic identity had been manipulated to become the prime trigger of tensions and conflict.[22] Political and economic elites are actively involved in the manipulation of ethnic identities and often resort to the use of armed militias composed of mostly young people. This aligns with Mesfin Getachew's assertation that the politicization of ethnicity involves the preservation of ethnic groups and their distinctiveness and transforming them into political conflict groups.[23]

The proliferation of arms and the security dilemma

Security factors also contribute significantly to creating a cycle of conflict between the Wimbum and the Mbororo. There is a high circulation of illegal arms from Nigeria especially in the context of the

---

[21] Taras, R., & Ganguly, R. (2015). *Understanding ethnic conflict.* Routledge.

[22] Interview with George Ncham

[23] Getachew, M. (2006). Ethnicity and ethnic conflict in post-federal Ethiopia: a case of Mai'so District conflict between Oromos and Somalis. *EPU Research Papers*, *3*(6).

Anglophone separatist conflict.[24] Having this chance, many people got the opportunity to buy and own weapons. As Stanley Ehiane et al argue, the fundamental implication of small arms accumulation and circulation is in its tendency to pave the ground for higher risk of violent and/or armed conflict.[25] The supply of arms stimulates violence instead of dialogue and has many undesirable effects. Before the outbreak of the Anglophone conflict, Dane guns were used during Wimbum traditional ceremonies and at the time, having a gun was considered a symbol of wealth and respect. Therefore, to be respected and accepted by society every household capable of buying would have a gun. Having a gun was considered as a means of self-protection, protecting ethnic members, villages, and properties, and guaranteeing security. However, the situation became different in the context of the Anglophone conflict as separatists smuggled arms to fight against the government and those they considered sellouts or "blacklegs". As one Wimbum key informant claimed,

> there is a weak and inadequate security sector that can respond to conflicts in Donga Mantung. For example, the security forces were very late in preventing as well as managing violent clashes between the Wimbum and the Mbororo.[26]

In general, the easy availability of small arms is one of the contributing factors for Wimbum-Mbororo inter-ethnic conflict.

As United Nations Security Council (UNSC) Report (2015) indicates, the widespread availability of small arms and light weapons and their ammunition is a key enabler of conflict. In the study area, there is a weak legal and security system that can control the circulation of illicit arms. This means that the poor management and control of illicit arms escalated inter-personal clashes into inter-ethnic conflict. Regarding the issue, UNSC confirmed that poor weapons management is an area of alarming concern in today's world. Above all, the causes of Wimbum-Mbororo inter-ethnic conflict could be understood through the lens of the security dilemma. For instance, in 2019, because of the tensions between both ethnic groups, separatist fighters in Fuh shot and killed a Mbororo indigene at close range. The Mbororo in response strengthened

[24] Sunjo, E and Page, B. (forthcoming). Where politics and geography meet: security and conflict on the Cameroon-Nigeria border. *Routledge Encyclopedia of African Studies*

[25] Ehiane, S. O., & Uwizeyimana, D. D. (2018). Challenges in combating the proliferation of small arms and light weapons (SALW) in Nigeria: a human security perspective. *Journal of African Foreign Affairs*, *5*(3), 65.

[26] Interview with Stephen Nfor, retired teacher, Nkambe, 11 September 2020

themselves by arming young male fighters from their ethnic group. As a result, a violent and bloody conflict broke out that caused the death of several people not just in Mbongong and Fuh but also in other places such as Ngarbuh, Ntayi, Mayo Binka and Ntisaw.[27]

This implies that while one ethnic group strengthens in arming its members the probability of the conflict occurrence increased or for it to escalate if it was already there in the form of tensions. Barry Posen in his article "Dilemma and Ethnic Conflict" defines the security dilemma as:

> a situation in which neighbours wish to remain autonomous and secure; they will react by trying to strengthen their positions. This is the security dilemma: what one does to enhance one's own security causes reactions that, in the end, can make one less secure.[28]

Barry Posen thus contends that the security dilemma could also be applied to the intra-state level, that is, ethnic and intra-state conflict.

Inter-personal conflicts

In the study area, there are instances whereby conflicts between individuals can often quickly escalate into inter-communal conflicts. Some individual conflicts that result in theft, looting and beating occasionally extend into inter-ethnic conflicts. For example, when either of the two groups kills a person, the victimized family and ethnic group members are driven to take similar action or go beyond that. Two key informants of Wimbum and Mbororo maintained that inter-personal conflicts in the area are the triggering factors for inter-ethnic conflict. The 2018-2019 inter-ethnic violent clashes were triggered by the beating of the Fon of Mbipgo by Mbororo youths in Mbongong.

The major actors of the conflict

Youths: In today's world young people are primary participants in conflicts. There are different reasons why they participate in conflicts. These include lack of economic opportunities, political voice, and sense of belonging to their communities and are easily mobilized by others. In

[27] Ngeh, Roland; Balgah Sounders; Lotsmart Fonjong and Nformi Solange Chewe (2019). Understanding the nature, challenges and implications of land conflicts on local development in Ndu sub-division of Cameroon, in Lotsmart Fonjong (ed) *Natural Resource endowment and the fallacy of development in Cameroon*. Mankon, Bamenda: Langaa Research and Publishing CIG

[28] Posen, B. R. (1993). The security dilemma and ethnic conflict. *Survival, 35*(1), 27-47.

the Wimbum-Mbororo inter-ethnic conflict, youths are direct participants /actors of the conflict. They often take part in the frontline of the conflict between the two ethnic groups. At the same time, they have been impacted by the conflict directly and/indirectly. Key informants of both Wimbum and Mbororo affirmed that youth played a significant role in the conflict between the Wimbum and the Mbororo. Youth and adults are energetic and voluntarily participated in the inter-ethnic conflict.[29] As the participants of Wimbum and Mbororo FGD identified, the motives behind the participation of youths in the conflict include the desire to help their ethnic group members and the desire to enhance economic opportunity through conflict/violence.[30] For example, due to inter-ethnic conflicts, some grazing lands forcefully encroached on farms. As a woman from the Wimbum FGD argued, "the youths believe that controlling the grazing lands was a way of reclaiming their land which will result in more fertile farmlands for members of their ethnic group."[31] Apart from the above motive, another motive of youths to participate in the conflict is the culture of both ethnic groups. As many of Wimbum and Mbororo FGD noted, in both ethnic groups fighting with another group, considered as an enemy makes them have hero status and gain respect within their own communities.

Local Elites: Contemporary literature on theory defines 'elites' as actors who control resources, hold strategic positions, and relate with each other through power networks[32] The concept is now also closely associated to the Weberian understanding of power, as the capacity to enforce one's will, irrespective of the opposition they encounter.[33] This conception also resonates with Marxist idea of a ruling class, which derives its position from the ownership of the means of production. In the context of elite power however, attention is not only economic factors but more on political considerations. Thus, elites consist of prestigious and established leaders, top politicians, business persons, intellectuals, senior civil servants, senior military officers and relatively

[29] Interviews with Lamga Ernest, Notable, Nkambe, 29 December 2020; Alhadji Jalike, Cattle Herder, Nkambe, 12 September 2020.

[30] Focus Group Discussion with Mbororo youths, Mbongong, 08 September 2020; FGD with Wimbum youths, Nkambe, 12 September 2020

[31] Focus Group Discussion with Wimbum Women, Mpipgo, 10 September 2020

[32] Yamokoski, A., & Dubrow, J. K. (2008). How do elites define influence? Personality and respect as sources of social power. *Sociological Focus, 41*(4), 319-336

[33] Brennan, C. (2020). *Max Weber on power and social stratification: an interpretation and critique*. Routledge.

transitory and less individually known leaders of mass organizations and politically consequential mass movements.[34] In the context of the Wimbum-Mbororo inter-ethnic conflict, three major local elites have become identifiable as major actors: political elites, business elites, academics/intellectuals.

The political elite is a group of people, political parties and/or other kinds of organizations who manage and organize government and all manifestations of political power.[35] In the context of the Wimbum-Mbororo inter-ethnic conflict, political elites are government officials at different levels. One of the interviewees who was a political elite argued that politicians, play an unseen role in the Wimbum-Mbororo inter-ethnic conflict. Accordingly, they manipulate and instrumentalise the ethnic differences of Wimbum and Mbororo for their political benefit.[36] In line with such manipulation of ethnic identities, instrumentalist theorists view ethnicity as a means to some specific but sometimes hidden political end and self-serving goals of elites rather than the general good. Ethnicity is a mask of elite interest to attain certain objectives, as it is easy to mobilise people based on such group identity.[37] Local leaders and elites may play roles in aggravating the conflict by supporting the other side of the conflict, due to their inability/unwillingness to give immediate solutions to conflicts.

Academics/Intellectuals are the second type of elites and have played a key role in manipulating and/or mobilizing ethnic differences between the Wimbum and the Mbororo. In the context of the Wimbum and the Mbororo inter-ethnic conflict, this is a group of individuals are considered to have been enlightened and endowed with intellectual prowess above and beyond and the average person. Moreover, academics/intellectuals are those individuals who are respected and accepted by the ethnic group members due to their place in society. In the Wimbum-Mbororo inter-ethnic conflict, educated elites are among the major actors of the conflict in influencing the political situation of

[34] Higley, J. (2008). Elite theory in political sociology. *Texas: University of Texas in Austin http://paperroom. ipsa. org/papers/paper_4036. pdf.*

[35] Yamokoski, A., & Dubrow, J. K. (2008).

[36] Interview with Lamga Ernest, Notable, Nkambe, 29 December 2020

[37] Rothchild, D. S. (1997). *Managing ethnic conflict in Africa: Pressures and incentives for cooperation.* Brookings Institution Press.

the locality and often mobilise their ethnic group members, particularly young people.[38]

Traditional Leaders and Elders: A traditional leader is a person who by their ancestry who occupies a throne and is appointed following the customs and tradition of the society/ethnic group. In other words, a traditional leader/ruler is the traditional head of an ethnic unit who is the holder of a title recognized by the ethnic group members. Their primary function is to regulate and control the relationship and social behaviour within a community.[39] Both Wimbum and Mbororo discussants of FGD depicted the fact that both ethnic groups are structured and attached in the traditional system that binds the ethnic group members. In both ethnic groups, traditional authority emanates from the values and culture of each ethnic group. In the Wimbum-Mbororo inter-ethnic conflict, the traditional leaders were actors of the conflict and to some extent involved in conflict management.

However, their role in conflict management and resolution diminished over time.[40] As remarked by one of the interviewees, even though their role of conflict management and/or resolution is diminishing, the traditional leaders are closest to the people.[41] They are also accepted by their ethnic group members because they act as guardians of their ethnic group culture. The Wimbum and the Mbororo traditional leaders play a minimal role in conflict management and/resolution. The informants also revealed the fact that traditional leaders were actors of the conflict indirectly through supporting their ethnic group members.

Women: It is increasingly recognized that, although women are not directly involved in inter-ethnic conflicts, their role is significant as every man who carries a gun has a woman in his life. Women are not only victims of the conflict but also actors that can influence their husbands and act as a catalyst of conflict. In the Wimbum-Mbororo inter-ethnic conflict women are one of the actors that play a key role in stimulating

---

38 Ngenge, R. T. (2021). Party politics and intra-ethnic conflicts in the Nkambe central subdivision of Cameroon in the 2013 legislative election. *International Journal of New Economics and Social Sciences IJONESS*, *13*(1), 197-211.

39 Mthandeni, E. D. (2002). Traditional leaders and new local government dispensation in South Africa. In *Rencontres scientifiques franco-Sud-Africaines de l'innovation territoriale* (p. 6).

40 Sunjo, E. (2020). Traditional authorities and land conflict resolution in Nso, Cameroon: a historical appraisal. *UB Law and Political Science Quarterly*, Vol, 1, No. 1, 71-91

41 Interview with Eveline Nye, Teacher, Mbongong 08 September 2020

the conflict. However, they do not directly engage in the violent attacks. Both Wimbum and Mbororo FGD participants affirmed that women were one of the actors of the inter-ethnic conflict. The major roles of women as actors include preparing food, encourage their husbands and sons, helping victims, disseminate messages about the conflict around villages, take care of their children and property.

The impact of the Wimbum-Mbororo conflict

In economic terms, ethnic conflict dismisses the very bases of development and discourages the playing field for sustainable development.[42] The Wimbum and the Mbororo interviewees confirmed that the inter-ethnic conflict had damaged the economic resources of the area. Moreover, individual houses of both Wimbum and Mbororo were burned, and the people were displaced from their homes/residences. According to Roland Ngeh et al,[43] houses have been burnt, cattle theft increased, targeted attacks on tribal and ethnic increased and some women resorted to using chemicals as a weapon of war. Those chemicals were sprayed on the grass along cattle routes which led to loss of cattle, leaving a negative economic impact on the Mbororo.

In addition, the Wimbum-Mbororo ethnic conflict has affected economic activities (such as agriculture and trade). Because of fear of insecurity caused by the conflict, economic activities of the community were hindered. This in turn negatively impacted the livelihood of the people in the conflict area. Based on the livelihood assessment carried out by United Nations World Food Programme (WFP) in March 2021, the area is highly susceptible to food insecurity due to population pressure and environmental degradation. Food insecurity was further exacerbated by the Wimbum-Mbororo inter-ethnic conflict. Clashes between the two groups have impacted agricultural activity in places like Mbongong, Ntayi and Ntamru and in some cases interrupted. Apart from the interruption of agricultural activities, the trade relationship between the Wimbum and the Mbororo was greatly reduced due to fear of moving from place to place. Consequently, it endangered the flow of agricultural produce and goods that profoundly reduced the incomes of traders and farmers.

---

[42] Bisram, V. (2015). Impact of Ethnic Conflict on Development: A Case Study of Guyana.

[43] Ngeh, R. et al., (2019).

In general, the loss of lives and properties in the conflict posed a serious challenge to the economic development of the area. However, contrary to the impacts above, the Wimbum-Mbororo inter-ethnic conflict allowed arm dealers and brokers to take advantage of smuggling small arms and light weapons into the conflict area.

Apart from its economic impact, the Wimbum-Mbororo inter-ethnic conflict has resulted in social impacts. The loss of human life was the first social impact. Karl Cordell and Stefan Wolff have argued that the most severe outcome of violent ethnic conflict is its social cost such as loss of human life.[44] Even though, accurate data is not mentioned, the tensions between the Wimbum and the Mbororo have caused untold suffering to many as some were injured, left homeless, displaced, and killed. In the conflict, most of the victims were also women, apart from youth and adults (front fighters).

Moreover, the frequent Wimbum-Mbororo inter-ethnic conflicts weakened and destroyed the social bonds between the two communities. Inter-ethnic marriage links were disturbed as the conflict replaced cooperation with hatred and grievance. Nevertheless, there is no clearly shown data about broken marriages because of the conflict. At the same time, both Wimbum and Mbororo key informants indicated the fact that some Wimbum-Mbororo marriages survived despite the inter-ethnic conflict between the two ethnic groups.[45]

There are equally political ramifications of the conflict between the Wimbum and the Mbororo. Because of the recurrent nature of the conflicts, ethnic difference has been politicised and weaponised by the local political elites. This has in turn diminished the credibility and responsibility of local officials in making decisions related to managing and resolving the conflict. The two ethnic group representatives maintain a hidden agenda of supporting their ethnic group rather than being responsible government officials. Existing mistrust and suspicion between the two communities makes it difficult for any conflict management attempts to succeed. In general, ethnic politics between the Wimbum and Mbororo endangers the institutional capacity of the government to respond to the conflicts.

---

[44] Cordell, K., & Wolff, S. (2009). *Ethnic conflict: causes, consequences, and responses*. Polity.
[45] Interview with Abdul Mousa, Cattle Herder, Njema, 12 September 2020; Interview with Lamga Ernest, Notable, Nkambe, 29 December 2020

Conflict management and peacebuilding efforts

Conflict management is an intervention towards preventing the escalation and negative effects of violent and continuing conflicts. It is the reduction, containment, and elimination of the propensity of conflict to violence by enhancing positive behavioural changes among the actors of the conflict.[46] However, in conflict resolution root causes of conflict will get addressed, so that the situation is no longer violent, hostile and exploitative.[47] Thus, multiple sources of data revealed that the Wimbum-Mbororo inter-ethnic conflict is not addressed at the grassroots level. However, the conflict was managed, and peacebuilding efforts were made through both traditional and formal mechanisms.

Representatives of the central government at the local level have been at the forefront of managing/resolving the inter-ethnic conflict between the Wimbum and the Mbororo. In line with this, Wimbum participants of the focus group discussion argue that the mechanisms at the sub-divisional and divisional levels are not fair enough.[48] They argue that cases between the Mbororo and the Wimbum taken to the Divisional Officer have always ended up in favour of the Mbororo, who are in the minority. The Wimbum accuse the administrative authorities of corrupt practices such as collecting cows from Mbororo to rule in their favour. In line with this, some Wimbum people have lost trust in the administrative authorities and sometimes prefer to handle issues by themselves which often results in violent clashes.

Peacebuilding is the creation of structures to promote sustainable peace by addressing the root cause of conflict. Peacebuilding comprises multidimensional responsibilities/activities from disarming of armed groups to the building of political, social, judicial, and civil society organizations.[49] Based on this conception, it is difficult to say there is sustainable peace in the area. However, efforts have been made by Community Based Organizations (CBOs) such as the Farmer-Herder Dialogue Platform (FHDP), an initiative of Mbororo Social and Cultural Development Association (MBOSCUDA). Based on a Mbororo key

---

[46] Miller, R. (2019). Managing Regional Conflict: The Gulf Cooperation Council and the Embargo of Qatar. *Global Policy*, *10*, 36-45.

[47] Wallensteen, P. (2018). *Understanding conflict resolution.* Sage.

[48] Focus Group Discussion with Wimbum Men, Mbongong, 08 September 2020

[49] Barnett, M., Kim, H., O'donnell, M., & Sitea, L. (2007). Peacebuilding: What is in a name. *Global governance*, *13*, 35.

informant, the FHDP is made up of both Wimbum farmers and Mbororo herders.[50] The platform provides an equal opportunity for the committee to assess and evaluate cases of farmer-herder conflict and pass judgment that is so far considered fair. To further strengthen relations with each other, the committee came up with an initiative called Farming Alliance (FA). Based on this initiative, a farmer can agree with a herder to keep cows on his or her farm during the dry season for to cows eat the remains of dry corn stock while sleeping in the said farms. In return, the farmer benefits manure from the cow droppings which renews soil fertility, leading to higher yields. This has been initiated in some communities in Nkambe Central Sub-Division such as Binshua and Binjeng.[51] There are hopes that such initiatives could help in restoring trust and friendship which was enjoyed by both parties before 1996.

Conclusion

Even though efforts have been made to manage the conflict as well as build peace in the area there remain significant hurdles. Some of the key challenges include lack of gender consideration in the management of the conflict, lack of preventive or early warning mechanisms and conflict-sensitive development projects as well as state institutional weakness. The participation of women in conflict management and peacebuilding was highly limited compared to men. For example, as all research participants stated, during the peace committee meetings, the role of women was only limited to the preparation of foods and drinks. The peace committees were male-dominated. The voices of women were left unheard meanwhile women are key actors in Wimbum-Mbororo inter-ethnic conflict. The approach of the government has been more reactive than preventive (proactive). Most of the initiatives and activities have been undertaken after deadly clashes have occurred. Moreover, in the area, conflict-sensitive development programming that can create harmonious and peaceful relationships are limited.

More concerning, tensions between the Mbororo and Wimbum communities in the Donga Mantung Division are worsening significantly in the context of the anglophone separatist conflict. The separatists have often accused the Mbororo of cooperating with the government. The

---

50 Interview with Mbuldi Admu, Cattle Herder, Nkambe, 12 September 2020
51 Interview with Ngoina Oumarou, Cattle Herder, Binshua, 12 September 2020

separatists have also accused the government of arming the Mbororo and claimed that pro-government militias pose as separatists and attack Mbororo populations to sow discord between the Wimbum and the Mbororo communities.[52] This came to a boiling point when in February 2020, military officers with the help of armed Mbororo militia men stormed the village of Ngarbuh and massacred 21 Wimbum people, including 13 children and one pregnant woman.[53] This has seen the gains made in the preceding years reversed. The polarisation and weaponization of ethnicity continue to pose a serious threat to the peaceful coexistence of Wimbum and Mbororos in the area. Political entrepreneurs must desist from using the ethnic differences, inadequate land for both farming and cattle rearing as opportunities to incite violence and make political gains.

---

52 Willis, Roxana, J. McAulay, N. Ndeunyema, and J. Angove. "Human Rights abuses in the Cameroon Anglophone crisis." (2019).
53 Ben, O. M. (2021). Role of Women Organisations of Cameroon in Peacemaking: An Exploratory Study.

Indigenous Approaches to Conflict Resolution in Contemporary African Societies

Fabrice Tambe Endoh

Lecturer, Faculty of Laws and Political Science,
University of Buea
Email: fabriceendoh21@gmail.com/tambe.fabrice@ubuea.cm

Abstract

The political debacle facing African societies has been the prevalence of ethnic, cultural and religious conflicts within their environment. The inevitability of these conflicts has remained a worrying concern to both scholars and activists. Despite the adoption of innovative approaches, most of the conflicts plaguing the continent have continued to defy resolution. In line with this contention, traditional conflict resolution experts among others have raised the pointing question-what are the core issues flaming conflicts within the continent and calling for attention during the conflict resolution time line? The paper adopts the phenomenological approach to discuss how phenomenon's common in African cultural practices influence conflict resolution in contemporary African societies. It is recommended that the relevant conflict resolution systems common within and across African communities and used to resolve previous conflicts be adopted as blueprints for the maintenance of peace and security across African societies.

Key words: Indigenous communities, conflict resolution, reconciliation, rehabilitation, and reintegration

1. Introduction

Conflicts prevailing in African societies have persisted amid well-established conflict resolution systems designed to lead conflict management in an era of modern civilization. Generally, it is perceived that Africa is trapped in a never-ending cycle of ethnic conflicts.[1] Apartheid South Africa, The Rwandan genocide, Darfur, Northern Nigeria, Ivory Coast, and the violent aftermath of the controversial Kenyan elections, among other cases, seemingly substantiate this perception. This coinage of human misery accumulates grievances that motivates never ending reprisals. The centuries-old inertia behind these animosities, moreover, defies resolution.[2] The seeming implication is that Africa's complicated ethnic diversity leaves the continent perpetually vulnerable to devastating internecine conflicts which in turn, cripple prospects for resolution and subsequent economic development. This write-up challenges that notion arguing that a re-diagnosis of the underlying drivers to ethnic violence can lead to more effective and sustainable responses. In this regard, the author probes into value systems common among African traditional practices with a view to determine and probably expose their strength in advancing the conflict resolution agenda.

Conflict prone communities across Africa often portray elements of hatred, bitterness and avoidance for the mere violation of a right perceived by conflicting parties as fundamental to their existence. These rights are considered by such parties as a form of heritage which they possess by virtue of their ethnic origin.[3] Such rights therefore become important not because of their mere existence, but because of their influence in advancing the human agenda. From a logical perspective, the impact of these rights on conflict resolution rest not in the

---

[1] Report prepared for the Africa Conflict Prevention Pool (ACPP), Conflict Trends in Africa, 1946-2004: A Macro-Comparative Perspective, Available at: http://www.systemicpeace.org/africa/AfricaConflictTrendsMGM2005us.pdf. Accessed 10 February 2022.

[2] C. Aapenguo, "Misinterpreting Ethnic Conflicts in Africa", *Africa Security Brief* No. 4, April, 2010.

[3] O. Bamikole, "Nkrumah and the Triple Heritage Thesis and Development in Africana Societies", *International Journal of Business, Humanities and Technology*, Vol. 2, No. 2, 2012, pp. 19- 15.

undisputed interdependence of the peace and rights paradigm, but on the hypothesis that society's efforts to stabilize peace within ethnic communities in Africa will be influenced by its performance on ethnic and cultural values throughout the conflict continuum.[4] In other words, the transformative process from belligerent to collaborators can be achieved by appropriating cultural values into the conflict resolution process. This article deliberates on the values inherent in African cultural practices and how such values can be appropriated into the conflict resolution process to foster reconciliation and peace building within and across ethnic communities in Africa.

Given that cultural values are significant in the conflict resolution process, it is important to discuss the values common in African cultural practices and how they inform conflict resolution within the continent. Projecting culture as a set of values, rather than a strict repository of norms, evokes a deeper understanding of its transformative quality. While the rigid prescriptive approach is conditioned to the strict observance of standards, the value approach is versatile and flexible. In this regard, values could be viewed as representing the desirable aspirations that may be varying in importance but which, nonetheless, "serve as guiding principles in people's lives".[5] Rokeach observed that a value is, "an enduring belief that a specific mode of conduct or end-state of existence is personally or sociably preferable to an opposite or converse mode of conduct or end-state of existence".[6] Therefore, values motivate behavior, which would be consistent with a preferable sociable condition irrespective of rewards or sanctions that may be consequential to the behavior.

In Rokeach's orientation, values instigate uniformity in behavior and may therefore lead to shared responses and the establishment of a value system. If culture is viewed as a value system, then its enduring quality and sociable attributes must be appreciated. After all, values are

[4] F. Acquah, "The impact of African traditional religious beliefs and cultural values on Christian-Muslim relations in Ghana from 1920 through the present: A case study of Nkusukum- EkumfiEnyan area of the Central Region". PhD thesis, University of Exeter, UK.
(https://ore.exeter.ac.uk/repository/bitstream/handle/10036/3473/AcquahF.pdf?sequence=3)19 June 2018.
[5] Sagiv and Schwartz, "Values proprieties and readiness for out-group social contact" *Journal of Social & Personal Psychology,* 1995, pp. 437.
[6] M. Rokeach, *The Nature of Human Values,* Free Press, 1973, pp. 5

themselves sociable and enduring. Swartz defines values as "desirable state, objects, goals, or behavior transcending specific situations and applied as normative standards to judge and to choose among alternative modes of behavior".[7] In multicultural contexts, the value system must take on a democratic flavor that allows for negotiation of acceptable meanings of specific values. In conflict, such negotiation will occur within the framework of positive transformation that yields to peacefulness. It follows that accepted values should motivate behavior that supports peace.

Although the value approach seems ideal towards achieving peace, its relationship with conflict resolution is yet to be established. It is argued that the value approach is multicultural and will inform positive behavior depending on the culture's specific dynamics.[8] The human rights culture among others, generate a set of values upon which human rights norms have been established. The norms provide rules that guide and direct conflict resolution practitioners in their quest to restore peace. Given that the value system illuminates the conflict resolution agenda, and that their successful implementation to retain peace in the face of conflict can be fostered by human rights activism, the following questions have emerged: What are the values inherent in African cultural practices? To what extent can such values promote the conflict resolution process? Who are the primary beneficiaries protected by the norms inherent in such values? The answers to these questions will address the conflated issues of conflict resolution prevailing in ethnic communities across Africa. The write-up is a composition of five sections inter-linked with each other to form the chronological order of the text. Section one provides the general introduction which captures the background information based on which the article is constructed. Section two composed of the methodology and provides the notochord linking the article from introduction to conclusion. In sections three and four, indigenous patens of conflict resolution common in African traditional practices are diagnosed and elaborated upon to achieve the main objective of the article. Section five recounts the main points raised in the text to provide a brief conclusion of the article.

---

[7] Swartz, "Universals in the context and structure of value: Theoretical advances and empirical tests in 20 countries" in Zanna (eds) *Advances in Experimental Social Psychology*, 1992, pp. 1 65.

[8] L. Juma, "Dignified Existence: Reflections on Aspects of Culture and Cultural Rights Debate in Africa", *Speculum Juris, South Africa,* 2008, pp. 1-22.

2. Methodological approach

It is essentially important to engage different category of leaders whose participation in community affairs promote the values inherent in traditional conflict resolution systems across African communities. Notwithstanding, factors beyond human control, including the devastations imposed by the current COVID-19 pandemic could not support this exercise and therefore, face to face interview with community leaders from Uganda and other regions could not be conducted. However, the exercise was carried out in South Africa and primary data was obtained from eight leaders across various communities, including Zululand, North West, Free State and portions of the Eastern Cape. Data obtained from these audiences was categorized into two stratum and the first strata constituted six leaders who supported an African centered paradigm to conflict resolution and focusing on African cultural values. This cluster of respondents are survivors of the outdated apartheid system, and their day-to-day survival serves as a testimony to the legacy of apartheid. The second strata constituted two respondents who contradicted the African centered paradigm to say, modern conflict resolution systems can be more beneficial given that they provide sanctions to perpetrators and deter them from further engagements with wrongful conducts. Though different in approaches, both category of respondents emphasized the need for effective resolution to guarantee sustainable peace.

Table 1: Distribution of respondents

Areas Visited	Respondents in favour of an African Centered approach to conflict resolution	Respondents in favour of a Western Centered approach to conflict resolution
Zulu Land	2	-
North West	2	-
Free State	-	2
Eastern Cape	2	-
Total responses	**6**	**2**

Source: *Fieldwork, 2021*

The table above signifies responses obtained from respondents in different regions across South Africa. Two participants from Zululand voted for an African centered approach to conflict resolution in Africa. Respondents from North West and Eastern Cape also pledge their support for an African approach to conflict resolution. For Free state, approach to conflict resolution that imposes sanctions for the purpose of deterrence. To sum it up, six participants prefer African centered approaches to conflict resolution as opposed to two participants from the Free State who preferred a Western approach. This feedback is indicative of racial division motivated by the fact that residents of The Free State are predominantly whites as opposed to their black counterparts in the other regions. Consequently, the ideology of a black African remains different from that of their white counterparts in terms of addressing societal issues.[9]

In addition to the method of data collection discussed above, empirical qualitative survey[10] was utilized as an alternative to face-to-face interview and primary information was obtained from media platforms like emails, BOTIM, whatsapp and many more. To ensure conformability, primary data obtained from the sources discussed above was analyzed concurrently with secondary data obtained from journal articles, textbooks and news feeds. The current compilation reflected as a manuscript is a result of data collection and analysis from the multiple sources discussed above. The paper also prioritizes ethical concerns by strictly adhering to the principles of research which prohibit misconducts like fabrication, misinformation, falsification, and plagiarism in analyzing, reviewing and reporting research. Data obtained from multiple sources have been acknowledged by way of citations and complete references.

3. Ethnic communities and the dynamics of escalating tensions in Africa

Africans live in multi-ethnic societies exhibiting different cultural heritage and customary practices. Indigenous communities exhibit a kind of structural order based on the respect for cultural values and unity is

[9] K. Rwebangira, Conflict Transformation in Post-apartheid South Africa from 1994 – 2013, Masters thesis, University of Kwazulu Natal, South Africa, 2013.

[10] Empirical qualitative survey is typified in the diverse methods of collecting qualitative data which could include various platforms like online mediums serving as enablers to facilitate the process of data collection in challenging situations. The method is particularly suited for this article given that the exercise of data collection was conducted during the peak of the COVID-19 pandemic. The impossibility of the writer to meet with the relevant participants was a call for concern. This inevitable drawback encouraged the writer to utilize the empirical qualitative survey method to obtain data using the various media platforms stated above. For more on empirical qualitative survey, see H. Jansen, The Logic of Qualitative Survey Research and its Position in the Field of Social Research Methods, *Forum: Qualitative Social Research*, Vol. 11, No. 2, 2010.

informed by unanimity in terms of traditional beliefs between and among ethnic tribes. Despite numerous challenges posed by ethnic diversity and the dynamics of cultural interplay, ethnic communities continue to stay united by the force of social cohesion.[11] The logic is, people make meaning out of life by associating themselves with cultural groups within their communities. In doing so, they advance the notion that no man is an island. The identity of an African indigene is determined by the community in which he or she belongs, the culture they practice and the custom they respect. Indigenous Africans show respect for community values more than any civilized system and are driven by the belief that any form of disrespect for such values breaches the substratum upon which the community is formed.[12] When this occurs, defaulters face sanctions according to established rules and regulations enforced by the community. For fear of community sanctions, people often obey community rules as well as living in peace and harmony with their neighbors.[13]

Despite the relevant regulations enforced by community leadership, linguistic and religious differences, including the struggle to identify themselves within the context of a multi-cultural environment continuously provoke social, ethnic and religious tensions. These factors have flamed violent conflicts in many regions across the continent. Among others, Nigeria has suffered from interfaith conflict for decades. The country hosts most of its Muslim population in the North while most Christians are stationed in the South. Due to the quest for legitimization, these two factions have remained in conflict for close to 65 years and human casualties; including the destruction of classic infrastructures have become a common phenomenon.[14] The conflict has been exacerbated by the uprising of the Islamic movement, the Boko

---

11 C. Madukwe and N. Madukwe, "African Value Systems and the Impact of Westernization: A Critical Analysis", *International Journal of Research in Arts and Sciences*, Vol. 2, 2010, pp. 264-274.

12 O. Ezenweke and K. Nwadialor, 2013, "Understanding human relations in African traditional religious context in the face of globalization: Nigerian perspectives", *American International Journal of Contemporary Research* Vol. 3, No. 2, 2013, pp.61-70.

13 S. McCarthy, Globalization and Education, in B. William (Ed.). The book of virtues. New York: Simon and Schuster, 2004.

14 O. Adeyanju, 2013, *The Implications of the Christian 'Golden Rule' for African Christianity in the Context of the Yoruba Concept of Omoluwabi*, in Fatokun, S. A, (Ed.), Christianity and African Society: A festschrift in Honour of Pastor (Dr.) Gabriel Oladele Olutola at 80, Ibadan: BookWright Publishers, 2013, pp. 176-187.

Haram which completely rejects western philosophies in favor of Islamic believes. The consequence of the Boko Haram movement is evident in the political, social, religious and cultural divide among Christians and Muslims, including the forced disappearances of young school children on regular basis. Most often, the captives are used by their captors to demand ransom from the government as a form of compensation for their release.[15] These activities have strained the government of Nigeria as it continues to find a lasting solution to the interfaith conflict affecting the country.

The Darfur region of The Sudan also experienced ethnic tensions between the Arabs and black Africans who engaged in serious competitions over grazing land and scares resources. The indigenes of Darfur also complained of systematic marginalization by the ruling government, even though most of the country's wealth comes from the region.[16] The Darfur conflict provoked spontaneous rebel groups like the Justice Equity Movement (JEM) and the Sudan's People Liberation Movement (SPLM) who organized themselves to fight against the purported marginalization. In response to such developments, the government's backed *Janjaweed* militia launched a bloody crackdown to disarm the rebel movements. Confrontations between the rebels and the militias have resulted to the death of approximately 400,000 Darfur indigenes, including the destruction of private properties and other valuables.[17] Although efforts have been made by the international community to remedy the situation, residence in these areas still experience ethnic tensions on regular basis. The Darfur region of the Sudan remains one of the areas most affected by escalating ethnic tensions in Africa.

Besides Nigeria and Sudan, South Africa experienced decades of racial injustices perpetrated against the black majority through the established policy of 'Apartheid'.[18] The practice was manifested through

---

[15] A. Adesoji, "The Boko Haram Uprising and Islamic Revivalism in Nigeria", *African Spectrum*, Vol. 45, No. 2, 2010, pp. 95-108.

[16] D. Unruh and A. Abdul-Jalil, "Constituencies of Conflict and Opportunity: Land rights, narratives and collective action in Darfur", *Political Geography*, Vol. 42, 2014, pp. 104-116.

[17] D. Unruh, "Land and legality in the Darfur conflict", *African Security*, Vol. 5, No. 2, 2012, pp. 105.128.

[18] A. Wizarat, "Apartheid and Racial Discrimination in South Africa— An Overview of the Control Network, Pakistan" *Horizon*, Vol. 33, No. 4 (Fourth Quarter, 1980), pp. 84-87.

the adoption of discriminatory laws including among others, 'The Group Areas Act',[19] 'The Separate Amenities Act',[20] 'The Bantu Education Act',[21] 'The Job Reservation Act'[22] and many more. These laws disadvantaged black Africans over their white counterparts and the consequence is visible in today's class distinction within the modern state of South Africa.[23] Although the democratic constitution of 1994[24] purported to eradicate the scares of Apartheid, the falcon still lives but in another form called 'Xenophobia', which extends the bitterness to foreign nationals.[25] In an attempt to provide a more pro-active approach to address these differences, South Africans chose to utilize a local conflict resolution mechanism known as 'Ubuntu' (togetherness). This local remedy is characterized by societal values that generally promotes the interest of the community. The subsequent sections will detail the practice of Ubuntu as exercised in South Africa and elsewhere.

Other African countries have experienced deadly conflicts whose consequences resulted to the rise of rebel movements. Such movements continue to threaten the peace and security of the continent. Among others, reference can be made to long standing grievances expressed by

---

19 The Group Areas Act No. 41 of 1950 was enacted by the Parliament of South Africa under the Apartheid regime to assign racial groups to different residential and business sections in urban areas in a system of urban apartheid.

20 The Separate Amenities Act No. 49 of 1953, constituted part of the apartheid system of racial injustices. The Act legalized the racial segregation of public premises, vehicles and services in favour of white citizens. Only public roads and streets were excluded from the Act.

21 The 1953 Act was purposefully adopted to consolidate Bantu education, i.e. education of black people, so that discriminatory educational practices could be uniformly implemented across South Africa.

22 The Job Reservations Act expressly excluded black employees from the definition of an employee. Only white and coloured workers were permitted to form and join registered trade unions.

23 Apartheid was a system of conscious discrimination perpetrated by the white minority of South Africans over heir black counterparts who constituted approximately 70% of the county's total population. The practice rubber stamp selective advantage in the areas of job and education, including which, blacks were not allowed to visit white communities or use properties reserved for whites. Also, intermarriages between white and blacks were not permitted.

24 See the Bill of Rights Under the 1994 Democratic Constitution governing the modern State of South Africa.

25 P. Khan, "South Africa: from apartheid to xenophobia", *Institute of Race Relations*, Vol. 63, Issue 1, 2021, pp. 3–22

citizens of Northern Uganda against the ruling government.[26] For failing to address issues of systematic marginalization, a spontaneous movement referred to as the Lord's Resistance Army (LRA) has taken up arms against government of Uganda and numerous efforts to reverse the circle of violence affecting this region has proved futile.[27] Consequently, Ugandans have invoked their traditional conflict resolution mechanism known as the 'Mato Oput' reconciliation system. This system has also been diagnosed in the section below.

Most often, judicial efforts and conflict resolution mechanisms initiated by governments fail to deal with the root causes of conflicts emanating from African communities. These conflicts exhibit certain characteristics that stem from the dynamics of cultural beliefs and common among them are issues of ethnicity, language differences and religious disparities, including issues relating to marginalization. Simply put, most conflict emanating from Africa are linked to ideological differences and conflict resolution efforts initiated by governments rarely pay attention to such differences.[28] These are some of the reasons why language, ethnic and religious conflicts still persist across many African countries. Government's efforts towards finding lasting solutions have continuously failed because the focus is often geared towards politics and power rather than practical differences which perhaps, may be the root cause of such conflict. While organized conflict resolution mechanism have continued to be unproductive, some traditional conflict resolution systems emanating from the continent have provided more

---

26 The conflict in northern Uganda has continued for over two decades, and there appears to be little end in sight. Over 1.4 million people have been displaced, tens of thousands more have been killed, raped or abducted, and the war has spread into other districts. Human Rights Watch, Stolen Children: Abduction and Recruitment in Northern Uganda, New York, 15(7), March 2003.; R. Will, 'Lord's Terror', *BBC Focus on Africa.* 14(2), April-June 2003, pp. 20-21.

27 T. Ajayi and O. Buhari, "Methods of conflict resolution in African traditional society", *African research review*, Vol.8, No. 2, 2014, pp.138-157.

28 R. Love, "Religion, Ideology & Conflict in Africa", *Review of African Political Economy*, Vol. 33, Issue 110, 2006, pp. 619-634.; A. Olaosebikan, "Conflicts in Africa: Meaning, Causes, Impact and Solution", *African Research Review*, Vol. 4 (4), Serial No. 17, October 2010, pp. 549-560.

practical solutions to the people.[29] The next section will throw more light on such initiatives.

4. African initiatives towards conflict resolution and peace building

Previous sections of this article highlighted that Africans mostly identify themselves with their cultural beliefs. To them, life is meaningful depending on one's cultural affiliation. These cultures probe into the deep meaning of life by posing questions like; what does it mean to be human? What is –or ought to be-the nature of human relations? Better still, what is the purpose of existence? These questions define their attitude and the values they cherish which in turn determine how they interact with one another. In general terms, cultural values establish social norms through which ethnic communities are govern. These values are shared among community members and handed down to future generations as a legacy through which the community is subsequently identified with a particular cultural image.[30] To re-establish peace in conflict communities across Africa, African conflict resolution mechanisms should prioritize social cohesion and respect for cultural heritage. By this strategic approach, indigenes try to identify themselves with their cultural image, respecting the norms and values of their culture and find reasons to coexist as one people.[31]

In the Northern part of Somalia also referred to as Somaliland, traditional leadership institutions, including traditional methods of solving community disputes have been used to unite different clans and create government legislative structures. By bringing together traditional structures and government institutions like parliament, Somaliland has been able to maintain a degree of relative peace and stability.[32] Also,

---

[29] B. Brock-Utne, Indigenous conflict resolution in Africa, A draft presented to week-end seminar on Indigenous Solutions to Conflicts held at the University of Oslo, *Institute of Educational Research*, 2001, pp. 23-24.

[30] T. Murithi, "Practical Peacemaking Wisdom from Africa: Reflections on Ubuntu", *Journal of Pan African Studies*, Vol.1, No. 4, 2006a, pp.25-34.

[31] S. Mwenda, Paradigms of alternative dispute resolution and justice delivery in Zambia, PhD thesis, University of South Africa, 2009. (http://uir.unisa.ac.za/bitstream/handle/10500/2163/thesis.pdf) Accessed, 19 June 2021.

[32] T. Murithi, "African Approaches to Building Peace and Social Solidarity", *African Journal on Conflict Resolution*, Vol. 6, No. 2, 2006b, pp. 9-34.

post-conflict Mozambique encouraged traditional healing and reconciliation practices which enable combatants, particularly child soldiers to be re-integrated into their communities. Ghana, Niger and Chad have also used traditional institutions in the past to deal with low intensity conflicts that affected their respective regions.

Another good example is the traditional justice and reconciliation system in Rwanda known as 'Gacaca'. The system was established to enable judgment against persons accused of being the mastermind of the 1994 genocide.[33] Although the Gacaca tribunals where largely criticized based on their operational efficacy, advocates of the system argue that the use of indigenous and/or traditional approaches to administer justice in a modern nation state will always challenge established western principles. They further debated that, while the system was open to criticisms, lessons could be learned for future conflict resolution efforts across African communities.[34] The Gacaca system was organized on the basis of community involvement. The local community participated actively towards encouraging the perpetrators to acknowledge their wrongful acts, as well as encouraging, but at same time, providing guidance for the victims to determine what reparations ought to be made for purposes of reconciliation and re-integrating the perpetrators into the society. The Gacaca tribunals fostered a system based on community values and cultural norms and the system was seemingly effective in the respective communities. The fact that the Rwandan government made use of the Gacaca system was an indication that African indigenous approaches play a vital role in restoring lasting peace and promoting reconciliation and social cohesion across indigenous communities. Besides Gacaca, a culture that has brought more solidarity and social cohesion among Africans is 'Ubuntu'.

4.1. The culture of Ubuntu

The culture of Ubuntu is commonly applicable across Southern African countries. It is built on aspects of generosity, hospitality, friendliness, caring attitude and compassionate behaviors. The idea of Ubuntu is informed by the philosophy that 'no man is an island' or 'no

---

[33] A. Corey and S. Joireman, "Retributive justice: the Gacaca courts in Rwanda", African Affairs, Vol. 103, 2004, pp.73-89.
[34] Ibid.

single tree can make a forest'.[35] Hence, we exist because others exist and therefore, we are one another's keeper. Those who practice the culture of Ubuntu possess characteristics of love, trust, togetherness, harmony and forgiveness. Such inherent characteristics can advance peace building and foster reconciliation in conflict societies. Archbishop Desmond Tutu mentioned that the principles underpinning the culture of Ubuntu helped towards directing the thoughts and actions of perpetrators and victims who came before the South African Truth and Reconciliation Commission (TRC) to confess and forgive.[36] Such actions build the impression that much can be learned from African indigenous approaches to conflict resolution and peace building.

While indigenous approaches can be considered to have imparted positively towards peace building across African communities, one must bear in mind that some African cultures are gender bias and as such, they do not propagate the ideals envisaged by the broader international human rights system. Therefore, in promoting indigenous approaches to conflict resolution and peace building, we must reflect on customary practices and cultural values that generally appreciate the essence of humanity. By doing so, Africans will have the opportunity to re-construct their communities and build on a legacy. Desmond Tutu analyzed that while serving as chairman of the South African Truth and Reconciliation Commission (TRC), he applied both Christian and cultural values to guide perpetrators and victims.[37] In particular, he made use of the principles underpinning the culture of Ubuntu during the Commission's hearing. He pointed that Ubuntu speaks to the very essence of humanity which includes aspects of love, forgiveness, generosity, hospitality, caring and being compassionate.

Ubuntu emphasize the importance of peacemaking through the principles of reciprocity, inclusivity and a sense of shared destiny between and among people. It provides rationality for sacrifices and the need to let go of past wrongs. Ubuntu provides the moral guidance for governments to legislate and set up laws that promote reconciliation and peace building among communities. Simply put, the culture of Ubuntu re-informs practical efforts towards building peace as well as healing traumatized communities. It is important to note that the principles

---

35 D. Prinsloo, 'Ubuntu Culture and Participatory Management' in Coetzee, P. H, & Coetzee, A. P, (Ed.), *The African Philosophy Reader*, Psychology Press, 1998, pp.41.

36 D. Tutu, *No Future without Forgiveness*, Rider Publishers, 2000, pp. 1-244.

37 *Ibid*

underlying Ubuntu are common across African cultures and their purpose is to unite members of the human family through essential values that foster cooperation and collaboration for purposes of peacemaking and peace building.[38] Ubuntu communities simply make use of a form of legal order to govern and sustain the peace of their environment. Such communities place a high value on communal life, imposing positive relations within the society as a collective task in which everyone is involved[39]

Ubuntu communities are built on collective security and the willingness to protect such that an act against one is considered an act against all.[40] Therefore, the safety of each member of the community is the responsibility of other members. The strength behind the idea of Ubuntu is that parties are obliged to show remorse for their wrong deeds followed by genuine repentance. After these two conditions are fulfilled, reconciliation is initiated to rebuild and maintain social cohesion and trust among community members with the view to suppress retribution. Admittedly, some lessons have been learned from the culture of Ubuntu. First, the importance of public participation is emphasized throughout the peacemaking and peace building processes to strengthen social cohesion among community members. Secondly, the unity of purpose towards supporting victims and encouraging perpetrators as they go through the difficult process of peacemaking is appreciated. Thirdly, the sense of acknowledging guilt and to show remorse, including the granting of forgiveness to achieve reconciliation is highly appreciated. Lastly, the importance of constantly referring to the values of humanity upon which the culture of Ubuntu is built is noted with emphasis.

4.2. The Mato Oput system

Owing to decades of escalating tensions in Uganda, indigenes of the Acholi community invoked their customary conflict resolution system known as Mato Oput. In the past, the system served as an institution for maintaining law and order within the Acholi community. The Mato Oput resolution system derived its strength from customary practices that placed high value on communal life. Although the system existed

---

38 Prinsloo, *op. cit.*, pp. 41

39 Murithi 2006b, *op. cit.*, pp. 9

40 Penal reform international, 2000, Access to Justice in Sub-Saharan Africa: the role of traditional and informal justice systems. (http://www.gsdrc.org/docs/open/ssaj4.pdf) Accessed 12 June 2021.

before colonization, its values were systematically undermined by colonial and post-colonial regimes.[41] Notwithstanding, efforts are being made to revive the system and promote sustainable peace within and across African communities. The system allows community members to share their views and air out their opinions at all stages of the resolution process. Before the resolution commence, a panel dominated by the council of elders and referred to as 'Kacoke Madit' is assembled to supervise the entire process.[42] The main duty of the panel is to analyze multiple opinions from community members who have been authorized to pose questions to the perpetrators, the victims and their witnesses. In the end, a resolution is issued to the satisfaction of all community members, including the disputants.

To complete the Mato Oput resolution process, five key requirements must be complied with.[43] In the first instance, perpetrators are encouraged to acknowledge their guilt owing to credible evidence obtained from victims, witnesses and the public and investigated by the council of elders. Secondly, perpetrators are oblique to show remorse for their wrongful conduct. The third requirement involves the victims who are called upon to show mercy by forgiving the perpetrators. After compliance with the first three requirements, perpetrators are directed by the council of elders to pay adequate compensation as a symbolic gesture that seeks to reinforce their genuine remorse. The process concludes with an act of reconciliation between representatives of the victims and representatives of the perpetrators. The reconciliation process is finalized through an official ceremony known as the Mato Oput, involving the drinking of a bitter tasting herb obtained from the Oput tree. This process signifies that the victim has swallowed the bitterness caused by the perpetrator and has moved on to embrace a new life filled with forgiveness, love and happiness.

Within the context of Acholi communities, the Mato Oput resolution process covers all category of offences, be it simple theft or aggravated crimes that may cause the death of a community member. The essence is

---

41 V. Warikandwa and S. Amoo, *African Law in Comparative Law: A Case of Undermining African Jurisprudence and Promoting a New World Agenda?* In Warikandwa, T. V, (Ed.), Social and Legal Theory in the Age of Decoloniality: (Re-) Envisioning Pan-African Jurisprudence in the 21st Century, Langaa Publishers, 2018, pp. 299-326.

42 Kacoke Madit 2000, The Quest for Peace in Northern Uganda, London: Kacoke Madit, 2000, www.km-net.org 29 June 2021.

43 Murithi 2006b, *op. cit.*, pp. 9

to regulate the way offenders respond to their wrongdoers. To make sure they do not consider retribution as a form of justice against the perpetrator/s, particularly in situations where a death penalty is likely to be the outcome.[44] Although some cases may seem difficult to handle, imposing retribution through death penalty as a form of justice will rather traumatize the community and hinder the possibility of re-establishing an environment conducive for human habitation.[45] If the offence in question is too severe, say for example, cases involving murder, the Mato Oput reconciliation process divides the council of elders in to two groups. The first group composed of the male elders is called 'Rwodi Moo' while the group of female elders is referred to as the 'Rwodi Mon'. The Rwodi Moo and Rwodi Mon ensure a two-phase final blessing to mark the end of the conflict.[46]

The essence of the Mato Oput reconciliation process is to ensure reconciliation between the perpetrator and the victim, including the re-establishment of trust and social cohesion within the community.[47] This is the reason why the process always involves the perpetrators, victims, their representatives, and the public. The role of public consensus is to make sure disputed parties do not breach established agreements after the resolution process is complete, for such acts may be interpreted as an offence against the community. The Acholi's Mato Oput resolution process simply explains the role of culture in the resolution of violent conflicts and the process of healing through which the community is re-established as it where before the conflict occurred.[48]

5. Conclusion

This article does not in any way undermine organized government structures and institutionalized mechanisms of conflict resolution. Rather, it provides viable alternatives to such systems particularly in circumstances where belligerent parties proof adamant to comply with government protocols. It is a fact that indigenous communities across

---

44 R, Mac Ginty, "Indigenous peace-making versus the liberal peace", *Cooperation and conflict*, Vol.43, No. 2, 2008, pp.139-163.
45 Mac Ginty *op. cit.*, pp. 139
46 Murithi 2006b, *op. cit.*, pp. 9
47 J. Osamba, "Peace building and transformation from below: Indigenous approaches to conflict resolution and reconciliation among the pastoral societies in the borderlands of eastern Africa", *African Journal on Conflict* Resolution, Vol.2, No. 1, 2001, pp.22-28.
48 Murithi 2006b, *op. cit.*, pp. 9

Africa continue to experience conflicts resulting from ideological differences linked to ethnicity, language, religion and culture. These factors which are the consequence of minor disagreements have gradually become the main drivers of ethnic conflicts across the continent. From East, West, North, South and Central Africa, communities have experienced disruptions because of the push factors contextualized herein. The worrying concern is the effect of such conflicts negatively impact the smooth functioning of organized government structures. Most often, judicial interventions merely provide partial settlement without taking into consideration the perceived grievances expressed by conflicting parties. Under such circumstance, the conflicts appear to be resolved but failing which, critical issues are left unaddressed. These issues rooted from ethnic, religious and cultural values have become the main reasons for which the said conflicts continue to persist. It is argued that, to give to Caesar what is Caesar's, traditional conflict resolution mechanisms which characterize the values common in African cultural practices should be adopted as a measure to address the root causes of conflicts affecting indigenous communities across the continent.

From a comprehensive point of view, the traditional systems of conflict resolution discussed above portray elements of collectivity, public participation, and acceptance of guilt, showing remorse for wrongful conduct, forgiveness, love, unity, harmony, peace building and most importantly, the possibility of re-integrating perpetrators in to the communities where they truly belong.[49] These characteristics play in favour of Africans by helping them to build trust and social cohesion among themselves. The Gacaca system advocated for justice based on public participation and collective decision making while Ubuntu emphasized the need for forgiveness, reconciliation and social cohesion. The Mato Oput system simply appreciates the Gacaca, and Ubuntu approaches and guarantees reconciliation and re-integration to ensure sustainable peace within ethnic communities. This article recommends that conflict resolution efforts across the continent should prioritize these cultural values in the interest of indigenous communities.

---

[49]Ibid

The death of George Floyd beyond America: Rethinking America's moral legitimacy to lead the world

Gabsa Wilfred Nyongbet

Secretary General in the Ministry of Higher Education and Professor of Political Science, Department of Political Science, University of Yaounde II, Soa

and

Suh I Fru Norbert

Department of Political Science and Comparative Politics, University of Buea

Abstract

The purpose of this research is to identify and analyse various shifts in perceptions about American State and society beyond America, following the death of African American George Floyd and its aftermath. We use the event analysis approach as we consider the death of George Floyd an event that caught worldwide attention and that influenced perceptions about America. It is assumed that reactions to the death of George Floyd represent shifts in perceptions of America's moral legitimacy as world leader. Across the world there are feelings that post-racial America is not over, extralegal police violence is not uncommon, target Black killing is an institution, violence is still a technique of domestic politics and America remains a frightening society. America's worldwide reputation as leader has plummeted as it identified and promoted values across the world it did not implement or did so only to an extent.

Keywords: America, Black, Democracy, rule of law, Police, George Floyd,

1. Introduction: context and background

The politics of identity in America is also defined in Black quest for dignity through the civil rights movements of the sixties that demanded that America fulfils the promise of racial equality in the Declaration of Independence and written in the Constitution at the end of the Civil War.[1] In June 1964, the American Senate voted a bill on civil rights and worldwide reaction was general satisfaction. It was satisfaction because the passage of the bill was perceived to decrease worldwide criticism of race relations in America, a significant triumph of Black cause and a strong signal that all men are created equal. Since then, ironically, Blacks have continued to be object of targeted state-society and police violence.[2]

When Barack Obama was declared America's first black president in 2008, it was believed that America had entered at long last an age of post-racial politics, in which democracy will not be distorted by issues of race.[3] This political event was no doubt a turning point in American political history since it was the first time a Black man assumed the highest office in a country in which just half a century ago refused to recognise constitutional right of Black people. However, it never meant an end to white supremacist feelings and a sustained command of black leadership and power.[4] At best, racial equality is a loose form of improvement and when thought of in this way, racial justice gets reduced to a charitable enterprise—a practice by which white people 'do good' for black people.[5]

---

[1] Fukuyama, Francis. *Identity: The Demand for Dignity and the Politics of Resentment*, (New York Farrar, Straus and Giroux: 2018), p. 90.

[2] For example, just few weeks (July 1964) after the bill was voted a riot broke out in Harlem after police shot and killed a Black teenager, notwithstanding events of similar nature.

[3] Marable, M. and Clarke, K. (Eds.) *Barrack Obama and African American Empowerment: The rise of Black America's new leadership*, (New York, Palgrave Macmillan: 2009), p.2.

[4] For example, although the door remains open for resurgence in support of Black Nationalism, Obama's election appears to be less fertile for Black Nationalist activism so long as discrimination and inequality persists. See Price, Melanye T. *Dreaming Blackness: Black Nationalism and African American Public Opinion*, (New York, New York University Press: 2009), p. 179.

[5] Glaude, Eddie S Jr. *Democracy in Black: How Race still Enslaves American Soul*, (New York, Crown Publishers: 2016), p. 3.

The killing of George Floyd by a White Police officer indeed comes to remind us that discrimination and inequality against Blacks persists and that not even the Obama administration was able to do something about it. The death of George Floyd and the popular outrage that ensued pose real questions which penetrate close to the heart of American democracy and rule of law. Indeed, how can we understand that amid a dominant liberal culture Blacks are still subject of systematic police violence? How can we make sense out of repeated violence in American society and how has this affected perception of America's moral legitimacy as world leader?

The world could not have been indifferent to what occurred to George Floyd given that America is the presumptive leader of the free world. Just like African American Jimmy Wilson who, in 1958 was sentenced to death for stealing less than two dollars and was at the center of international attention in the heart of the Cold War[6], Floyd has also brought to the surface international anxiety about the State of American race relations and democracy. America is recognised as a leading democracy that had been the architect of modern liberal international order as it, at least, led the neoliberal revolution under Ronald Reagan—unfortunately, it appears to be turning away from this.[7] It is far more unexpected according to Fukuyama that threats to democracy should arise from within established democracies themselves including America under Trump.[8] Repeated, almost routine threats to Black life in America are testimony of the limits of American leadership and authority in the promotion of worldwide democratic values. From this perspective, American calls to end human rights violations and other nondemocratic practices may go unanswered despite the threat of sanctions that can come with it. The death of George Floyd marks another period of upsurge of anti-Americanism and perhaps even more significant than previous ones.[9]

Domestic and international reactions to it speak of the perceptions that have developed across the world about America a world leader. Indignation to the event reveals the extent to which the incident was

---

[6] Dudziak, Mary. L. *Cold War Civil Rights Race and the Image of American Democracy: Politics and Society in Twentieth Century America*, (Princeton, Princeton University Press: 2000), p.11.
[7] Fukuyama, 2018, *Ibid.*
[8] Ibid., pp. 7-8.

unable to control collective emotion. Life video of the 'graphic' scene was powerful than the ability of the world to contain its emotion as it created uncontrollable sensations. His death implied several things that could not leave the world indifferent: that Blacks continue to be a 'systematic target' of the police shows racial discrimination and injustice is still a practice in American society and this is far from the image of a 'just' society this country tries to project across the world; the fact that the police is recurrently accused of murder and violence against Blacks could leave the impression that the institution of the police was a political arrangement to control Black life—if that be the case, then it is a case of institutionalised abuse of power and authority, away from expectations of order-maintenance and protection of life and property; that the emergence of protest movements (first in America and later across the world) is an indication that Black people are *still* struggling for genuine/substantial freedom perhaps not only in America, for Black power and against all forms of formal and informal discrimination against Black people, that the Pan African dream is an ongoing struggle and that the institutionalization of equality between Blacks and Whites is still in the making. All of these reveal the inadequacies of the American system of governance of democracy and rule of law.

The purpose of this paper is to show how the incident of George Floyd represents a credible threat to America's moral legitimacy to lead the world as it shaped peoples' perception of America across the world to feel that post-racial America is not over, extralegal police violence is not uncommon, target Black killing is an institution, violence is still a technique of domestic politics and America remains a frightening society.

1.1. Background to America's (Moral) legitimacy as World leader

Why is America said to possess the moral legitimacy to lead the world? What are the foundations of America's moral legitimacy as world leader? Sources of America's international leadership strength are multiple and diverse. America's role in world politics from the period after WWI through to the WWII, the Cold War and into 9/11 and beyond was remarkable. During these periods America was able to put itself at the forefront of international missions and actions.

The values for which America stood and promoted seems to have garnered appeal beyond its borders. Fukuyama describes America as:

> consistently more antistatist, individualistic, laissez-faire, and egalitarian than other democracies...There has been only one American regime...as the world's oldest continuously existing democracy...imbued with an almost religious reverence that Europeans with more ancient sources of identity find peculiar.[10]

American leadership always believed in the strength of its system; that rests on constitutional democracy and has always thought of it as *best practice* for political systems beyond. For Americans, their Declaration of Independence and Constitution are not just the basis of a legal-political-order on the North American continent; they are the embodiment of universal values and have significance for humankind that goes well beyond the borders of the United States.[11] Europe endorsed American leadership during the Cold War by accepting it as desirable,[12] although it was for strategic reasons. Kagan Robert argues that it was not international law and institutions but the circumstances of the Cold War, and Washington's special role in it that conferred legitimacy of America, at least within the West. Kagan further explains that it was the threat posed by Communism, with the stationing of thousands of Soviet troops in the center of Europe which created the understanding that only Washington possessed the power to deter Moscow.[13] Thus the legitimacy America largely enjoyed during the Cold War period and from the West derived for the most part on the self-interest of the allies—that of doing away with communism. Whatever, America's leadership was also the making of American businessmen, engineers, production managers and workers both men and women who built the most awesome military machine in history: the arsenal of democracy that armed the Allies and defeated the Axis.[14]

American leadership finds political pride in its political system so that it is ready to severe its relationship with any other system that is not founded on constitutional democracy. Thus, for American leadership, any State that is not democratic in the American leadership sense of the term might not only be a dictatorship and breathing ground for communism (from after WWI to Cold War and early 2000s), but also

---

[10] Fukuyama, Francis. *State Building, Governance and World Order in the 21st Century*, (Ithaca/New York, Cornell University Press: 2004), p. 113.

[11] *Ibid.*, p. 113.

[12] Kagan, Robert "America's crisis of legitimacy", *Foreign Affairs*, (82 No. 2: March/April 2004), pp.65-83.

[13] Ibid.

[14] Herman, Arthur. *Freedoms Force: How American Business Built the Arsenal of Democracy that won World War II*,(New York, Random House:2012), p. 3.

and most especially, a breathing ground for terrorism and violent extremism (after 9/11), all of which are threats to the American system. Americans tend not to see any source of democratic legitimacy higher than the constitutional democratic State that it claims to be.[15] This belief prompted America to take the initiative to democratize the world by way of dissuasive persuasion and dissuasive force after 9/11.[16] Any State that is not democratic is a weak state at least and a danger to world peace and security at best, so American leadership predominantly believes. In 2003, Bush set up an extraordinary agenda to transform the politics of much of the Middle East including progress in the Arab-Israeli conflict and the promotion of pluralism in the rest of the Arab world and beyond.[17] In execution of the plan Iraq was invaded in March 2003, as part of its project to democratize the world.

It was also on the premise of this geostrategic philosophy that America spearheaded humanitarian interventions across the world; sometimes alone, sometimes in coalition of primarily European countries.[18] Without doubt it was America that promoted the League of Nations, the United Nations, the Bretton Woods Institutions, the general Agreement on Tariff and Trade (GATT), the World Trade Organisation and a host of other international organisations.[19] Paradoxically, though, this belief and *good practice* is sometimes at odd with part of the reality on the ground as, the world has sometimes seen Americans cajole and cooperate with dictatorships in some serene manner and also not doing anything to rescue societies in crises.

1.2. American race relation as determinant of foreign leadership

A major determinant of American leadership in world affairs is the struggle for (racial) equality through civil rights reform. A study conducted by the United States Intelligence Agency (USIA) reveals that the Black man is the focus and symbol of human rights in America to the world and that the topic of American race relation attracted world-wide interest amongst the most influential segments of the American population.[20] Earlier on, Tocqueville saw the danger that Black presence in America will pose. He writes that the most formidable of all the evils

[15]Fukuyama (2004), *Ibi*d, p.109.

[16] American Presidents always perceive America as more civilized than others and hence their mission across the world as a civilizing one.

[17] Fukuyama (2004), *Ibid.* p.95.

[18] Ibid, p. 97

[19] Ibid, p. 106.

[20] Dudziak, *Ibid*, pp. 208-209.

that threaten the future of the United States arises from the presence of Blacks on their soil. When you seek the cause of present troubles and future dangers of the Union, you almost always end up at this first fact, from no matter where you start.[21]

The issue of Black status in America is likely to capture viral awareness and concern than any other across the world. A USIA report showed that 85% of educated elite in Asian and African countries described themselves as being aware of recent racial incidents in America and 91% was the figure in Europe and Latin America.[22] A September 1965 study of residents of Lagos, Nairobi and Dakar found that a high proportion of literate persons had a bad or very bad opinion of the treatment of Blacks in America.[23]

American foreign relation is determined by the extent to which it shows it can therefore handle racial challenges. This was particularly an issue in the bipolar Cold War context—however, it is relevant today. Africans could not have been happy seeing their racial folks being mistreated in America and this could be a rationale for shifting relationship to Russia, America's major rival. One of President Johnson's missions was to re-conquer international trust following the assassination of civil rights reformers and activists such as Kennedy, Martin Luther King, etc. and to do so; he had to move forward on civil rights.[24] However, parallel challenges like the Vietnam War and the eruption of domestic violence made it clear that the problem of inequality could not be fully solved by the President's civil rights agenda. Whatever, once violence occurs and when it is presumed to be premeditated against Blacks or Black supporters, as the case was with George Floyd and many others we cannot name here, that moral authority in world affairs is obviously questioned.

1.3. The Incident

On May 25, 2020, in Minneapolis, America, a White police officer, Derek Chauvin, was caught live on video, pressing his knee against the neck of a Black man called George Floyd, for about nine minutes. The

---

21 De Tocqueville, Alexis, *Democracy in America*, (Chicago, The University of Chicago Press:2000), p. 549.
22 Dudziak, Ibid, p.209.
23 Ibid.
24 Ibid.

unarmed black man was handcuffed, and his face was down as he repeatedly said to the police officer he cannot breath. It took place in the midst of bystanders some of whom pleaded with other officers for help. Other police officers stood by and watched around, paying less attention to what their colleague, Derek Chauvin, himself, irresponsive to the call of the defenceless Black man, was doing to him. After about nine minutes, the White man took his knee off the neck of Floyd and from the video footage, Floyd had ceased to breathe as his neck was uncontrollably swinging left right up down. Few minutes later, an Ambulance drove to the scene and the presumably lifeless body of the Black man was carried along. That was the end of the video footage and also the end of the life of George Floyd! He was later reported dead.

The video of the incident went viral on social media and other media outlets, provoking a stampede of anti-Black racial manifestations and a police response. The protesters denounced racial injustice and police atrocities across America. It is also important to note that the storm of protests that followed the death of George Floyd occurred during the Corona virus pandemic (Covid-19), with little or no respect for the barrier measures to limit the spread of the 'deadly' disease. Protests and reactions to the incident were not only limited to America as, in other parts of the world (Europe, Asia, Middle East, Africa, etc.) similar manifestations were observed.

2. Reactions beyond America

2.1. Theoretical considerations

How and why have foreign governments and society reacted to the death of George Floyd? How has the death of George Floyd affected worldwide perception of America? Worldwide indignation to the death of George Floyd represented the international dimension of what could be considered a domestic affair. American foreign policy is a substantial part of American society and life and for that reason; the world could not have been indifferent.

Categories of international actors who expressed their views on what happened in America include: States, inter-governmental organisations (IGOs), non-governmental organisations (NGOs), civil society/ movements, and individuals of some international standing.

Reactions were determined by the nature and degree of connection between a particular category and America. Categories concerned with the promotion of democracy and rule of law across the world condemned in 'strong' terms what happened in America and used affirmative action to express indignation. Those found in this category include NGOs and most especially civil rights and other rights protection groups and movements like the Black Lives Matter (BLM), the most prominent of all. Categories directly connected to Black citizenry condemned and expressed disappointment. This category is to be dominant in Africa, the cradle of Black descent. Normative reactors consist of those in formal ties of partnership and cooperation with America. The release of official statements to condemn human rights violation in terms that are diplomatic in a sense without necessarily questioning America's moral legitimacy as world leader was common among this category. Other reactors were driven by international power struggle and include America's power rivals and competitors, who saw in what happen and opportunity to expose America's weaknesses. China, Russia and some countries of the Middle East were found in this category.

Categories of reactions can be grouped into two: conventional and nonconventional reactions. Nonconventional reactions are protest demonstrations characterised by (un)authorized (physical and symbolic) violence from demonstrators and police. The violence can be explained by the emotionally charged character of this form of reaction. The reaction in the conventional category is issuance of release statements expressing sympathy, grieve, dissatisfaction, disappointment, and condemnation. State and governmental officials have particularly reacted through their tweeter accounts. In a nutshell there are variations in the reactions of foreign categories regarding the killing of George Floyd and its aftermath.

2.2. Reactions from Europe

In Europe, reactions randomly came from states, European Union (EU) and civil society (through their representatives). The EU's diplomatic chief condemned the "abuse of power" saying that Europe is "shocked and appalled" by police killing of African-American George Floyd. In addition, the EU parliament unlike the AU, which just contented itself with a release statement from its chair, adopted a resolution in which it strongly condemned the "appalling death of George Floyd" and similar practices across the world, white *supremacism* and called on the American government to address its racist practices.[25] The EU parliament also denounced episodes of "looting, arson, vandalism and destruction of public and private property caused by some violent demonstrators" and demanding at the same time that the disproportionate use of force and racist tendencies in law enforcement be publicly denounced wherever and whenever they occur. Boris Johnson of the UK saw the incident as a form of racist violence that he condemned arguing that it "has no place on our society" and that he was "appalled and sickened" by the footage. The chief executive of the Federal Republic of Germany, Angela Merkel did not hesitate to qualify the incident as a murder case stating that "this murder of George Floyd is something very, very terrible". Her foreign minister Heiko Maas expressed German support for demonstrators with the hope that the demonstrations "...won't slide further into violence, but even more than that...that they will make a difference in the United States". In Ireland, the morality of America was questioned as Irish Taoiseach Leo Varadkar said the death of George Floyd meant an "absence of moral leadership" in America. Turkey thought of America as a fascist state as its leader Recep Tayyip Erdogan blamed the death of Floyd on a "racist and fascist approach" in practice in America.

Overall, the death of George Floyd and its aftermath was perceived in Europe as a case of continuous racism, breakdown of morality, power abuse by the police, human rights abuse, etc. The dominant reactions were the issuance of release statements (mostly from governments), mass demonstrations and occupation of public places in protest of what happened. Except for very few cases, most European governments did not use affirmative action to express indignation. Scotland was one of the few examples where affirmative action was used when its Parliament voted a bill to end the export of rubber bullets, tear gas, and riot geared to America, to limit potential of police violence on protesters.

2.3. Reactions from America's Power rivals: Russia and China

Russia and China are traditionally known to be America's super power rivals and competitors. In the Asia and Pacific, China was among the first States to condemn what happened in America. Its foreign

[25] The resolution was adopted with 493 votes to 104 and 67 abstentions. Available at https://www.europarl.europa.eu/news/en/press-room/20200615IPR81223/parliament-condemns-all-forms-of-racism-hate-and-violence-and-calls-for-action, accessed November 20, 2020.

ministry spokesman called out American racism as a "chronic disease of American society". Chinese State and social media have also given extensive coverage of the protests in American cities as if to expose to their audience the weaknesses of the American democracy. However, has the incident further affected Sino-American relations in any substantial way, is what matters the most. Chinese reaction has prompted some American authorities to think of China as a foreign instigator of violence and unrest, along with other American rivals like Russia and Zimbabwe. For example, Robert O' Brien who is also President Trump's National Security Adviser accused China of "taking pleasure and solace in the chaos in America" and added that they will not "get away with it".[26]

Russia made the case of not being surprised with what happened arguing that human rights abuse is systematic in American history and society. The effect of Russia's reaction prompted a feeling of foreign conspiracy among American authorities. They have reinvented foreign conspiracy against the American people. President Trump and some of his collaborators have blamed the unrest in America following the death of Floyd on outside agitators and "foreign adversaries" like Russia.

The reaction from Russia and China is obvious. America has hardly accepted the political system in Russia and China as a constitutional democracy. It was therefore logical for Russia and China to use this crack in the American system to expose the weaknesses of American democracy and rule of law.

2.4. The Middle East:

The Middle East is a hotbed of variations in anti-Americanism. Iran's foreign ministry spokesman Abbas Mousavi invited America to stop violence and told the American people that "...the world has heard [their] outcry over the state of oppression. The world is standing with you." He also called on the American officials and police to allow Americans

---

[26] See AA News Broadcasting System "Zimbabwe summons US ambassador over Floyd's death" https://www.aa.com.tr/en/africa/zimbabwe-summons-us-ambassador-over-floyds-death/1860769

[26] Sharro Karl, Lebanese British satirist resident in London, personal communication with Los Angeles Times, d(June 3, 2020) "As America rages, the Middle East watches with surprise and some schadenfreude", available at https://www.latimes.com/world-nation/story/2020-06-03/america-george-floyd-protests-middle-east-watches-surprise-schadenfreude, accessed November 10, 2020.

"breathe". Iran's Supreme leader, Ali Khamenei also expressed fears about the life of black demonstrators in a retweet.

In fact, memories of American double standard game in the region resurrected and, in some cases, analysts saw no difference between America and some Middle Eastern countries in terms of human rights and abuse of State power. One of the analysts was quoted in the Los Angeles Times as saying, "What you have in the US and what you have in the Arab world are exactly the same: a pauperized citizenry rising up against a militarized state and system...And the system has responded with more security and force, curfews, the National Guard—and of course the president eggs them on".[27]

2.5. From Latin America

A reaction came from the President of Peru describing the killing as a "sign of racism and discrimination" that has to be ended. In Venezuela Nicolas Maduro accused President Trump of using the military against American people claiming that demonstrators were simply demanding an end to racism and police violence. There is a normative explanation to this reaction because relations between Venezuela and America are traditionally known to be tensed.

2.6. From Africa

It was in Africa that the incident had a special resonance however, with reactions from the African Union (AU), the continent's supranational body and from individual countries. Africa is the genetic home of Black people and for obvious reasons the continent could not have been indifferent to an abuse of Black people anywhere in the world. Floyd's case resurrected three key issues: anti-black racism, racial discrimination and the Whiteman's (especially British) colonial legacy. Anti-police violence also constituted part of the protest demonstrations in Africa that was a result of Floyd's death case.

The chairperson of AU commission, Moussa Faki Mahamat condemned the killing of George Floyd, and urged the American

[27] Sharro Karl, Lebanese British satirist resident in London, personal communication with Los Angeles Times, d(June 3, 2020) "As America rages, the Middle East watches with surprise and some schadenfreude", available at https://www.latimes.com/world-nation/story/2020-06-03/america-george-floyd-protests-middle-east-watches-surprise-schadenfreude, accessed November 10, 2020.

government to intensify efforts to ensure the total elimination of all forms of discrimination based on race and ethnic origin. He also expressed wishes of condolence to the bereaved family. The AU also reaffirmed and reiterated the continent's rejection of the continuing discriminatory practices against Black citizens of America.[28]

These are obvious statements expected from an inter-governmental organisation bound by the Principle of Human Rights following its resolution on Racial Discrimination in America made by African Heads of States and governments in 1964, Cairo, Egypt during the OAU's First Assembly Meeting. However, a stronger action (perhaps encouraging a continent's widespread anti-racial protest) would have been expected given that victims of police violence in America are blacks whose ancestral origin is from Africa. It is also the historic responsibility and political duty of Africa through the AU to take affirmative action to protect Blacks wherever they are against all forms of discrimination. Having a Charter condemning racial discrimination is good but effectively overseeing that something that makes a difference is done when Black lives have been abused is much better. A counter-reaction from the American Mission to the AU, however, joined America, Africa and the world not only to condemn the killing of George Floyd, but insisted that the American is taking the matter seriously, notably with the arrest of the police officer for murder and manslaughter charges, and the conduct of a criminal investigation by the American Attorney's Office for the District of Minnesota, the American Department of Justice Civil Rights Division, and the Federal Bureau of Investigation (FBI).

Individual African States have reacted too although they mostly came from English-speaking African countries. In West Africa, Ghana's President, Nana Akufo-Addo said Black people across the world were "shocked and distraught" by the killing of George. He added that the Ghanaian people "stand by their kith and kin in America in this difficult moment".[29] In a protest that brought together some 100 people, Julius Malema, leader of South Africa's radical left party, the Economic Freedom Fighters, at the American embassy in Pretoria on June 8 said

[28] African Union, "Statement of the Chairperson following the murder of George Floyd" available at https://au.int/en/pressreleases/20200529/statement-chairperson-following-murder-george-floyd-usa, accessed November 10, 2020.

[29] CGTN, "Ghanaian president seeks justice for George Floyd" available at https://news.cgtn.com/news/2020-06-02/Ghanaian-president-seeks-justice-for-George-Floyd-QZbIGhctbO/index.html, accessed November 15, 2020.

"Enough with police brutality on our black bodies".[30] They also paid tribute by taking a knee and observing 8 minutes 46 seconds of silence, the time it took for Floyd to die under the knee of White police officer. In Kenya, portraits of Floyd were plastered on walls across Nairobi, the capital city, where, about 200 people demonstrated against police violence in the Mathare slum—with some of the young people and mothers carrying placards with names of friends, neighbours or sons killed in recent times by the police.[31] In Zimbabwe, Floyd's death seems to have given the opportunity to Zimbabwean authorities to speak out their mind and to take affirmative action against a country that has not been supportive of their policies. Their reaction was a counter-reaction to allegations that the American government accused Zimbabwe of taking advantage of the incident to fuel unrest in America. The government of Zimbabwe summoned the American ambassador to the country over remarks by a senior American official accusing it of stirring anti-racism protest following Floyd's death. In an interview over ABC news, the American national security adviser Robert O'Brien referred to Zimbabwe and China as "foreign adversaries" who use social media to promote unrest and "sow discord" after the killing.[32] In the Corniche des Almadies in Dakar, Senegal some 50 people representing various associations of Senegalese civil society gathered to pay tribute to George Floyd. In other African countries, symbols of colonial legacies became objects of violent targets. Some five days after the incident, the Rhodes Stable located at the Matobo National Park in Southern Zimbabwe was burnt down by unknown persons. In South Africa, BLM targeted statues of colonial legacies. Although it is not the first time artefacts of colonial domination were being vandalised in the continent, Floyd's death renewed debate over these symbols of white domination: whether they should be removed or preserved.

30 CNA, Reuters "South African opposition leads Black Lives Matter protests outside US missions", available at https://www.channelnewsasia.com/news/world/george-floyd-protests-south-africa-12816384, accessed January 10, 2021.

31 Halima Gikandi, "Police filling of Georege Floyd strikes a cord in Kenya", *The world*, available at https://www.pri.org/stories/2020-06-04/police-killing-george-floyd-strikes-cord-kenya, accessed January 10, 2021.

32 Jeffrey Moyo, "Zimbabwe summons US ambassador over Floyd's death", *World, America, Africa*, available at https://www.aa.com.tr/en/africa/zimbabwe-summons-us-ambassador-over-floyds-death/1860769, accessed January 10, 2021.

2.7. From The UNO

The UNO through Michelle Bachelet, High Commissioner for Human Rights condemned the act, called on American government to take "serious action" and urged protesters to express their demands for justice peacefully and the American police to refrain from the excessive use of force. No resolution was passed by an assembly as was the case with the EU. Few days later, on June 5, 2020 a group of 66 UNO experts called the killing as modern-day "racial terror" African-Americans, they pursue, "continue to experience racial terror in state-sponsored and privately organised violence".[33] The UN in its reaction recognised that American society is short of the capability of effectively protecting Black live, and by extension human rights. By qualifying the act as racial terror, UN experts are recognising the vulnerability of Black minority and indeed that State terrorism in America is a structural reality.

3. Effects of reactions: shaping perceptions and images of the American State and society

The various worldwide indignations to what happened in America could be linked to forms of perceptions and images about America across the world. The puzzle in the minds of people is whether America can still claim an international leadership role when it comes to mentor respect for democracy and rule of law. The shift in perception about America from moral legitimate leader to doubtful capacity to morally lead seems to be what comes out of the various reactions. America cannot substantially claim international mentorship for democracy and rule of law values because of the multiple 'negative' perceptions and feelings generated across the world about the state of American society following the death of George Floyd and aftermath.

Key perceptions and images generated from worldwide reactions are: 1) that post-racial America is not over, 2) extralegal police violence is not uncommon, 3) target Black killing is an institution, 4) violence is still a technique of domestic politics and 5) America remains a frightening society.

---

[33] The Guardian, "UN experts condemn modern-day 'racial terror' lynching in US, available at https://www.theguardian.com/world/2020/jun/05/un-human-rights-monitors-us-modern-racial-terror-lynchings, accessed January 10, 2021.

3.1. Post-racial America is not over

Prior to the death of Floyd, many people outside America would have thought that post-racial America is over.[34] This perception is under threat of erosion by the events of May 25, 2020. The death of George Floyd seems to have resurrected the feeling that post-racial America is not over. The optimism that the election of Barack Obama, for example, raised was dashed away when it was found that in spite of his ascension to power, black people continued to suffer tremendously under a police that was on what seems like a rampage—killing young black people at alarming rates.[35] Floyd incident just adds to the repertoire of the ugliness. The murder of George Floyd, the existence of rights movements and the emergence of anti-racial demonstrations are indicators that post-racial America is far from being over. A movement like the Black Lives Matter (BLM) became popular following the death of Floyd and is rethinking its strategy of anti-racial struggle as a repair of what previous movements failed to do or did wrongly.[36] Repeated police violence on Blacks and the (re)emergence of anti racial movements sound like racial discrimination and violence is design of American society. Former American President Bill Clinton in a release statement confessed that "In the days since George Floyd's death, it is impossible to feel grieve for his family—and anger, revulsion, and frustration that his death is the latest in a long line of tragedy and injustice, and a painful reminder that a person's race still determines how they will be treated in nearly every aspect of American life".[37] He further made it clear that as white your chance to survive under similar situation is greater when he states: "No one deserves to die the way George Floyd did. And the truth is, if you're white in America, the chances are you won't" We can also feel that racial violence is a fabric of American society and life when we follow President Trump's

[34] This feeling of a 'perfect' American society was also influenced by a 'poisitivist' literature that was able to display American prowess and exceptionalism. See for example American *exceptionalism* ideology in Brendon O'Connor, *Ibid.*

[35] Glaude, *Ibid*, p. 21.

[36] Clark, Amanda & Dantzler, Prentiss & Nickels, Ashley. "Black Lives Matter: (Re) Framing the Next Wave of Black Liberation", (2018: 10.1108/S0163-786X20180000042006) and Lebron, Christopher J. *The making of black lives matter: A Brief history of an idea*, (Oxford, Oxford University Press: 2017).

[37] Chas Danner, "Read what presidents Obama, Bush, Carter, and Clinton have said about George Floyd" *Intelligencer*, available at, https://nymag.com/intelligencer/2020/06/obama-bush-carter-george-floyd-protests.html, accessed August 1, 2020.

statement: "We condemn in the strongest terms this egregious display of hatred, bigotry and violence. On many sides, on many sides it's been going on for a long time in our country. Not Donald Trump, not Barrack Obama. This has been going on for a long time. It has no place in America."[38] What could have been considered an isolated incident is in fact revealing in the eyes of the world that racial discrimination is not forgone but it is strong and alive, perhaps even, it may survive for long.

3.2. Extralegal police violence in societal control

Although police activity is recent in American society, the number has grown tremendously within the last century. Its increasing number indicates the central role this institution plays in American politics. However, the killing of George Floyd by a police and the manner in which the self-same police handled anti-racial protests linked to the incident has raised the question of the role of the police in societal control worldwide.

There is some feeling among people across the world that the American police is using extralegal violence to control society. Images of the brutal suppression of protesters, in some streets of American cities, following the death of Floyd, sent shocking waves across the world. The American police came under attack for using what is perceived as extralegal violence in societal control although some felt that what followed the killing of George Floyd was an overreaction to police wrongdoing.[39] Of what use is the police in American society? Why was the police institution designed? Is there any reason to believe that the police were designed to control Black life and protect White supremacy? We ask these questions to understand why fatal police violence on Blacks is enduring.

The police department was created in the mid-nineteenth century but became a major part of urban politics after about a hundred years after the creation of the republic and with industrialization. Prior to that

---

[38] Woodward, Bob, *Fear Trump in the White House*, (London, New York, Toronto, Sydney, New Delhi, Simon and Schuster: 2018), p. 228.

[39] For example, Guiliani, former mayor of New York is cited in The Washington Post, as saying that "...99 percent, if not more of the police contact with the public is appropriate". He further claimed that "...more police officers are shot and killed, shot and killed by blacks than police officers shoot and kill African Americans. The unarmed shooting which are the ones that are troublesome there are only nine of them against blacks. Twenty against whites in 2019. So that will give you a sense. Meanwhile there were 9000 murders of blacks, 7,500 of which were black-on-black" For details of the interview see https://www.washingtonpost.com/politics/2020/06/17/giuliani-falsely-claims-that-black-people-kill-more-police-than-vice-versa/

order-maintenance was vested in the institutions of slavery and proprietorship, whereby farmers were dedicated to and contented with their small properties and thus unlikely to challenge socio-political order, while slaves were under the personal authority of private masters.[40] Slave patrols[41] existed (although not in all colonies), along with other forms of order-maintenance such as night watch and hiring for protection. Until the creation of modern police, policing essentially took the form of policing communities to check for immigrants and to control slaves.[42]

Police violence in America is not a new phenomenon in Black communities.[43] With the end of slavery and slave trade in 1865, police institution adapted itself to maintain white supremacy through force and racial terror by making slavery and servitude illegal.

What is interesting to note here is that modern police institution also emerged from the slave economy and was intended to protect private property owners—with the private property being Black slaves. This breathed the perception that it was on racist sentiments that police department was created. It is remarkable to realize that, they target Black people, interrupt Black families, and continue to further the notion that Black people are to be punished and watched, and are certainly not to be trusted.[44] The modern police was understood as a professional apparatus, publicly funded, permanently constituted, and acting with the authority of the people themselves,[45] to use disciplinary, welfare and repressive functions that the state exercises in order to guarantee social order.

---

[40] Mitrani, Sam. *The Rise of the Chicago Police Department: Class and Conflict, 1850-1894*, (IL: University of Illinois Press, 2013), p.13.

[41] Slave patrols were created to chase and hunt escaped slaves and to release terror on slave communities to prevent riots and keep plantation owners in check. The patrol was usually made up of three to six men riding horseback and carrying whips, ropes and even guns. For details see Ben Fountain, "Slavery and the origin of American Police State" available at https://gen.medium.com/slavery-and-the-origins-of-the-american-police-state-ec318f5ff05b accessed November 13, 2020.

[42] For details on racial explanation of police origin see Gourevitch, Alex "Police Work: The Centrality of Labor Repression in American Political History" *Review Essay Perspective on Politics,* (American Political Science Association; 2015), Vol. 13/No. 3, pp. 762-773.

[43] Alicia Garca, "Foreword" In Schenwar, Maya., Macare Joe., Price, Alana., *Who Do You Serve Who Do You Protect: Police Violence and Resistance in the United States*, (Chicago, Haymarket Books: 2016).

[44] *Ibid.*, p. 13.

[45] Gourevitch, *Ibid.*

Although modern American police has been lauded for positively responding to shootings and terror attacks, and for enforcing the disenfranchisement laws against the socio-political and economic emancipation of Black people, protests against the police across the world following the death of Floyd remind us that something is wrong with police treatment of citizens worldwide and especially, people of colour in America.

3.3. Violence as technique of domestic politics

We have examined a first form of violence which is extralegal police violence whose scope is limited to the police. We now turn to another form of violence: that which is used as political instrument and whose scope is inclusive. This violence can be used both by the police and other social forces.

In modern American political history, the period after World War II (WWII) was the peak of violence as political instrument. This period was referred to as the 'crisis of the seventies' in which violence was considered as an American way of life. Murder for example, as technique of domestic politics is a description of American politics and society borrowed from Arthur Schlesinger to describe a series of systematic physical violence that culminated in random assassinations of political figures in the decade after WWII. As early as the 60s and 70s America was described as the "domestically most murderous nation in the world" so much that any act of violence beyond American borders, such as the drop of the atomic bomb was barely thought of as an accident.[46]

It was also within this period that Schlesinger raised alarm that 'violence and the politics of the deed' were becoming emerging patterns of American way of life following the killing of three men in the spring of 1968 (John F. Kennedy, Martin Luther King and Robert Kennedy) who greatly embodied the idealism of American life.[47] The presence of the police everywhere in American life suggests impulses of violence rooted in American society. During the 1968 presidential campaign, for example, "At every rally, the police were everywhere. There were cops [also police] on rooftops...in helicopters...in mufti...to control the people,

---

[46] Schlesinger, Arthur M. Jr. "Violence as an American way of life" In. Young James, Consensus *and Conflict: Readings in American Politics*, (Dood, Mead & Company, Inc.: 1972), pp. 17-22, p.20.
[47] *Ibid*, p. 21.

to herd them about, to insulate the candidate against them". Beyond political assassinations and target police violence on Blacks, lynching was also a common form of structured societal violence prior to WWII.[48] Blacks were victim of lynching particularly between 1890 and 1940. Although it was uncommon, it was singular in that it generated a certain form of fear and horror that overwhelmed all other forms of violence.[49] During those years, lynching stood as the primary representation of racial injustice and oppression as a whole and it was expressed in terrifying images of white power and black helplessness refracted not only into black homes and communities but across the American racial landscape.[50] However, it had been on a decline since early 20th century thanks to the activities of National Association for the Advancement of Colored People (NAACP) and other anti-lynching activists.

The death of Floyd is target Black killing that represents in some way a technique of domestic politics. Although Floyd was not a politician per se, the fact that it involved a Black unarmed victim and a white police assailant obviously shaped people's thinking of it as attempt to protect White supremacy by way of illegal force. In any case, violence as an American way of life is rooted in the very foundation of the United States of America. America obtained independence from bloodshed and seemingly, blood is still a major determinant of power relations, in spite of its wide condemnation. As technique of domestic politics violence is used against political adversaries and to protect some predesigned value. Many people beyond America have come to perceive the use of violence as necessary tool to ensure White supremacy. There seem to be a kind of police anarchic murder of Blacks in the air so that theoretically, Blacks are perceived to be victims in America.

3.4. Target Black killing as an institution in America

We cannot talk about extralegal police violence without raising the issue of Black/White police victimization. There is a debate over whom between Blacks and Whites are the most victims of police violence. Some people are of the feeling that more Blacks die in hands of police than Whites while others think the other way round.

---

48 For details, see Wood, A.L *Lynching and Spectacle: Witnessing Racial Violence in America, 1890-1940*, (North Carolina, The University of North Carolina Press: 2009)

49 *Ibid.*

50 *Ibid*, p.2.

The killing of African American George Floyd shaped people's perception that American society is one in which target Black killing is somehow institutionalized. While our intuition may lead us to draw this conclusion, others believe that more Whites die in hands of police than Blacks. President Trump is of that opinion. He stated that although the killing of Floyd was 'terrible', more White people die at hands of police than Blacks.[51] However, Trump's failure to provide evidence has left the impression of an attempt by the President to deny allegations of a systematic target of Blacks by the police and in some way protect the police institution.

Declarations of disproportionate police violence against whites have not gone unchallenged by statistical evidence. Although it is true that between 2013 and 2017, the number of white people killed by the police was higher than Blacks, this was because whites represent a larger portion of the population. However, Black people are three times more likely to be killed than whites by the police.[52] The smell of deadly danger here and there in America turned it into a frightening society.

3.5. America as a frightening society

Atrocities committed here and then in America and beyond America by America left the impression that America is a frightening society. From a domestic standpoint living in America is a risk and this is particular so for Blacks and perhaps other races. Worries expressed by older generations about their children are real. Worries expressed by parents and relatives of immigrants to America are concrete. America is known as a nation of immigrant, but it is also a nation of xenophobia where in Chinese immigrants were excluded, Japanese incarcerated, Mexicans deported and the fear of Muslim, Latinos and the browning of the nation is ever growing.[53] Images of the live murder of George Floyd

---

[51] Interview with CBS Journalist, Catherine Herridge quoted in DeCambre, M. "President Trump says George Floyd's death was 'terrible' but says more 'white people die,' at hands of police than Blacks in U.S." available at https://www.marketwatch.com/story/president-trump-says-george-floyds-death-was-terrible-but-says-more-white-people-die-at-hands-of-police-than-blacks-in-us-2020-07-14.)

[52] Schwartz GL, Jahn JL "Mapping fatal police violence across U.S. metropolitan areas: Overall rates and racial/ethnic inequities, 2013-2017". PLoS ONE 15(6): e0229686, available at https://doi.org/10.1371/journal.pone.022968, accessed October 12, 2020.

[53] See Lee, Erika *America for Americans: A history of xenophobia in America*, (Basic Books: 2019).

must have left Black parents weary of America's capacity to secure the life and future of current and future generation. Hatred and acrimony have led to murder and assassination in America. Hatred for colour, religion, race, position, socioeconomic status, etc can provoke ghastly murder—in fact they have often been associated with crime. Fear is the outcome in societies with established patterns of hatred and acrimony. The institutionalization of fear is the product of domestic violence. Fear is not only expressed in the risk of being killed, it is also manifested in diminished feelings of credible belonging to the American State and society. As domestic violence increases, nationalism is adversely affected. Even if it is the dream of every immigrant to acquire an American nationality (Green card), it is more as means to survive than a substantial expression of love for the *fatherland.* After all, the Green card is not a protection from domestic violence.

From an international perspective dealing with America can turn out a fiasco. America threatened to and attacked foreign countries that were not seen to bear no proportionate relationship to its national security and interest. Vietnam and Iraq are examples. Beyond the symbolic dispensation of power and deterrence for which these attacks and threats could have been intended, smaller States would have to be weary enough about America, even though America has suffered *humiliating* defeat in some cases.

4. Conclusion, discussions and lessons

The death of George Floyd and what followed from it represents a threat to America's legitimate claim of moral authority as world leader. The shocking waves that the incident sent across the world provoked a stampede of reactions that represent ways in which America is perceived by its allies, friends and foes. When deduced from the reactions, post-racial America is not over, extra legal police violence is not uncommon, target Black killing is an institution, violence is still a technique of domestic politics and America remains a frightening society.

This paper provoked some questions related to American *exceptionalism*[54] and moral legitimacy to lead the world. Can these

---

[54] American *exceptionalism* is generally expressed as a belief that America is superior to other nations: a providential nation this is the greatest on earth with an exceptional role to play. See O'Connor Brendon, *Anti-Americanism and American Exceptionalsim: Prejudice and pride about the USA*, (London & New York, Taylor & Francis:2020), p.142.

perceptions make a difference on the way America is expected to behave? Can international indignation to the death of George Floyd help America rethink how to reshape its image abroad by ensuring Blacks are treated well and reducing abuse of police violence? Can they cause America to rethink its moral legitimacy as world leader? What discussions and political lessons can emerge from these perceptions? Is America still the last best hope on earth as Abraham Lincoln once thought? Has America lived up to consider the self-evident truth that all men are born equal as Martin Luther King predicted? Was Thomas Jefferson right in believing in the success of American democracy even though it was failing? Is the American democracy and rule of law system still the envy of much of the rest of the world?

Attempts to respond to these interrogations provide lessons that could be drawn from America and the practice of democracy and rule of law.

4.1. Lesson 1 on worldwide influence

America remains a force to reckon with only to the extent that it can use force to extend its influence worldwide. America can defend its geopolitical and geostrategic interest somehow, but it is hard for it to compel others to turn into what it pretends to be. It is most likely that other States embrace American-style democracy out of fear than out of genuine sheer will and conviction.

4.2. Lesson 2 on theory and practice of democracy and rule of law

America is not a disciplined practitioner of democracy—not being a consistent implementer of democratic values and norms. Implementing democracy is somewhat more or less an occasional moment in the political live thread of the American system.[55] Fundamentally, the State in America is struggling to interiorise racial equality. Democracy is the ability to conceal undemocratic attitudes and behaviours. That is the image America seems to display about democracy. So long as a State presumably democratic can conceal violations of democracy from international public eye, it remains presumably democratic. At best, democracy is a struggle without end.

---

[55] Putnam, Robert "Bowling alone: America's declining social capital" *Journal of democracy*, (January 1995), pp. 65-78.

4.3. Lesson 3 on Black and black place in American society

The American society has pretentiously accepted blacks. Black position in American society is precarious as Blacks remain vulnerable. Blacks have been accepted in American society but have not been genuinely considered.

4.4. Lesson 4 on repairing image abroad

The world now views contemporary America with consternation. International indignation is however necessary. An international eye could act as agent in detecting violent impulses in American society. In some way it can help America rethink how to shape its image abroad. America has to rethink its commitment made to the American people, friends and allies across the world—commitment to uphold and defend democracy, human rights, equality, justice and rule of law. If America does not want to rethink, then, it should be able to control technology to avoid the evasion of information about the atrocities committed in American cities. Unfortunately, this seems almost impossible. The much talk about reform of the police is a product of protest marches across America, which in turn, is a reaction to the murder of George Floyd. Taking concrete actions to reform the police can repair America's image abroad. America is sick and needs entrenched attitudes of accepting and considering the 'other' to get healed and to prevent the worst.

Cameroon's compliance with the international standard for combating the financing of terrorism: the road not taken

Patience Sone

Associate Professor of Law, Depart of English Law, University of Buea
Emial: pattysonem@gmail.com

and

Sona Mukete Gerald

Department of English Law, University of Buea
Email: sonamukete@gmail.com

Abstract

Terrorist acts require finances thus the best approach towards combating such acts is suppressing the means of funding to terrorist organisations. This study investigates Cameroon's compliance with the international standard for combating the financing of terrorism. Cameroon's commitment in suppressing the financing of terrorism is impeded by inadequate funds and intelligence. The system of blacklisting of individuals and organisations associated with terrorist groups which constitute a step in combating the financing of terrorism in Cameroon is problematic. The 2003 law on Money Laundering and Financing of Terrorism in Central Africa which is applicable in Cameroon lacks a review mechanism for targeted individuals and organisations to defend and seek redress against preventive measures or orders affecting them. The study adopts the qualitative methodology and the method used is content analyses of both primary and secondary sources. The study finds that Cameroon's commitment with the international standard in combating the financing of terrorism is impeded by inadequate funds and intelligence necessary for suppressing the financing of terrorism. To address the dearth of a review mechanism of blacklisting individuals suspected of associating with terrorists groups, it is recommended that the 2014 anti-terrorism law be amended to incorporate a designation process of individuals and organizations suspected of associating with terrorist organisations.

Keywords: Terrorism, compliance, Combating, financing, international, standard, Cameroon

Introduction

The first cause argument of the existence of God is to the effect that nothing causes itself to be. The existence of something is due to a chain of events or causes with an original cause which itself is unmoved.[1] This argument is a fundamental principle of insurance known as 'proximate cause'.[2] The analogy here is that acts of terrorism committed by perpetrators are fuelled by individuals or groups other than the direct perpetrators. These individuals or groups are 'hiding behind the veil'. These persons are obviously the original or proximate cause of terrorist acts. It therefore becomes imperative to prohibit not just the perpetrator of the terrorist acts but also those financing the acts. Krieger and Meierrieks[3] argue that "drying out the financial flow from terrorist financers to terrorist groups or from terrorist headquarters to terrorist cells can largely hamper terrorist capacities to attack". Investigation from the US government averred that at least $238,000 was sent into the US through wire transfers to facilitate the 9/11 attacks, of which $500,000 was estimated as the cost to execute the acts.[4] According to experts, the financial strength of Bin Laden made the 9/11 attacks possible.

There are a good number of methods through which terrorists derive funds. Chinedu[5] identifies two categories of such methods namely financial support and revenue generating activities. While the former is derived from donations, community solicitation and other fundraising initiatives, the latter constitutes income derived from criminal activities such as kidnapping, extortion, smuggling or fraud. Income gotten from legitimate

---

[1] T., Aquinas, *Summa Theologica*, Part 1a, Question 2, About God Whether he Exists, Article III., translated by Fathers of the Dominican Province,

[2] *Scottish Union* and *National Insurance Company v. Alfred Pawsey* and *Company* (Jamaica) Privy Council (16 Oct, *1908*) 16 Oct, *1908* ... [*1908*] UKPC 60. The proximate cause of a loss is its effective or dominant cause.

[3] T., Krieger and D., Meierrieks, Terrorist Financing and Money Laundering (June 8, 2011), p.2. Available at SSRN: https://ssrn.com/abstract=1860069 or http://dx. doi. Org / 10 .2139/ssrn.1860069, visited, 11/09/2019.

[4] A.D., Hardister, "Can We Buy a Peace on Earth: The Price of Freezing Terrorist Assets in a Post-September 11 World", *28 North Carolina Journal of International Law & Commercial Regulation*, 2002, vol.28, N0.3, p.605.

[5] C.E Chinedu, "Transnational Organised Crimes and Terrorist Financing in West Africa: Challenges and Strategies", *African Journal for the Prevention and of Terrorism*, 2011, vol.2, No.1, p.75.

economic activities such as diamond trading or real estate investment also fall within this category.[6]

Suppressing terrorist financing becomes necessary considering the difficulty in defeating terrorists physically. It is therefore the perfect way to suppress the means for doing harm and facilitates the penetration of organized groups by the law enforcement. The global action plan adopted at the World Ministerial Conference on Organized Transnational Crime,[7] also reiterates the need to suppress the financing of terrorism. It enjoins States to "ensure that the fight against organized transnational crime is based on strategies aimed at defeating the economic power of criminal organizations."[8]

In Cameroon and its neighbouring countries, Boko Haram[9] has committed terrorists' acts. These acts have negatively affected the social and economic activities in Nigeria, Cameroon and neighbouring countries as well as refugee crisis.[10] With regard to funding, how the Boko Haram Islamic Sect is being funded is a controversial issue which has not been agreed on. The US Treasury reports that the group is cautious and avoids making use of official banking systems. To them, funding of Boko Haram comes from 'sophisicated financiers' who avoid being tracked. Human couriers carry money around and move from one place to another and they hide their financial transactions with other terrorist groups.[11]

---

[6] *Ibid.* This category also include fund raising by the diaspora. For instance, Sri Lanka's *LTTE* (*Liberation Tigers of Tamil Eelam*) received donations from the diaspora. T., Krieger and D., Meierrieks, *op cit.* p.9-11.

[7] Naples, November 21-23, 1994. Report to the United Nations General Assembly on the World Ministerial Council on Organized Transnational Crime, A/49/748/1994.

[8] Political Declaration and Global Action Plan against Organized Transnational Crime, report to the United Nations General Assembly, *op.cit.*, para. 35.

[9] *Jama'atu Ahlis Sunna Lidda'awati Wal-Jihad* (the 'Association for propagating the Prophets' teaching and Jihad') commonly known as Boko Haram is among the most dangerous terrorist groups in the world that has caused insecurity and fear. Curbing Violence in Nigeria (II): The Boko Haram Insurgency Africa, International Crisis Group Report N°216, 3 April 2014, p.7.

[10] O., Faluyi, An Assessment of Nigeria's Counterterrorism Policies Against Boko Haram, Masters Thesis, University of KwaZulu-Natal, 2017, p.5, available at https://researchspace.ukzn.ac.za/handle/10413/14762, visited,03/03/2021.

[11] M., Fisseha, The Nexus between Religion and Terrorism: An Investigation into the Boko Haram Killing Activities in Nigeria, Unpublished Masters Thesis, Uppsala University, 2016, p.5-6, available at http://uu.diva-portal.org/smash/get/diva2:933994/FULLTEXT01.pdf, visited, 03/03/2021.

Establishing a framework for suppressing the financing of terrorism by a state is therefore the ideal for that state's duty of protecting the citizens and guaranteeing security. Apparently, Cameroon is not inactive in the global struggle to suppress the financing of terrorism. How committed is Cameroon with the international standard for combating the financing of terrorism is therefore what this article seeks to aver. In this light, the study examines the international standard for combating the financing of terrorism. The social contract theory is used to ascertain Cameroon's commitment with this international standard by analyzing the relevant domestic laws and enforcement machinery.

Theoretical foundations: the social contract theory

This study builds its argument on the social contract theory which maintains the notion that the state or specifically, civil society is the product of a contract, a covenant, an agreement, or a compact.[12] The theory states that human beings give up certain rights they have in a state of nature in order to obtain the securities and rights provided by civilization.[13] Advocates of the theory in its modern form are Thomas Hobbes, John Locke, Baruch Spinoza, Samuel Pufendorf, Jean-Jacques Rousseau and Immanuel Kant.

Locke's "contract of government" presupposes that the people had earlier given their mutual consent to the formation of society [14] and then, as members of society, they later chose their rulers to form their government, each party having specific duties and obligations. It becomes necessary to use the social contract theory to illustrate the commitment of the government of Cameroon in combating the financing of terrorism. Counter financing of terrorism measures undertaken by the government of Cameroon is an indication that it is committed in the social contract because the essence of these measures is to guarantee the security of the citizens. Whereas the inefficacy of counter financing of terrorism measures in Cameroon would obviously be a breach of the social contract.

---

[12] D., Alubabari, "The Social Contract Theory: A Model for Reconstructing a True Nigerian Nation-State", *International Journal of Humanities and Social Science,* vol. 2 No. 15, 2012, p.268.

[13]J., Rousseau, The Social Contract (1762), available at http://www. constitution. org/jjr/socon. htm; http:// www.iep.utm. edu/soc-cont/, visited, 23/03/2021.

[14] D., Alubabari, *op cit.,* p.270.

International standard for combating the financing of terrorism

Security Council Resolution 1267

The United Nations Security Council's (UNSC) Resolution 1267 counter-terrorism sanctions regime initially adopted in 1999, targets individuals and entities suspected of associating with Al Qaeda and/or the Taliban and it requires UN Member States to freeze their assets and implement travel bans.[15] The Resolution established the Al-Qaeda and Taliban Sanctions Committee which operates with the use of a "Consolidated List".[16]

The Committee has the mandate of overseeing the sanctions regime provided in the Resolution. It possesses discretionary powers to list and de-list targeted individuals.[17] States and regional organizations may propose names for listing and provide a statement of case in support of the proposed listing. Individuals and entities that are targeted have the privilege to submit a request for de-listing through the State of their residence or citizenship in the UN Secretariat. The Sanctions Committee makes decision on listing or de-listing requests by consensus.[18]As to June 2007, there were 142 individuals and one entity associated with the

[15]The sanctions regime has since 9/11 been modified and strengthened by subsequent resolutions, including resolutions 1333 (2000), 1363 (2001), 1373 (2001), 1390 (2002), 1452 (2002), 1455 (2003), 1526 (2004), 1566 (2004), 1617 (2005), 1624 (2005), 1699 (2006), 1730 (2006), 1735 (2006), 1822 (2008), and 1904 (2009) in consequence extending its scope to cover individuals and entities associated with Al Qaeda, Osama bin Laden, and/or the Taliban wherever located. See Consolidated Reference for OSCE Anti-terrorism Efforts, Organisation for Security and Cooperation in Europe, March 2018, p.5, available at https:// www.osce. org/files/ f/ documents /0/8/99765_0.pdf, visited, 10/10/2020.

[16]C., Michaelsen, "The Security Council's Al Qaeda and Taliban Sanctions Regime: "Essential Tool" or Increasing Liability for the UN's Counterterrorism Efforts?,"*Journal Studies in Conflict & Terrorism,* vol.33, Issue 5, 2010, abstract.

[17] *Ibid.* It is important to know how the blacklist's actually work. It is simple, under the 1267 Committee's 2002 Guidelines 8, any Security Council member may propose a name, which is then circulated among other members for five working days. If no member objects, then the name is included in the list. If an individual is listed, all States are required to freeze that individual's assets, prevent his/her entry into or transit through their territories, and prevent the direct or indirect supply, sale and transfer of arms and military equipment. R., Uruena, Beyond a Matter of Rights: The UN's 1267 Committee and the Hidden Role of International Law in Anti – Terrorist Policy, p.3.

[18]See the Guidelines of the Sanctions Committee, available at http://www. un. org/sc/committees 1267/ pdf/1267_guidelines.pdf, visited, 09/12/2020.

Taliban included in the consolidated list, as well as 223 individuals and 124 entities associated with Al-Qaida.[19]

The resolution 1267 sanction regime has been criticized for neglecting human rights and the due process of law. This is because the 1267 sanction review did not offer any recourse or review mechanism for individuals who argued they were wrongfully sanctioned. In the case of *Assin Abdullah Kadi and Al Barakaat International Foundation v. Council of the European Union and Commission of the European Communities,*[20] *the European Court of Justice challenged the* 1267 regime and held that it violated fundamental human rights, posing a potential threat to the legitimacy of the Council's larger sanctions enterprise. In consequence, review machinery for requests for delisting from sanctioned individuals or entities was established by the Council in 2009.

United Nations Convention on the Suppression of Financing Terrorism 1999

The International Convention for the Suppression of the Financing of Terrorism 1999 (hereafter referred to as the Convention on Terrorist Financing) is the major UN counter-terrorism Convention on combating the financing of terrorism.[21] Article 2(1) of the Convention describes the offence of financing of terrorism to include unlawful and willful provision or collection of funds with the intention that to commit acts of terrorism. The Convention on Terrorist Financing is criticized for the lack of an enforcement mechanism. This is a problem because implementation of its provisions is the discretion of member-states.[22] The problem was however addressed in Security Council Resolution 1373 (2001).

---

[19] R., Uruena, *op cit.*, p.3.

[20] (C402/05 P) and (C-415/05 P) [2008]. In this case, the Council of the European Union and Commission of the European Communities passed a regulation that froze the funds of Mr. Kadi and Al Barakaat (Appellants) pursuant to the Resolution 1267 sanction regime.

[21] Cameroon deposited its instrument of accession to this Convention on the 6th February 2006. The International Convention for the Suppression of the Financing of Terrorism 1999, available at https://treaties .un.org›Pages › ViewDetails, visited, 09/12/2020.

[22] A.D., Hardiste, *op cit*, p.624.

Security Council Resolution 1373 (2001)

Security Council Resolution 1373 which reaffirmed the Council's unequivocal condemnation of the terrorist acts of 11 September and call on all member States to criminalize the willful provision or collection of funds for terrorist acts and to freeze any financial assets and economic resources of those who commit or attempt to commit terrorist acts or participate in or facilitate the commission of terrorist acts and of persons and entities acting on behalf of terrorists.[23]

The resolution permits member states to designate persons and entities whose assets can be frozen.[24] So designation of persons and entities for association with terrorist organisations is done by member states and not the Security Council.

Resolution 1373 has more probative value than the Convention on Terrorist Financing 1999 reason being that states agree whether to make Conventions binding on them but do not have an option on UN resolutions which are binding on all UN member-states.[25] It therefore proffers a more effective framework for freezing terrorist assets than the 1999 Convention.[26]

Its binding nature is also seen in the establishment of enforcement machinery which is the Counter-Terrorism Committee (CTC). The CTC is made up of all 15 members of the Security Council and the mission is to monitor States' implementation of the resolution and, where necessary, to facilitate the provision of relevant technical assistance to Member States.[27] The mandate of the committee was expanded to include monitoring its implementation by the 2005 Resolution 1624 relating to the issue of incitement to commit acts of terrorism adopted on 14 September 2005 during the UN World Summit.

---

23 Security Council, press release, 28 September 2001, SC/7158.

24 K., Stroligo, Guidelines Regarding the Necessary Steps to be Taken for Effective Implimentation of the UN Security Resolutions on Terrorism, 25, April 2007, p.5, available at https://www. coe.int/t/dg1 /legalcooperation/economiccrime/MoneyLaundering/Projects/MOLI%20UA2/moliua2_Klaudio_Guidelines_UNSC_Resolutions_against_terrorism_eng.pdf, visited,23/03/2021.

25 See A.D., Hardiste, *op cit.*, p.625.

26 *Ibid.*

27 A Review of the Legal Regime Against Terrorism in West and Central Africa, United Nations Office on Drugs and Crime Vienna, Working Document, October 2008, p.6.

Resolution 1373 instituted a reporting system whereby states are to report to the CTC on the steps that they have taken to implement the resolution.[28] The basis of the Committee's work with Member States is therefore mostly seen in the reports.

Reluctance of the CTC to adopt coercive measures is a loophole of this institution. It has not been able to adopt sanctions against failures to comply with Res 1373 (both for material breaches or non-fulfillment of reporting requirements) and many indications show that the possibility of the imposition of these measures in the near future is very slim.[29]

Cameroon's compliance with international standards

Cameroon's compliance with the international standard for suppressing the financing of terrorism illustrates its commitment to the social contract. To what extent is Cameroon committed in the social contract in relation to combating the financing of terrorism is therefore the question that begs for answer. In 2002, Cameroon expressed commitment to UN's counter-terrorism legal framework by reporting its counter terrorism measures pursuant to Resolution 1373. Several measures were outlined by the government to curb terrorism.[30] It acknowledged the efforts towards the adoption of a specific legislation on terrorism but stated that it has a general legal framework that enables it to respond to terrorism, such as the Penal Code.[31] With regard the suppression of the financing of terrorism, the government referred to section 97 of the Penal Code that covers complicity.[32]

In its 2006 Report to the CTC, it pointed out the step it took in the adoption of a legislation for the prevention and suppression of terrorist

[28] Note verbale SCA/20/01(6).

[29] Three options were considered by the CTC in a policy document to deal with late or non-reporting members to wit: i) inviting the Permanent Representative to a meeting, ii) preparing a reminder letter, or iii) making a recommendation to the CTC to defer the deadline. CTC, Revised procedures for the Counter-Terrorism Committee's stocktaking of Member States' implementation of Security Council Resolutions 1373 (2001) and 1624 (2005), 11 March 2013, § 12, available at http://www.un.org/en/sc/ctc/docs/2013, visited, 23/03/2021.

[30] CTC (S/2002/277.

[31] Provisions cited include sections 9, 94,103,114, 227, 316-2, 275, 276,277, 278, 279, 280, 281,94, 229.

[32] *Ibid.* p.41.

acts,[33] the creation of a Technical Inter-Ministerial Commission by the Minister of State responsible for Justice Affairs to incorporate UN Counter-terrorism instruments as well as the organization of a Workshop with the United Nations Office on Drugs and Crimes (UNODC) which resulted to legislative changes geared towards making national legislation to reflect the UN Counter-terrorism instruments. The government also cited Regulation No. 01/03-CEMAC-UMAC-CM (4 April 2003) as the legal framework for combating the suppression of the financing of terrorism and money-laundering in Central Africa.[34]

The absence of a specific legislation on the financing of terrorism in particular and on terrorism in general in the reports, reiterate the inherent problem of reporting as an enforcement mechanism. Reporting is actually 'window dressing' and as such lacks a system of sanction. The reports only enable recommendations that states may choose to either obey or disobey. Nevertheless, Cameroon enacted a specific legislation on terrorism in 2014, the Law on Suppression of Acts of Terrorism 2014 (the 2014 anti-terrorism law). This law is actually a demonstration of Cameroon's commitment in the social contract given that it punishes severely terrorists' acts as well as the financing of terrorism.

Can the enactment of the 2014 law be attributed to the recommendations resulting from Cameroon's Report to the CTC? If the answer is in the affirmative, then the importance of state reporting as an enforcement measure cannot be overemphasized. Such importance has been recognized in scholarly works. Saunders[35] for example, asserts that "the work of reporting helps to 'socialize' or 'acculturate' states, ultimately nudging states to behave in conformity with the prevailing cultural norms the reports have helped shape (whether the states agree with the norms' content or not)".

---

33 A Review of the Legal Regime Against Terrorism in West and Central Africa, United Nations Office on Drugs and Crime Vienna, Working Document, October 2008, p.42.
34 *Ibid.*
35 P.Q., Saunders, "The Integrated Enforcement of Human Rights", *New York University Journal of International Law and Politics*, 2012, p.103.

Regulation No. 02/10–CEMAC–UMAC 2003 Relating to the Prevention and Suppression of Money Laundering and Financing of Terrorism in Central Africa

No.02/10-UMAC 2003 lays down rules with the aim of preventing, detecting, checking or suppressing the use of the financial system or other sectors of the economies of the CEMAC States for the purposes of money laundering; the financing of terrorist acts whether they are associated with money laundering or not.[36] Pursuant to article 5 of the regulation, persons liable include: "any individual or legal person that, as part of practice, carries out, controls, or advises on transactions involving deposits, exchange, investments, conversions or all other capital movements….".

These persons have the obligation to report 'suspicious transactions and funds intended to be used for financing of terrorism, terrorist acts or terrorist organizations to the National Agency for Financial Investigation.[37] The Regulation establishes a system of designation of persons, entities or organizations that may be subject to restrictive measures for association with a terrorist organization or involvement in financing of terrorism. According to article 37 of the Regulation, the Counter Terrorism Committee/Sanctions Committee[38] is responsible for such designation while the Ministerial Committee[39] enlist persons, entities or organizations whose funds have been frozen by financial bodies or the other persons liable under the Regulation, "in conformity with the list of the Sanctions Committee and information gathered in the

---

[36] Article 4 of Regulation No. 02/10–CEMAC–UMAC 2003. Article 3(25) defines funds as assets of every kind, whether tangible or intangible, movable or immovable, however acquired, and legal documents or instruments in any form, including electronic or digital, evidencing title to, or interest in, such assets, including, but not limited to, bank credits, travellers cheques, bank cheques, money orders, shares, securities, bonds, drafts, letters of credit. For the definition of terrorism, see article 3(22) of the Regulation.

[37] Article 36 Regulation No. 02/10–CEMAC–UMAC 2003.

[38] It is the United Nations Security Council Committee composed of all members of the said Council set 5 up by Resolution No. 1373 adopted on 28 September 2001 by the United Nations Security Council concerning counterterrorism, to monitor implementation of the very Resolution No. 1373. *Ibid.* Article 3(11).

[39] It is the Ministerial Committee of the Monetary Union of Central Africa. *Ibid.* article 3(5).

Member States". From 26 June 2014, Boko Haram and its major leaders were listed pursuant to the designation process in the Regulation.[40]

The Regulation has however not provided a review mechanism for designated persons and organisations. It means the right to a remedy by an individual or organization whose funds have been frozen is suppressed. This is an infringement of the right to fair hearing which is an inalienable right. This is compounded in article 22 of the Regulation which gives immunity to 'persons liable' under the regulation from liability.[41] It is worth noting that the right to a remedy by designated persons is recognized in other supranational legal system for example, the European Union. According to Article 33 of Regulation (EU) 2018/1805 on the Mutual Recognition of Freezing Orders and Confiscation Orders,[42] "affected persons have the right to effective legal remedies in the executing State against the decision on the recognition and execution of freezing orders. The right is invoked before a court in the executing State in accordance with its law".[43]

The implication of lack of review machinery in the CEMAC Regulation is that a person or entity blacklisted may unjustly suffer and the suffering can even extend beyond the immediate victim. For instance, the freezing of the assets of the al Barakaat network led to the shutting down of the business.[44] This rendered workers unemployed and also affected those who simply used the business for remittance. Given that al Barakaat was the primary institution used by the Somali community to remit money to their family in Somalia, the freezing of its assets resulted to the loss of their life savings.

---

40 Synthesis of Activities of the Nafi in 2014, available at https://www.anif.cm/images/pdfanif/SYNTHESIS-OF-ACTIVITIES-OF-THE-NAFI--IN-2014.pdf,visted, 07/10/2020,p.18.

41 Article 22 states:….."no civil liability action may be brought, nor any professional sanction imposed for violation of banking or professional secrecy or in any other capacity against a financial body, its officials or employees that in good faith reported and carried out other procedures prescribed by this Regulation or blocked a transaction within the framework of this Regulation, notwithstanding that the investigations led neither to prosecution nor to conviction".

42 Regulation (EU) 2018/1805 of the European Parliament and of the Council of 14 November 2018 on the mutual recognition of freezing orders and confiscation orders.

43 See article 23(1)) *ibid.*

44 V., Ortblad, "Criminal Prosecution in Sheep's Clothing: The Punitive Effects of OFAC Freezing Sanctions", *Journal of Criminal Law and Criminology*, 2008, Vol. 98, Issue 4, p.1453.

Coercive measures for involvement in the financing of terrorism are enshrined in the Regulation.[45] These measures may be seizures or other provisional measures ordered by a competent legal authority.[46]Article 52 makes the financing of terrorism a criminal offence punishable with imprisonment of atleast 10 years and a fine that may exceed ten times the sums in question but not being below CFAF 10000000.[47]

It can be understood from the CEMAC Regulation that the freezing and confiscation orders involve both administrative and legal procedures. The administrative procedure is reflected in the blacklisting of suspected persons and organisations pursuant to UN Security Council Resolutions, while the legal procedure is manifested in the criminalization of terrorism.

Law on suppression of acts of terrorism in Cameroon 2014

The Law on the Suppression of Acts of Terrorism (the 2014 anti-terrorism law) is Cameroon's counter-terrorism legislation. It was enacted following the extension of the activities of the Boko Haram Islamic Sect to Cameroon.[48] Article 2(1) of the law provides a vague description of terrorism which may lead to the criminalization of groups whose aim is to peacefully protest such as labour, minority or human rights groups.[49] This is so because mere protest that takes the form of any of the acts mentioned in 2(1)for example, destruction of state property constitutes terrorism. The law prohibits the financing of terrorism. Section 3 provides:

> Whoever directly or indirectly: a. Provides and/or collects funds; b. Provides or offers or collects funds with the aim of financing acts of terrorism and by whatever means, shall be punished with the death penalty. The offence referred to in Section 3(1) above shall be deemed to have been perpetrated even where the funds, the material means and/or financial services have not effectively been used to commit the offence.

---

[45] *Ibid.* article 43. Article 43 concerns seizure of property of designated persons suspected to be used in terrorism while article 44 imposes seizure of property of designated persons on the ground of the presumption of the property being used for terrorism.

[46] These coercive measures once ordered may still be uplifted. *Ibid.*

[47] This article further provides that the punishment is only enforced if the funds are effectively used to commit the offence stated in article 3(22) of the Regulation.

[48] S.G., Mukete, "A Legal Perspective of the Definition of Defining Terrorism: The Case of Cameroon", *African Journal of Social Sciences,* vol.10, No.6, p.40.

[49] *Ibid.* p.42.

This provision shows that Cameroon has incorporated the U.N Security Council Resolution 1373 (2001) which call on all States to criminalize the willful provision or collection of funds for terrorist acts. Going by the 2014 anti-terrorism law, financing of terrorism is a punishable offence in Cameroon. This provision reflects the prohibition of financing of terrorism contained in article 2(1) of the Convention for the Financing of Terrorism 1999. Just like the Convention for the Financing of Terrorism, the 2014 anti-terrorism law prohibits the collection and provision of funds related to terrorism even if the funds are not actually used for terrorism.[50] However, in the Convention for the Financing of Terrorism, the collection and provision of funds must be unlawful and willful.

Going by the language of section 3, involuntary provision of funds can be cut up within its scope because section 3 does not include the requirement of 'willful' and 'unlawful' provision of funds. This means the prohibition of payment for ransom to terrorists is indirectly within the scope of section 3 of the 2014 anti-terrorism law. This is not the case with the Convention on Terrorist Financing. Bundy[51]asserts:

> The Convention's definition of terrorist financing as the provision or collection of funds "by any means, directly or indirectly, unlawfully and willfully with the intention or in the knowledge that they are to be used" in furtherance of terrorist acts might be read broadly to encompass finances exchanged for hostage release. However, the provision's application only to persons providing funds "unlawfully and wilfully" distinguishes the deliberate financing of known terrorist activities, prohibited under the Convention, from the legitimate interests of humanitarian undertakings. The exemption of the latter category of activities reflects the drafters' intent to preserve, among other humanitarian endeavors, the ability to negotiate for the freedom and safety of hostages.

The 2014 anti-terrorism law does not define the term 'funds'. It is therefore not clear if the term is confined to the literary meaning which is of course pecuniary benefit or extends beyond the literary meaning to cover assets of every kind, whether tangible or intangible, movable or

---

[50] This is the same position in Nigeria where the Nigerian Terrorism (Prevention) (Amendment) Act, 2011, (as amended) provides that a person is deemed to commit the offence of terrorist funding if he knowingly enters into or becomes involved in an arrangement as a result of which money or other property is made available, or is to made available, for the purpose of terrorism or for a proscribed organization. section 13(b). So, the violator is punished incurs criminal responsibility even if the funds have not been used.

[51] E.,Bundy, "Rescuing Policy and Terror Victims: A Concerted Approach to the Ransom Dilemma Ransom Dilemma", *Michigan Journal of International Law*, vol.37, issue.4, p.721.

immovable as defined in the Convention for Financing of Terrorism. For example, if a person provides an animal for the purpose of committing terrorism, can one say that it constitutes the offence of financing of terrorism as per the 2014 anti-terrorism law? The answer to this question will necessitate inspiration from other jurisdictions. Article 421-2-2 of the French Penal Code provides that the reference to the term "funds" includes "funds," "securities or property of any kind," and "advice."[52] In Japan, in article 2 of the Act on the Punishment of Financing of Offences of Public Intimidation, defines "funds" to mean "cash and monetary instruments easily convertible into cash." The scope of the definition has been extended by Ministry of Justice of Japan whose definition include "not only cash and other means of payment," but also "other kinds of assets that are provided or collected with the intention of gaining such cash or other means of payment as a fruit or to be converted into such cash or other means of payment."

From observation, the 2014 anti-terrorism law does not provide for the designation of individuals and organisations associated with terrorists to whom preventive measures such as freezing of funds could be imposed. To recall, Resolution 1373 permits member states of the UN to such individuals and organisations as a step in combating the financing of terrorism. This obligation is given statutory effect in some jurisdictions. For example, in New Zealand, the Terrorist Suppression Act 2000. Pursuant to section 22 of this Act, the Prime Minister may designate an entity as a terrorist entity if the Prime Minister believes on reasonable grounds that the entity has knowingly carried out, or has knowingly participated in the carrying out of, one or more terrorist acts. The Act makes it a criminal offence to have any dealings with such entities such as providing services, property or funds.[53]

However, the blacklisting of terrorists (individuals and entities suspected of terrorist acts) remains a measure in combating the financing of terrorism in Cameroon. From article 37 of CEMAC Regulation No. 02/10–CEMAC–UMAC 2003, one can deduce two aspects: first, the Resolution 1267 designation process is automatically applied in Cameroon and second, the government of Cameroon has forfeited its rights to designate terrorists to the Ministerial Committee of CEMAC.

---

52 H , Tofangsaz, *op cit.*, p.92.

53 See also articles L562-1 and L562-2 of the French Financial and Monetary Statute 2005.

Enforcement

Cameroon's commitment in the social contract vis-à-vis combating the financing of terrorism is also visible in its subscription to the 40 Recommendations and 9 Special Recommendations of the Paris Based Financial Action Task Force (FATF) against money laundering and financing of terrorism respectively.[54] FATF is an inter-governmental organisation whose establishment resulted from the G7 Summit in Paris in 1989 to enhance cooperation among states by developing and promoting policies that combat money laundering and terrorism financing.[55]FATFs 40 Recommendations on money-laundering and its Special 9 Recommendations on terrorist financing guarantee an effective global enforcement regime, specifically preventive measures by states to combat money laundering and terrorist financing in various financial institutions.[56]

By subscribing to FATF, Cameroon therefore enjoys the privilege of membership in the Egmont Group, an informal organisation of FATF regime compliant countries.[57] Cameroon is not on the FATF List of Countries that has been identified as having strategic Anti-Money Laundering deficiencies.[58] With regard to compliance with FATF

---

54 See C., "Okereke *et al.*, Terrorism in Africa: Trends and Dynamics", *African Journal for the Prevention and Combating of Terrorism*, 2016, vol.5 N° 1, p.98 who points out that several African states have subscribed to the 40 Recommendations and 9 Special Recommendations of the Paris Based Financial Action Task Force (FATF) against money laundering and financing of terrorism. Cameroon's membership in the *Groupe d'Action contre le Blanchisement d'Argent en Africa Centrale* (GABAC)is another plus in its commitment in combating the financing of terrorism.

55T., Cheludo, The Impact of the Financial Action Task Force Counter Terrorist Financing Measures on Women Rights Organisations in Developing Countries, p.3, available at https://www. researchgate. net/ public ation/32 93 1000 3_The _Impact_ of_ the_ Financial _Action_ Task_Force_ Counter_ Terrorist_ Financing _Measures_on_Women_Rights_Organisations_in_Developing_Countries/link/5c15e7 4592851c39ebf08c79/download, visited, 23/03/2021.

56 FATF, 2012.

57 The Egmont Group is a united body of 165 Financial Intelligence Units (FIUs**)**. The Egmont Group provides a platform for the secure exchange of expertise and financial intelligence to combat money laundering and terrorist financing (ML/TF). Available at https://egmontgroup.org/en/content/about,visited,05/10/2020.

58 Unlike Nigeria that was place by FATF in June 2001 on its list of non-cooperative countries and territories (NCCTS) in combating money laundering. S., Ghoshray, Compliance Convergence in FATF Rulemaking: The Conflict Between Agency Capture and Soft Law, 2015, 59, 1-25.

Recommendations, the 2008 Mutual Evaluation Report relating to the implementation of anti-money laundering and counter-terrorist financing standards in Cameroon was undertaken in 2008, found Cameroon Compliant for 0 and Largely Compliant for 10 of the FATF 40 + 9 Recommendation.[59]

National Agency for Financial Investigation

The National Agency for Financial Investigation (NAFI) is a creation of article 25 of Regulation No. 02/10–CEMAC–UMAC 2003. It is responsible for receiving, processing and, if necessary, forwarding to the competent judicial authorities' reports required of financial institutions and persons liable under the Regulation.[60] It has the power to freeze the funds of designated persons by the Counter Terrorism Committee or enlisted by the Ministerial Committee.[61]

Its establishment by Presidential Decree No. 2005/187 of 31 May 2005, on the Organisation and Functioning of the National Agency for Financial Investigations is a commendable crack in Cameroon's commitment with the international standard for combating the suppression of financing of terrorism. NAFI Cameroon is a financial information public service attached to the Ministry of Finance which fights against Money Laundering and Financing of Terrorism. [62] It is financially independent[63] and has decision-making authority in relevant matters of its competence. Its reports are submitted directly to the prosecution, which has an obligation to act based on such reports.[64]

NAFI has made strides in countering the financing of terrorism. From 2006-2014 for example, it reported 338 cases on proven suspicions of money laundering and the financing of terrorism to judicial authorities

---

59 https://www.knowyourcountry.com/cameroon1111, visited, 23/03/2021.

60 Article 25 Regulation No. 02/10–CEMAC–UMAC 2003.

61 *Ibid.* article 41.

62 http://www.minfi.gov.cm/index.php/en/bodies-under-supervision/nafi, visited, 23/03/ 2021.

63 Article 16.

64 Review by the Republic of Angola and the former Yugoslav Republic of Macedonia of the implementation by Cameroon of articles 15 –42 of Chapter III. "Criminalization and law enforcement" and articles 44 –50 of Chapter IV. "International cooperation" of the United Nations Convention against Corruption for the review cycle 2010-2015, United Nations Office on Drugs and Crimes, p.8.

throughout the national territory.[65] Its efforts in the suppression of the financing of terrorism are also visible in sensitization and awareness via seminars and training. For example, in 2014/2015, it conducted several training sessions, as well as annual working sessions and meetings with banks and microfinance institutions.

Problems

Cameroons' commitment in the social contract is questionable as far as suppressing the financing of terrorism is concerned. Impediments in measures to combat the financing of terrorism bespeak the veracity of this assertion. A worrisome issue already discussed is the dearth of review machinery for blacklisted persons and entities suspected of financing acts of terrorism in Cameroon.

A common problem with ensuring the implementation of Resolution 1373 is budgetary constraints.[66] The successful implementation of counter-terrorist laws and policies may be very expensive and demand considerable human resources. Highly skilled personnel as well as constant training are the assets necessary for monitoring the internet and tracking of financial transactions.[67] A state may fulfill the reporting obligation of Security Council resolution 1373 by disclosing the creation of legal and institutional infrastructure against terrorism and yet fail to enforce the law for want of funds or expert human resources. This is the case in Cameroon. It is documented that several countries in sub-Saharan Africa are constrained by inadequate resources to invest in combating the financing of terrorism.[68] Such inadequate resources include the weak institutional capabilities of the formal structures established to contain the financing of terrorism as well as lack of adequate training for the work force involve in this venture.[69]

---

65 Synthesis of Activities of the Nafi in 2014, available at https://www.anif.cm/images/pdfanif/SYNTHESIS-OF-ACTIVITIES-OF-THE-NAFI--IN-2014.pdf,visted, 04/03/2021, p.9.

66L., Hinojosa, A Critical Assessment of the Implementation of Security Council Resolution 1373, p.16, available at http:// digibug. ugr.es/ bitstream/ handle/ 10481/ 31650/ SC%20 Res%2 01373% 20Chapter. pdf;jsessionid = 70 D6 B16F 154 6631 AC6C C14C313782423?sequence=1, visited, 08/12/2020.

67 *Ibid.*

68C., Nna-Emeka *op cit.*, p.31.

69 *Ibid.*

Another problem in Cameroon's effort to suppress the financing of terrorism is the informal money transfer systems. The laws and enforcement measures for suppressing the financing of terrorism in Cameroon suggests that the focus has been on the formal method of money transfer, thus, neglecting the informal method of money transfer which terrorists make use of. The Informal money transfer systems are remittance systems that exist and operate outside of (or parallel to) conventional regulated banking and financial channels.[70] Christopher[71] notes that in some African countries, there is the prevalence of alternative remittance system, largely cash-based economies and informal procedures of foreign exchange transactions. According to him, this and other limitations have "continuously rendered the African space vulnerable to criminal syndicates engaged in money laundering and financing of terrorism".[72] Hinojosa[73] reaffirms Christopher's view by asserting that informal transfers, cash payments still provide numerous channels of funding to terrorists who, besides, do not need great quantities of money to perpetrate their attacks.

Conclusion

It has been averred that there is a legal framework for combating the financing of terrorism in Cameroon and measures to enforce the laws. Challenges however impede Cameroon's effective compliance with the international standard in suppressing terrorist financing. It is therefore recommended that policing the internet and tracking suspicious transaction should be given special consideration in the 2014 anti-terrorism law. The law should as well incorporate a designation process of individuals and organisations as terrorists for preventive measures akin to New Zealand. In New Zealand, pursuant to section 22 of the Terrorist Suppression Act 2000, the Prime Minister may designate an

---

[70] L., Buencamino and S., Gorbunov, Informal Money Transfer Systems: Opportunities and Challenges for Development Finance, DESA Discussion Paper Series, November 2002, p.1.

[71] C., Christopher, "International Extradition and Global Terrorism: Bringing International Criminals to Justice", 25 *Loyola of Los Angeles International & Comparative Law Review*, 2003, vol.25, p.494.

[72] *Ibid.* p.35.

[73] L., Hinojosa, A Critical Assessment of the Implementation of Security Council Resolution 1373, p.15, available at http://digibug. ugr.es/bitstream/handle/10481/ 31650/ SC%20 Res%2 01373% 20Chapter. pdf; jsessionid = 70D 6B1 6F1 546 631A C6CC 14C313782423? sequence=1, visited, 08/12/2020.

entity as a terrorist entity if the Prime Minister believes on reasonable grounds that the entity has knowingly carried out, or has knowingly participated in the carrying out of, one or more terrorist acts. The Act makes it a criminal offence to have any dealings with such entities such as providing services, property or funds. A review mechanism to challenge the blacklisting of persons and entities suspected of associating with terrorist groups should be incorporated in the law. This will help to protect human rights while countering the financing of terrorism.

The Law on Sustainable Usufructuary on Forest Resources with the Indigenous People of Cameroon

Nkweche Vitalis Mombeh

Lecturer, Faculty of Law and Political Science,
The University of Bamenda

Abstract

Sustainable development with indigenous peoples suggests that substantive measures exist which reliably permit indigenous people to enjoy forest resources. '*Customary rights*' to forest resources, require that indigenous people should harvest forest resources in accordance with their spiritual and material tenures. Regrettably, the exercise of *usufruct right* in Cameroon is complex and un-progressive, as it denies indigenous people the capacity to safely own valuable natural resources, making the State the only safe pair of hands for land and resource ownership. This paper adopts a socio-legal analytical research method; and is premised on the outcome that current development patterns recognise that the cultures and identities of indigenous peoples are inextricably linked to the lands on which they live and the natural resources on which they depend, but their economic, social, and legal status often limits their capacity to defend their interests in and rights to lands, territories, and other productive resources, and/or restricts their ability to participate in and benefit from forest resources.

Key words: sustainability; indigenous peoples; forest resources; usufructuary; usufruct right.

1. Introduction

Laws regulating natural resource management in Cameroon provide that the environment is a national common heritage and a global treasure to be safeguarded and sustained. They are based on the fundamental principle that supports an organised, transparent and sustainable system to access and use forest resources to improve on the political economy of the State, the wellbeing of the citizens, and the protection of the environment and biodiversity into the future. Where domestic law accords appropriate recognition and protection to the lands, territories and natural resources of indigenous peoples, their uninhibited collective well-being, enjoyment, use, occupancy and ownership rights are guaranteed. In Cameroon, the most commonly legally granted property rights of indigenous people is in the form of *usufructuary* and community management of natural resources over the national forest estate. Our focus is to examine whether State granted property rights meet the internal normative standards required for the exercise of a sustainable *usufructuary*. In indigenous worldviews, State granted *usufructuary* of indigenous peoples means the authorised collective or individual rights and/or interests of the group in relation with their traditionally owned or otherwise occupied and used lands, territories and resources and the possibility to uphold their responsibilities to future generations in this regard.

The methodological framework highlights the use of both data collection and the analytical framework. To arrive at the desired results, the design to collect data was the doctrinal and socio-legal methods. Data analysis combined legal exegesis and casuistry and gave prominence to the relationship between the law and indigenous peoples.

2. Context of the right

This affirmation lies on the premise that the forest estate cover is found on land that remains the property of the State, from where beneficial rights arise.[1] The State of Cameroon, on the one hand, has

[1] Note that the classical conception of the right to property usually refers to three elements namely: the right to use the thing that is the subject of the right (*usus*), the right to enjoy the fruit thereof (*fructus*) and the right to dispose of the thing, that is, the right to transfer it (*abusus*). In the case of *African Commission on Human and Peoples' Rights*

granted indigenous customary communities *usufruct rights* over forest resources and equally put in place mechanisms of supervision for the exercise of these rights and the sustainable conservation of the national forest estate. On the other hand, it exercises exclusive ownership of the said resources while the indigenous and customary communities are left at certain periods to use and enjoy the fruits on condition that they do not damage or diminish the quality of the forest.

Thus, for the State to be able to determine the fate of these natural resources, it is *inter alia* not only necessary that indigenous people enjoy the corollary rights permitting them to regulate the use and exploitation methods - either the *pre-* or *post-*authorisation phases - but, to further adopt an ever-emerging concept of sustainable development as the corner stone of governance agenda. In no way will indigenous people be left behind despite the increasing challenges for the State to fulfil her obligation under the international and domestic laws.

3. Relationship of indigenous people to Forest resources

The strong sense of solidarity and social relations of indigenous peoples takes the form of collective or communal management of natural resources found within their lands and territories. This communal stewardship results from their way of life, form of tenure and the nature of their cultural and spiritual connection with the mother earth and the collective nature of this relationship. Under state authorised property regimes (either formal or informal), this communal stewardship takes the form of personal and real manifestation on natural resources, which can be properly described as collective proprietary rights *in personam* and *in rem*.

3.1. Collective proprietary rights in personam on forest resources

Resource tenure laws clearly lay down the rights and duties of indigenous people, customary communities and government rights and prerogatives in the management of natural resources. In Cameroon, there is no specific legal recognition of indigenous people's rights to

---

V. The Republic of Kenya, (The 'Ogiek case'), Application 006/2012, Judgement, May 26, 2017, para.201, the African Court on human and Peoples' Rights recognised for the *Ogieks* a number of rights to their ancestral land, namely, the right to use (*usus*) and the right to enjoy the produce of the land (*fructus*), which presuppose the right of access to and occupation of the land.

their traditional lands, which can give them exclusive ownership of the forest resources therein. Resource tenure laws hold that the State is the beneficial owner and guardian of natural resources and the people beneficial users. The exercise of these legal rights and prerogatives over resources are subject to restraints imposed by public law aspect of property law, which is driven by political, economic, social and the cultural policies of the State. In this sense, use is not more than a general liberty of the populations to do what they like with their own but is much more in the nature of some kind of residual rights granted after all other relevant rights and restraints have been duly discounted. This is the subject of the State granted proprietary interest over natural resources, which are clearly manifested in the form of usufruct right of traditional communities, including other entitlements which are exercisable individually and/or collectively.

Thus, different rights and obligations arise as far as the exercise of interest or claims to natural resources are concerned. For as legally conceived, a *usufructuary* cannot be possessor of property, but one who merely uses and enjoys the fruits from another's property. To understand the real nature of a *usufructuary*, we have to examine the understanding given to proprietary rights under Cameroonian resource tenure. Since indigenous people neither own nor possess natural resources in Cameroon, the proprietary acts of the State are the best way to describe the extent of their *usufructuary*.

Proprietary rights *in personam,* therefore, entails the obligations of the State towards indigenous and customary communities in the form of intangible recognitions which guarantees them certain rights on forest resources. It arises from the personal conditions of indigenous people as influenced by their philosophies, spiritual traditions, cultural, economic, and political situation and their right to survival.

3.1.1. Legal guarantee of usufruct right

The English word 'usufruct' derives from the Latin word *usus* and *fructus* (use and enjoyment). A usufruct right refers to a right for a certain period to use and enjoy the fruits of another's property without damaging or diminishing it but allowing for any natural deterioration in the property over time.[2] The fundamental rights appertaining to

[2] Garner (B., A) (Ed). *Black's Law Dictionary*, 9th Edition, West Publishing Co, 2009. p. 1684.

ownership consist of the right to dispose (*jus disponende*)[3], right to use (*jus utendi*)[4] and the right to the fruits (*jus fruendi*)[5]. Of the above-mentioned substantive rights, the combination of *jus utendi* and *jus fruendi* are called usufruct and the remaining right, *jus disponendi* is the essence of what is termed naked ownership.[6] In a usufruct, only the *jus utendi* and the *jus fruendi* over the property are transferred to the *usufructuary*. The owner of the property maintains the *jus disponendi* or the power to alienate, encumber, transform, and even destroy the resources.[7]

The 1994 Forestry Law of Cameroon clearly provides that in the management of the national forest estate, favourable conditions must be put in place for the local population to exercise their usufruct rights.[8] Although entitlements range from usufruct rights, servitudes,[9] easements,[10] and *profit à prendre;*[11] the most important one identified under 1994 Forestry, Law is the usufruct right. The State is the owner of all resources; its ownership is burdened with a real right of enjoyment and use. The State maintains full ownership over the private forest estate (state forest, council forest) and naked ownership over the communal

---

3 *Ibid.*, p.938. *Jus disponendi* (Latin, right of disposing). The right to dispose of property, the power of alienation.

4 *Ibid.*, p.945. *Jus utendi* (Latin, 'right of using'). The right to use another's property without consuming it or destroying its substance

5 *Ibid.*, p.939. *Jus fruendi* (Latin, 'right of enjoying'). The right to use and enjoy another's property without damaging or diminishing it. N.B. The term fruits is traditionally referred to replenishable commodities on the property such as, for example, fruits, rodents, vegetables and livestock.

6 Naked ownership or imperfect ownership, is ownership of property subject to usufruct interest held by another. *Ibid.*, p.1215.

7 *Hemedes vs. CA*, 316, SCRA, 347, 1999. The facts of the case are available at http://sc.judiciary.gov.ph/jurisprudence/1999/oct99/107132.htm. (Accessed on August 12, 2019).

8 Article 29(1) of Law N°94/01 of 20th January 1994 to lay down Forestry, Wildlife and Fisheries Regulations.

9 Servitude is an encumbrance consisting in a right to the limited use of a piece of land or other immovable property without the possession of it; a charge or burden on an estate for another's benefit. See GARNER (B., A) (Ed). *Black's Law Dictionary,* 9th Edition, West Publishing Co, 2009, p. 1492.

10 Easement is an interest in land owned by another person, consisting in the right to use or control the land, or an area above or below it, for a specific limited purpose. *Ibid.*, p. 586.

11 Right to take, '*profit à prendre*' (French) is a right or privilege to go on another's land and take away something of value from its soil or from the products of its soil (as by mining, logging, or hunting); it is also termed right of common. *Ibid.*, p. 1330.

forest estate.[12] It is so because the State grants restrictive use and enjoyment rights on forest products over its private forest estate and an unlimited right of use and enjoyment over the communal forest domain. Although the State controls natural resources, it has no right to arbitrarily prevent or evict indigenous people from their ancestral territories.[13] To this effect, she grants indigenous people *usufruct right* which is the right to enjoy natural (forest) resources and is essentially their '*customary right*' to use such resources as prescribed under article 8(1) of the 1994 Forestry Law that: '... *logging or customary right means the right which is recognised as being that of the local population to harvest all forest, wildlife and fisheries products freely for their personal use except the protected species.*' It is obvious that Cameroon's forest resource tenure recognises the existence and use of traditional forest use rights such as collecting secondary forest products, notably raffia, palms, bamboo, cane or foodstuff and firewood and services to the people and entities that meet the criteria set by law.[14]

The Revised African Nature Convention, under article XVII (1) prescribes that State Parties should take legislative and other measures to ensure that traditional rights and intellectual property rights of local communities are respected.[15] The way this usufruct right is presented under the 1994 Forestry Law and its 1995 Implementation Decree, is the source of ambiguity in the very existence of this right. Under these laws, this right is presented variously as the logging, customary and/or hunting rights of the local population to harvest all forest, wildlife and fisheries

[12] The formulae with respect to full ownership, usufruct and naked ownership is as follows: full ownership equals naked ownership plus usufruct. Naked ownership equals full ownership minus usufruct. Usufruct equals full ownership minus naked ownership.

[13] In Uganda, the Benet, a small hunting-gathering community living in the northeastern part of the country, were evicted when the forest in which they lived was turned into a protected area. The Benet took the case to the High Court complaining that their ancestral territory had been denied them and that they had no means of livelihood. On 27 October 2005, the Ugandan High Court ruled that '*the Benet Community ... are historical and indigenous inhabitants of the said areas which were declared a Wildlife Protected Area or National Park.*' The Court ruled that the area should be de-gazetted and that the Benet are '*entitled to stay in the said areas and carry out agricultural activities including developing the same undisturbed*'. See ILO. *Indigenous and Tribal Peoples' Rights in Practice: A Guide to ILO Convention No. 169*, International Labour Organisation (ILO), Programme to Promote ILO Convention No.169 (PRO 169), International Labour Standards Department, 2009, p.103.

[14] Article 26 of Decree N°95/531/PM of 23rd August 1995 to determine the Conditions of Implementation of Forestry Regulations.

[15] Revised African Nature Convention, (adopted on March 7, 2017).

products freely to meet their diverse welfare needs. The first issue is the use of the word *'logging right'*, as encompassing the right to harvest Non-Timber Forest Resources (NTFRs). Both *'customary right'* and *'logging right'* have two separate ordinary meanings and/or one is dependent on the other. In fact, *'logging right'* is properly granted as an equitable servitude (easement by necessity) under article 26(2) of the 1995 Forestry Implementation Decree. This *'servitude'* is of an individual or collective nature and last for as long as that community survives and when they do not exceed their *usufructuary* rights.[16] The law recognises the exploitation of building timber by the local population, for the fulfilment of their *'customary right'*.[17] Secondly, the meaning of the word *'customary right'* is limited in scope, and, therefore, misleadingly used under these laws. Generally, *'customary rights'* to lands and resources refer to patterns of long-standing community land and resource usage in accordance with indigenous peoples' customary laws, values, customs, and traditions, including seasonal or cyclical use, which may or may not be recognised by the State.[18] It reflects the close ties indigenous peoples have to their land, forests, water, wildlife, and other natural resources which are vital for the sustainability of their cultures and livelihoods.[19] Thus, in the context of the 1994 Forestry Law, it should have been interpreted as the right of indigenous people to harvest all forest, wildlife and fisheries products freely for their personal use, except the protected species, in accordance with their cultural and spiritual values, hopes, vision and aspirations.

---

[16] Article 8(2) of Law N°94/01 of 20th January 1994 to lay down Forestry, Wildlife and Fisheries Regulations, provides that the Ministers in charge of forestry, wildlife and fisheries may, by reason of public interest, and in consultation with the populations concerned, temporarily or permanently suspend the exercise of logging rights, when necessary. Such suspension shall be done in consonance with the general regulations on expropriation by reason of public interest.

[17] Servitudes could be for conservation purposes such as restrictive or affirmative obligations by the state to protect the natural, scenic or open space values of real property, ensure its availability for agricultural, forest, recreational, or open-space use, protect natural resources and habitat, maintain or enhance air or water quality or preserve the historical, architectural, archaeological or cultural aspect of the real property.

[18]WORLD BANK OPERATIONAL MANUAL. <<*Operational Manual 4.10: Indigenous Peoples*>>, 2013, Available at https://policies.worlbank.org/sites/ppf3/PPFDocuments/090224b08f89d5.pdf., (Accessed on July 5, 2019).

[19] *Ibid.*

Although the government retains the ultimate responsibility for the management of forests, wildlife and fisheries resources, it has implicitly incorporated indigenous customary law practices within State legal system concerning land and natural resources through the legal recognition of the '*customary right*' of customary communities. It has further adopted and recognised a national policy on management and sharing of natural resources, in the best interest of indigenous people and based on their culture and subsistence. It implies that autonomous indigenous resource systems that apply indigenous customary law should be formally defined within State legal systems or even if not formally recognised within the State legal regimes, exist *de facto* and capable of regulating the lives of members of indigenous communities and provide continuity and cohesion for those communities. *De jure* recognition means existing as a matter of right or according to law.[20] Rights that originate from the government or are defensible through the formal legal process are referred to as *de jure* rights.[21] *De facto* means the right is actual, that is to say, existing in fact, having effect even though not formally or legally recognised.[22] Rights that have originated among indigenous peoples either through their formalised local institution or through long usage and norms are referred to as *de facto* rights. *De jure* or *de facto,* resource recognition are relevant to determine the rights of indigenous peoples, thereby making them to be in control of their own destinies.

Under article 8(1) of the 1994 Forestry Law, hunting, gathering, fishing and other livelihood rights are protected, not only as a symbol of the protection of the traditional subsistence economy, but also the symbol of protection of indigenous spiritual and material tenure. In fact, article 8(1) of the 1994 Forestry Law has triple political, socioeconomic and cultural implications. Firstly, that indigenous people are traditional and current users of their traditional lands, territories and natural resources; secondly, that they have the legal right to harvest forest, wildlife, fisheries resources that flow from their traditional and current

---

[20] GARNER (B., A) (Ed). *Black's Law Dictionary,* 9th Edition, West Publishing Co, 2009, p. 490.

[21] SCHLAGER (E) and OSTROM (E). <<*Property-rights, regimes and natural resources: A conceptual analysis*>>, Land Economics, Vol.68, Issue 3, 1992, pp.249-262. Also see BREMNER (J) & LU (F). (2006). '*Common Property among Indigenous Peoples of the Ecuadorian Amazon',* Conservation Society Vol. 4, Issue 4, 2006, pp. 499-521. Available at http://www.conservationandsociety.org/text.asp?2006/4/4/499/49278, (Accessed on March 30, 2019).

[22] GARNER, (B). *Op. Cit.,* p. 479.

use; thirdly that indigenous knowledge in the management of forest, wildlife and fisheries resources, complements State management systems, particularly that which contributes to sustainable development. Article 8(1) guarantees the *de facto* respect for indigenous spiritual interest and cultural views and values, including the recognition of the fact that collective gathering and hunting traditions are still the basis of the subsistence economy of indigenous peoples who continue to maintain strong ties to the land. It further implies *de facto* that indigenous people should enjoy a certain degree of self-government, participation and decision-making through their own institutions or representatives chosen by them. These institutions have the right to regulate the use and enjoyment of natural resources, ensuring that hunting and gathering traditions respect their spiritual and traditional tenures. To grant indigenous people greater control of their own traditional subsistence economy and life style are the bases to determine their own economic, cultural and social development rights. This automatically warrants them the right to benefit from profits in the sale of resources on their traditional lands and territories. Thus, it may be suggested that in Cameroon, indigenous people have unlimited rights of access, control, use, enjoyment, withdrawal and management of forest resources in accordance to their own worldviews. The extent of such a right cannot be restricted or prohibited whatsoever, except for the protected and special forest products or for specific public purpose/interest, subject to appropriate redress.

It is important to point that a usufruct is a real right on the property itself and not merely a right in relation to the property's profits.[23] So, it is a real right by virtue of which the people granted the right to enjoy the property are under an obligation to preserve its form and substance, unless the title constituting it, or the law provides otherwise. Indigenous Peoples' natural resources management practices have a long-term sustainability history. Despite this characterisation, usufruct remains a right with personal and temporal features since it is linked to the life of the *usufructuary*. As such, if indigenous and local communities abandon their traditional lifestyles and habitats, they lose their '*customary right*'. It is

---

[23] VERBEKE (A)., VERDICKT (B)., & MAASLAND, (D). *The many Faces of Usufruct*, Book Chapter, p.36. Available at https://lirias.kuleuven.be/handle/123456789/359493. (Accessed on August 12, 2019).

so because, this right is intrinsically linked to the role indigenous individuals and groups play in the community.

3.1.2. Right of pre-emption

The right of first opportunity granted indigenous peoples as a matter of state policy to manage forest resources because of their closeness to the forest estate. It is the opportunity to obtain at specified conditions a right of pre-emption on the forest estate for their economic and social welfare. In Cameroon, the establishment of community forest is one of the major innovations of the 1994 Forestry Law. It provides for the possibility of local communities to manage community or local council forests through a contractual relationship with the administration. Article 37(1) clearly provides for the management of forest resources by local communities who so desire. By this singular act, it adopts the right of local communities to pre-empt neighbouring forests from being allocated to other forest exploiters. More specifically, Order of December 21, 2001, to institute the right of pre-emption,[24] guarantees pre-emptive powers over local forest resources to local communities. More precisely, concerning community forestry, the role is that those communities situated nearest or on the outskirts of a forest, are those given priority in the allocation of any community forest.[25] In addition, the law further grants communities the right of pre-emption in the event of alienation of products found in their forests.[26]

Worth noting is the fact that the 1994 Forestry Law and Order of 21 December 2001, fail to mention the deep-seated implication and special relationship indigenous people have with mother earth, as the grounds for the grant of the right of pre-emption. The unique culture and traditions of indigenous peoples form the essence of their survival and heritage and should have formed the bases of the grant of this right of pre-emption. Indigenous peoples' culture and spirituality and the collective nature of the relationship depends on the protection of their lands, territories and natural resources. This singular conception on

---

24 Order No.01/518/MINEF/CAB of December 21, 2001, to Determine the Conditions for Attributing, in Preference, to Surrounding Village Communities, Any Forest Likely to Acquire Community Forestry Status (to institute the right of pre-emption)

25 Article 27(2) & (3) of the Decree N°95/531/PM of August 23, 1995 to determine the Conditions of Implementation of Forestry Regulations.

26 Article 37(7) of Law N°94/01 of January 20, 1994 to lay down Forestry, Wildlife and Fisheries Regulations.

indigenous customs, philosophies, and way of life, as a matter of state policy, should determine the extent and choice of exercise of this right and the bases of attribution of community forest, to obtain meaningful sustainable development with indigenous peoples. In fact, Justice Dow in her judgement in the landmark case of *Sesana & Others v Attorney General*[27] in Botswana subscribes to the Cobos 'wisdom' on the special relationship of indigenous peoples to their traditional lands and holds that it should be the basis for state policy and direction in dealing with indigenous peoples' traditional lands.[28] However, in Cameroon, the vision of the state is that of state solidarity and largesse on indigenous societies and not a matter of obligation for the protection of their lands, territories and natural resources.

3.2. Collective proprietary rights in rem on forest resources

Proprietary rights *in rem* refers to the existence of the various rights directly concerned with the physical use and enjoyment of natural resources. Generally, it refers to a right that can be protected and controlled by law enforcement and administrative officials during the normal and legal use and enjoyment of natural resources by indigenous people. These rights over State property have a physical material existence right exercisable by indigenous people over a material thing or that thing itself. It is a usufruct right, a right on a property itself (connected to a particular resource), if it is authorised by the law.[29]

Therefore, focusing on the State granted proprietary rights *in rem* and emphasising the significance of boundaries and exclusion in the defence of the interest of indigenous forest people is primordial to ascertain their survival in the present Cameroonian context. Note that property rights over State resources come in various degrees and one influential model for understanding that fact has been the *'bundle of rights'* idea of property associated with the work of John Commons and the legal realists.[30]

---

27 *Sesana & others v Attorney General*, (52/2002) [2006] BWHC1 (Botswana).

28 WACHIRA (G). <<*Indigenous Peoples' Rights to land and natural resources*>> in DERSSO (S). (Ed). *Perspective on the rights of Minorities and Indigenous peoples in Africa*, Pretoria University Law Press (PULP), 2010, p.304.

29 ZENATI-CASTAING & REVET, *Les Biens*, p.494, Cited in VERBEKE (A)., VERDICKT (B)., & MAASLAND, (D). *The many Faces of Usufruct*, Book Chapter, p.36.

30 FENNELL (L). <<*Ostrom's Law: Property in the Commons*>>, International Journal of the Commons, vol. 5, N° 1, Igitur Publishing, 2011, p. 14. It should be noted that Henry Maine first conceptualized *bundles of rights* in his classic book, *Ancient Law*, published in 1861.

These bundles of rights include access, withdrawal, management, exclusion, and alienation rights, which are mutually intrinsic; meaning to hold some of these rights, imply the possession of others. For example, the exercise of withdrawal rights is not meaningful without the right of access; alienation rights depend upon having rights to be transferred.[31] Asserting these rights which are available only in functional meaningful combinations warily represents the interests on indigenous people that the existing laws have failed to establish. Seemingly, the Cameroonian natural resources laws have identified the manifestations of these rights as a cumulative scale moving from the minimal right of access through possessing full ownership rights. Though these rights have been conceptualised as made up of two components: operational rights and collective choice rights, where the main difference between the operational level and collective choice level is that at the operational level users simply exercise individual rights, whereas at the collective-choice level, users participate in governance.[32] The ramifications as guaranteed under the natural resource laws are relevant.

3.2.1. Access and control rights

Access right is defined as the right to enter a physically defined area to harvest forest resources. On the one hand, control is aimed at maintaining the ecological balance, by preserving and conserving the natural forest ecosystem. Access and/or control of natural resources is not only important for sustainable management, but also for indigenous communities as an important means to meet both individual and collective subsistence needs like food, health and shelter. Indeed, indigenous communities are known to practice sustainable harvesting of forest resource because of their traditional ecological knowledge. It is held that the strong communal dimension of indigenous peoples' cultural life is indispensable to their existence, well-being and full development, and includes the right to the lands, territories and resources which they have traditionally owned, occupied or otherwise used or acquired.[33]

Access and control guarantee the most observable type of usufruct right, which is *use rights*, either to consumptive or non-consumptive use

---

[31] *Ibid.* pp.14-15.

[32] SCHLAGER (E). & OSTROM (E). (1992). <<*Property-rights, regimes and natural resources: A conceptual analysis*>>, Land Economics, Vol 68, Issue 3, 1992, pp.249-262.

[33] See the UNCESR, General Comment No. 21, Right of everyone to take part in cultural life (article 15, para. 1a of the Covenant on Economic, Social and Cultural Rights),

of the resources. Use rights are as varied as are uses of a unit of land and the natural resources it contains. For example, use rights to a parcel of land may include the right to farm, to pasture, to plant trees, to cut trees, to build a house, to establish a non-agricultural enterprise, to exploit the land as a quarry, or any combination of such rights. Use rights to trees may include fruit or leaf gathering, honey collection, removal of bark or branches, or removal of the tree itself. Use rights to a body of water may include drinking, bathing, washing clothes, watering livestock, fishing or irrigation.

In this light, article 8(1) of the 1994 Forestry Law establishes the *'customary right'* of local population to harvest all forest, wildlife and fisheries products freely for their personal use. The exercise of this right is not subject to any approval.[34] The 1994 Forestry Law clearly defines resource access right between the different users who have multiple and overlapping rights. Usufruct rights are not allowed in some State forest because of their objective such as integral ecological reserves, protection forest, recreation forest, teaching and research forest just to name these.[35] In another case, it provides for an unlimited access to communal forest and restrictive access to State production forest and plantation forest because an excessive exercise of *'customary right'* might jeopardise the purpose of such forest. Under the community forestry, Cameroon has made it possible for village communities to have an unlimited access to forest resources under the community forestry programmes.[36] In the case of registered individual property rights, all the forest products there belong to the owners.[37]

However, the appellation *'local population'* is of a general application and includes indigenous forest dwellers, village and neighbouring communities around the national forest estate. It does not only refer to members of a particular customary community, but any local person of Cameroonian nationality. In fact, article 37 of the 1994 Forestry Law is particularly clear on this matter when it identifies those entitled to usufruct right as *'citizens'*. The word *'citizens'* attaches enormous obligation on those authorised to extract forest resources.

---

[34] See article 35(3)(d) of Decree N°95/531/PM of August 23, 1995 to determine the Conditions of Implementation of Forestry Regulations.
[35] *Ibid.* Article 3.
[36] Articles 37 & 38 of Law N°94/01 of January 20, 1994 to lay down Forestry, Wildlife and Fisheries Regulations.
[37] *Ibid.*, article 39 *et seq.*.

Therefore, granting secure access to and control over land and natural resources for all indigenous people can generate critical incentives for conservation and sustainable use, management and governance of natural resources. It is generally held that insecure, unclear, limited or short-term access rights can inhibit sustainable land and natural resource management and discourage indigenous people from acting as long-term stewards of land and natural resources.[38] The control of forest resources rest on the local populations and the State under the auspices of the Ministry in charge of Forestry, Wildlife, Fisheries and the Ministry of Environment, Nature Protection and Sustainable Development who in return control the activities of the local populations. As such, the usufruct right of the local population can be suspended in case of necessity.[39] However, this can lead to the violation of the fundamental human rights of indigenous peoples if such suspension leads to changes in their way of life. In the case of the *African Commission on Human and Peoples' Rights V. The Republic of Kenya*, the African Court on Human and Peoples' Rights held that the restrictions put in place by Kenya on the right of the *Ogiek* people to access their land and natural environment, to some extent, violated their right to practice their culture under article 17 of the ACHPR.[40] Similar conclusions were arrived at by the Inter American Court on Human Rights in the case of *Sawhoyamaxa Indigenous Community v Paraguay.*[41]

3.2.2. Withdrawal right

Withdrawal right refers to the right to obtain and use a specified resource. The right to withdraw is perhaps the most important right for communities that are dependent on forest resources for their livelihoods. The purpose of withdrawal right is to enjoy the benefits and derive all advantages from the property because of normal use and exploitation. Withdrawal right may be for subsistence or commercial purposes and requires the harvesting of natural fruits from the national forest estate. Natural fruits are spontaneous products of the earth, that is to say, the

---

[38] AGGARWAL (S) & ELBOW (K). <<*The Role of Property Rights in Natural Resource Management, Good Governance and Empowerment of the Rural Poor*>>, Prepared by ARD Inc for USAID, 2006, p.1.

[39] See article 8(2).

[40] *African Commission on Human and Peoples' Rights V. The Republic of Kenya, (The 'Ogiek case')*, Application 006/2012, Judgement, May 26, 2017, paras.186 & 190.

[41] See IACtHR, Case of the *Sawhoyamaxa Indigenous Community v Paraguay*, Judgment of 29 March 29 2006 (Merits, Reparations and Costs) paras 73(3) - 73(5).

ordinary natural products from the State property.[42] The fruits must be separable from the property, for the *usufructuary* only becomes the owner once they are separated from the State property. It, therefore, means that natural fruits belong to the *usufructuary* only upon harvest. The fact that indigenous people can extract, use and control property from the forest under usufruct right, makes the produce their property.

In Cameroon, the forestry legislation differentiates between the right to harvest timber and the right to harvest Non-Timber Forest Resources (NTFRs) by customary communities, by clearly stating that they shall maintain their usufruct right in addition to felling the number of trees commensurate with such needs, which they are bound to use thereof and in no circumstance may they sell or exchange timber from the forest.[43] Considering the aforementioned, besides article 8(1) of the Forestry Law which states that local communities shall '*harvest all forest, wildlife and fisheries products freely for their personal use,*' it is clear that under the guaranteed usufruct right, the legislators have defined the destination of the fruits from the forest, which is basically for subsistence purposes.

In accordance with the law, *usufructuary* communities have the right to use and enjoy the State property and its fruits, while preserving the substance of the property. To achieve these objectives, the legislators have taken a number of measures. It has classified forest products into wood and non-wood products as well as wildlife, and fisheries resources derived from the forest. It has further enlisted certain forest products such as ebony, ivory, wild animal horns, as well as certain animal, plant and medicinal species or those which are of particular interest as '*special*' and subject to control.[44] Concerning wildlife products, the 1995 Forestry Implementation Decree specifies that traditional hunting shall be carried out using weapons made from materials of plant origin.[45] To further protect nature and biodiversity, some areas are declared out of bound such as ecological fragile areas and areas classified as protected State

---

[42] GARNER (B). (Ed). *Op. Cit.*, 2009, p. 470.

[43] Article 26(1) &(2) of Decree N°95/531/PM of August 23, 1995 to determine the Conditions of Implementation of Forestry Regulations.

[44] Article 9 of Law N°94/01 of January 20, 1994, to lay down Forestry, Wildlife and Fisheries regulations.

[45] Article 2(20) of Decree N°95/466/PM of 20th July 1995 to lay down the Conditions for the Implementation of Wildlife Regulations.

forest, full nature reserves or wildlife sanctuaries.[46] The raison d'être is to make sure that the collection of fruits of the forest do not change nor diminish the substance or the primitive value of the forest, including the physical and social environment.

3.2.3. Alienation rights

In Cameroon, ownership of forest resources remains the property of the State, who maintains the right to dispose the property *(jus disponendi)* or the power to alienate, encumber, transform and even destroy the same. The 1994 Forestry Law provides that the State, local councils, village communities and private individuals may exercise on their forest all rights that result from ownership, subject to restrictions provided by the law.[47] Usufruct right is granted on both permanent and non-permanent forests and accordingly, the *usufructuary* cannot dispose of the property for commercial purposes without the consent of the right holder (naked owner). The law authorises the *usufructuary* to use and enjoy the property for their personal use and in no case may it be sold or exchanged for commercial purposes.[48] This does not however, mean that the local population cannot exchange (sale) with other vital products which are not obtainable from the forest, and which are essential for their immediate survival.

In certain circumstances, like in the community forestry, where the State has transferred full ownership of the resources to the local population, the latter has the right of pre-emption in the event of alienation of products found in their forest.[49] In every circumstance, the people and the donor-*usufructuary's* actions must respect the destination of the property. In the latter case, the conditions of use of products derived from the forests are laid down in the management convention of

---

[46] Article 17 of Law N°94/01 of January 20, 1994, to lay down Forestry, Wildlife and Fisheries Regulations.

[47] *Ibid.*, Article 7.

[48] Concerning forest products, see article 26 of Decree N°95/531/PM of 23rd August 1995 to determine the Conditions of Implementation of Forestry Regulations. Concerning wildlife products, see article 24(3) of Decree No.95/466/PM of July 20, 1995, to lay down the Conditions for the Implementation of Wildlife Regulation. Concerning fisheries resources, see article 117(1) of Law N°94/01 of 20th January 1994 to lay down Forestry, Wildlife and Fisheries Regulations.

[49] Article 37(7) of Law N°94/01 of January 20, 1994, to lay down Forestry, Wildlife and Fisheries Regulations.

the said forest. The purpose generally is for the welfare and development of the said community.

For the sustainable conservation and use of the resources from the forest, hunting and fruits picking must be done in such a way that the intended booty remains part of the forest estate for a long time. The *usufructuary* is bound to manage the property in accordance with its intended purpose which is for their personal use and a further obligation to maintain the primitive value of the forest for natural deterioration. For their personal use, the local population can perform all acts of alienation and disposition, in so far as these acts are in accordance with the destination of the property. The destination is consumption and consumption imply alienation. It is worth noting that not in every circumstance, alienation is compatible with the destination of such property and does fall within the competence of the *usufructuary*. The *usufructuary* can, therefore, only dispose of the property with the consent of the naked owner. The modern face of usufruct is thus characterised by a relative and functional prohibition against alienation of property from ecologically fragile areas, protected forest, full nature reserves or wildlife sanctuaries.[50]

3.2.4. Exclusion right

Exclusion right refers to the power that property right holders have to deter others from using the resources with respect to a usufruct. A *usufructuary* generally has the following rights of action, with respect to usufruct right. Actions to protect the usufruct and the exercise of the usufruct. Exclusion mechanisms are at the core of such rights and refer to the determination of who has access, and withdrawal rights and whether they may be transferred. In fact, to have the rights of access, control and withdrawal of resources from a property are the most basic resource tenure rights and are closely linked to their opposite; the right to exclude or deny another party access and withdrawal to a particular resource.[51]

In Cameroon for instance, the State can temporary or permanently suspend the exercise of usufruct right of customary communities for

---

[50] *Ibid.*, Article 17.

[51] RIGHT AND RESOURCE INITIATIVE (RRI). *What Rights? A comparative Analysis of developing Countries' National Legislation on Community and Indigenous peoples' Forest tenure rights'*, Washington DC, Rights and Resource Initiative, 2012, p.15.

public purpose.[52] This is subject to the declassification instrument which determines the category and objective of the forest.[53] It is evident that usufruct right has a temporary character, so long as the State has not put the property into other use for the general interest. So, it is of a temporary nature or duration, not perpetual otherwise it could become an *emphyteusis*.[54] This exclusion mechanism is essentially for the sustainable management and conservation of the forest resources and use thereof. Here, in classifying a forest, the instrument must take into account the social environment of the local population as no forest may be completely or partially declassified unless a forest of the same category and equivalent area in the same ecological zone is classified.[55] The fact remains that though the State and the *usufructuary* do not co-own the property in undivided shares, each party has independent rights over the property; the actual powers of each party are determined and limited. Neither the State nor the *usufructuary* owner can act as if they were full owners. Each party must respect the interests of the other party while exercising its own rights. In this case, there exists a fiduciary relationship between the two parties. Logically, classifying an equivalent area would permit the local population to continue exercising their usufruct rights; given that the compensation mechanism provided for in article 27 of the 1994 Forestry Law does not include the hunting and gathering of NTFRs. This is a serious imbalance in the way usufruct right is practiced.

The 1994 Forestry Law authorises the State to restrict or extinguish '*customary right*' in the national forest estate when they are contrary to the objectives assigned to the specific forest.[56] In the event of compensation, there is no comprehensive legal procedure for calculating compensation for the loss of '*customary right*', and the regulations outlining review of compensation claims by Local Advisory Committees do not obligate the

---

52 Article 8(2) of Law N°94/01 of January 20, 1994, to lay down Forestry, Wildlife and Fisheries Regulations.

53 *Ibid.*, Article 25.

54 An *emphyteusis* is a contract by which one person delivers to another (the *emphyteuta*) a tract of land, either in perpetuity or for a long period of time, in exchange for the obligation to cultivate the land and to pay annual rental. Although the *emphyteusis* was alienable, the owner had to consent to the sale. Unlike a usufruct, *emphyteusis* did not terminate with the death of the *emphyteuta*. Perpetual *emphyteuta* was abolished in the 18th century. See GARNER (B). (Ed). *Black's Law Dictionary*, 9th Edition, West Publishing Co, 2009, p. 602.

55 Article 28(2) of Law N°94/01 of January 20, 1994, to lay down Forestry, Wildlife and Fisheries Regulations.

56 *Ibid.*, Article 26.

Ministry of Forestry and Wildlife to do more than review the claims the committees deemed admissible.[57] Following the provisions of article 23 of the 1994 Forestry Law, this compensation does not effectively include compensation for the loss of '*customary right*' and fallow lands, which are important livelihood resources. Compensation is authorised in accordance with article 7 of Ordinance of July 6, 1974, to establish rules governing State lands, which permits compensations only on buildings, plantations, and farms lands.

3.2.5. Management rights

Management rights refer to the right to create regulations concerning how, when, where and what stakeholders and users of resources have to do with respect to exploration and exploitation of forest resources. It equally consists of the right to organise and assign use rights. Article 8(1) of the 1994 Forestry Law circumscribes the management responsibilities of indigenous and customary communities. It provides for the '*customary right*' of the local population, meaning that management rights are supposed to be done in accordance with '*indigenous management systems*'. Management rights belong to the whole community of users and are exercised against them. It requires the participation and consent of all those concerned with the enjoyment of the resources. The State has to establish rules regarding the sustainable harvest of forest resources, making decisions about the impact of such activities on the physical and social environment and minimising the depletion of resources. The *usufructuary* is not responsible for deterioration of resources that results from the normal exercise of the usufruct. However, management in line with the usufruct right are twofold. The *usufructuary* must behave as a prudent and reasonable man and bear in mind that they must maintain the forest cover and ecological balance during their exercise of the usufruct. Secondly, the State has to determine the geographical boundaries and objectives of its forest estate in order to establish and define the exploitation areas of the local populations in keeping with its biodiversity conservation strategies. It further includes the duty to draw up an inventory and a management plan and the duty to provide security against damage to the national forest estate.

---

[57] This committee examines and make recommendations on any possible reservations or claims forwarded by the population or by any other person concerned, during forest classification or declassification operations. See Articles 19 & 23 of Decree N°95/531/PM of August 23, 1995, to determine the Conditions of Implementation of Forestry Regulations.

It should be noted that under the 1994 Forestry Law, management means the:

> ... carrying out certain activities and investments based on previously established objectives and on a plan for the sustained production of forest products and services, without affecting the primitive value or compromising the future productivity of the forest nor causing any damage to the physical and social environment.[58]

From the abovementioned, it is obvious that this definition is in the likes of the definition on sustainable development propounded in 1987 by the Brundtland Commission; meaning exploitation in such forest must abide to those standards. Secondly, for any activity to be carried out in the national forest estate, it must be subjected to a previously established objective and management plan approved by the competent authorities; meaning that in the exercise of the '*customary right,*' of the local population, the authorities in charge of forest resources typically have the power to make management decisions and over see their implementation for the various use right holders.

The obligation to preserve the substance of the forest imposes a serious limitation on access, control and use of the resources. These duties are imposed by the law. Generally, the 1996 Environmental Code provides that a sustainable natural resource management and biodiversity conservation can be obtained through an inventory of existing species, particularly those that are endangered, management plan of species and the preservation of habitat, and a system on the control of access to genetic resources.[59] More specifically, the 1994 Forestry Law clearly provides that forest management is the concern of the Ministry in charge of Forestry, which shall ensure the following management activities: inventory, re-afforestation, natural or artificial regeneration, sustained forestry exploitation and infrastructure.[60] These, if properly applied will allow for the sustainable exploration and exploitation of forest resources.

Concerning forest inventory, it is the evaluation of forest resources to ensure a sustained forestry management. Depending on the objective pursued within a forest, there are management inventories and

---

[58] Article 23 of Law N°94/01 of January 20, 1994, to lay down Forestry, Wildlife and Fisheries Regulations.

[59] See article 64(1) of Law No.96/12 of August 5, 1996, relating to Environmental Management

[60] Article 63 & 64 of Law N°94/01 of January 20, 1994, to lay down Forestry, Wildlife and Fisheries Regulations.

exploitation inventories. The former consists in evaluating, in a quantitative or qualitative basis, the resources which constitute a given forest, with a view to ensuring the rational management of all resources, while the latter consist in an exhaustive enumeration of all commercial species on a given geographical area.[61] This management technique, if properly applied, has to define the livelihood needs of the indigenous people, in the course of granting an exploitation right. It is worth noting that no forest activity can take place without a management plan drawn up by the ministry in charge of forestry or with their assistance, which depends on the results of the management inventory drawn up for each forest.[62] This management inventory provides the guidelines for drawing up a management plan, which in accordance with article 29(1) of the 1994 Forestry Law, indicates the conditions under which the local population may exercise their usufruct right. Exploitation right holders are bound to respect regulations laid down in a management plan for each forest management unit, failing which, they are subject to sanctions.[63] Unfortunately, the management plan demanded from exploitation rights holders does not clearly take into consideration the requirement of the '*conditions necessary for local populations to exercise their usufruct rights*'. Rather, the management plan simply provides for the logging programme, the available equipment or equipment to be used, anticipated yield, per product per budgetary year, the size of the workforce and the training programme thereof etc.[64]

Cameroon has also adopted a system of biodiversity conservation through the protection of fauna and flora and the creation and management of natural reserves and national parks.[65] These ecologically protected areas are subject to limitations as provided for in article 17 of the 1994 Forestry Law which is directed at the sustainable conservation and use of the said resources and of the various ecosystems. It further assures the sustainability that protects the welfare of indigenous people through Environmental Impact Assessment (EIA) and Environmental

---

[61] Articles 42 & 43 of the Decree N°95/531/PM of 23rd August 1995 to determine the Conditions of Implementation of Forestry Regulations.

[62] *Ibid.*, Article 45. Equally see article 29(3) of Law N°94/01 of January 20, 1994, to lay down Forestry, Wildlife and Fisheries Regulations.

[63] Article 46(4) of Decree N°95/531/PM of 23rd August 1995 to determine the Conditions of Implementation of Forestry Regulations.

[64] *Ibid.*, article 65(h).

[65] *Ibid.*, article 64(2).

Auditing (EA).[66] Such EIA and EA must be carried out in such a way that do not deprive the local population of forest products or jeopardise their survival when their lifestyle is dependent on the forest in question.[67] In most cases, these right holders fail to recognise the traditional ways of managing natural resources practiced by indigenous people or other communities, talk less of protecting their subsistence use. Also, the participation of the local communities is most envisaged in the management of forest resources, particularly when it concerns the implementation of the social policies of the State by the exploitation right holders. In fact, article 51(2) of the 1994 Forestry Law is to the effect that the State has the obligation to define the welfare work envisaged for forest communities in collaboration with the people concerned. Even if this is true, the atmosphere during public consultation is never amiable for local populations to express their concerns, given that it is never on a level playing ground.[68]

3.2.6. Alteration right

Alteration right refers to the right to maintain and preserve the primitive value of the environment and its substance. The *usufructuary* has the obligation to preserve the primitive value of the environment and substance, except the law provides otherwise; in this case, the law allows for improvements in the form of farmland, plantations and infrastructure. For any improvements to be considered, it must be of such a nature as to prevent over exploitation, abuse and impairment on the natural environment. Article 17(2) of the 1974 Land Tenure Ordinance permits situations where the local population can continue to peacefully occupy or use land without title as identified in article 2 of this law. The foregoing provides the possibility wherein, traditional communities can alter the use accorded a particular national forest estate. Alteration involves the complete transformation of the resource from its current state in ways that may be positive or negative depending on perspective and the outcome of interest, for example, administrative leniency where the local population continue to clear a forested area for

66 Article 16(2) of Law N°94/01 of January 20, 1994, to lay down Forestry, Wildlife and Fisheries Regulations.

67 Article 9(2)(a) & (b) of Decree N°95/531/PM of 23rd August 1995 to determine the Conditions of Implementation of Forestry Regulations.

68 Imagine the intimidating presence of administrative authorities like the Divisional Officer and his *État* majors, the different relevant decentralised authorities to indigenous communities.

agriculture, planting of trees or developing plantations on national lands. Curious enough, the 1994 Forestry Law allows for compensation in case of investment on such lands.[69]

The issue with alteration right is the impossibility to restore something that is consumed by its use. The State has to restore what is consumed even if it is impossible to restore it. An uncontrolled exploitation of forest resources leads to extinction. Since the destination of the resource is consumption and restoration cannot relate to particular forest resources, the obligation to preserve a resource is thus channelled towards conserving forest resources in ways that are compatible with its destination. As such, the State and other stakeholders in forestry management have been encouraging indigenous people to establish settled villages, as a means to avert the unforeseen dangers with harvesting forest resources. It is worth noting that the law provides for the clearing of all or part of state or council forest for purposes other than forestry[70] and the establishment of farmlands and ranches.[71]

3.2.7. Transfer rights

Transfer rights refer to the authority to assign or reassign both management and use rights (*abusus*). A transfer of rights may be definitive and absolute and may include all rights relating to the exercise of usufruct rights. The ability to definitively transfer rights over forest resources are atypical feature of Cameroon's resource tenure. Here, the national forest estate is continually classified and declassified, which continually affect the rights of the local populations.[72] Though the instrument classifying forest must take into consideration the social environment of the local population, public purpose is the determining factor. Declassification can, therefore, lead to a corresponding transfer of rights to a new destination. Worth noting is the fact that the security provided in case of transfer of rights, where a limitation is imposed by the public purpose of the forest envisaged, like a protection area is not commensurate to the rights lost. Under article 26(2) of the 1994 Forestry Law, usufruct right is lost in the name of compensation right. In fact, the

[69] Article 27 of Law N°94/01 of January 20, 1994, to lay down Forestry, Wildlife and Fisheries Regulations.
[70] *Ibid.*, Articles 15 & 16.
[71] *Ibid.*, Article 103.
[72] *Ibid.*, Article 28.

compensation law does not provide for a possibility of reparation in case of loss of rights over forest resources.

3.2.8. Extinguishability of rights

Extinquishability of rights becomes operative when the beneficiary-*usufructuary's* rights of use, withdrawal and management are terminated. It is accepted that a usufruct is a right with personal and temporal features, since it is linked to the life of the beneficiary-*usufructuary*.[73] It is impossible to constitute a usufruct which is permanent or unlimited in time. Its temporary quality is a rule of law which cannot be challenged. The extinction of this right is a major determinant in the management of forest resources. It can come about as a result of death, damage to the resources, or even fungible with change in ownership. Under the 1994 Forestry Law, an extinction of usufruct right can only be obtained when public interest is at stake, and in consultation with the people concerned. This aspect still creates a serious vacuum, given that such suspension is done in consonance with the general regulations on expropriation.[74]

Unfortunately, under the law, it is not clear whether a *usufructuary* can vindicate (*jus vendicandi*) or recover the lost resources subject to a suspension for public interest. The fact remains that the compensations payable under article 8(2), gives the local population the right to bring an action for inadequate compensation and not for the deprivation on the use and enjoyment of forest products. The latter is a matter of administrative prerogative and not subject to public action; given that usufruct right is considered as an aspect of State solidarity over its property. In this light, it is worth noting that the local population have to exercise their usufruct right with care and prudence, failing which the State can establish their liability and suspend their usage, based on the destruction of the natural environment. The controversy is that in Cameroon, indigenous peoples' rights to their traditional lands which are intrinsically linked to their right to natural resources are '*extinguishable*' when development affects their traditional areas and claims arising from such extinguishment usually are satisfied, in the best of cases, by a simple relocation and establishment of settled villages. For example, the relocation of the indigenous people of Mboro is particular, given that

---

[73] See VERBEKE (A), VERDICKT (B) & MAASLAND (D). *Op. Cit.*, p.36.

[74] Article 8(2) of Law N°94/01 of January 20, 1994, to lay down Forestry, Wildlife and Fisheries Regulations.

their relocation site was chosen by them to permit for the continuous exercise of their cultural practices.[75]

4. Conclusion

The State of Cameroon is increasingly developing a system of natural resource management based on the fundamental principles that support a more organised, transparent, and sustainable system for accessing and using forest resources to improve on the political economy of the State, the wellbeing of the citizens, and the protection of the environment and biodiversity into the future. Cameroonian laws guarantee the legal capacity for the exercise of the '*customary right*' of the local population. Thus, for the State to be able to determine the fate of its natural resources, it is *inter alia* not only relevant that it enjoy the corollary rights permitting her to regulate the use and exploitation methods, but to further adopt the ever-emerging concept of sustainable development as the corner stone of its development.

Sustainability with indigenous peoples requires that there should be a clear reconciliation between environmental protection and other development dimensions, which were till sometime, considered in isolation.[76] It represents a definitive and strong-impact entry of environmental and indigenous issues into the life of political, economic and social world. At the centre of this natural resource management system, there exists the *usufructuary* interest of indigenous peoples, defendable by the existing national framework in the form of the usufruct right of indigenous people. Understandably, sustainable development implies a concern for cultural integrity, social equity between generations, concerns that must be logically extended to equity within each generation.

By so doing, in no way will indigenous people, in the exercise of their usufruct right, be left behind, as their indigenous material and spiritual tenures must form an important part of the blueprints for action.

[75]The Mboro pygmies have been displaced from their present site of the Kribi deep sea port to their new village. See CAMEROON TRIBUNE of August 18, 2016, p.16. Interview with Sub Director in charge of the Socio-Economic Development of Indigenous Peoples, Ministry of social Affairs.

[76] In 1992, i.e. 20 years after the 1972 United Nations Conference on the Human Environment held at Stockholm, a summit on Environment and Development (Earth Summit) redefined the global development strategy.

Therefore, focusing attention on indigenous issues has implications that go beyond national policies, but the extent to which it is integrated in the political, economic, social, environmental, cultural frameworks of a country depends on the largesse of the national framework and resources available to them. It must provide the stimulus to augment the appreciation of '*customary rights*' and the flow of resources from the different stakeholders to the local population. Proof is that unless appropriate action is taken, indigenous people will continue to suffer rather than benefit from the new emphasis on sustainable development.

Government appropriation of crisis communication frames in health pandemics: the case of the COVID-19 pandemic in Cameroon

Ndang Godiva Fuai

Ph.D. Student, Department of Journalism and Mass Communication, University of Buea, Cameroon

and

Kingsley Lyonga Ngange

Deputy Vice Chancellor for Research Cooperation and Relations with the Business World, Associate Professor and Head of Department, Journalism and Mass Communication, University of Buea, Cameroon

Abstract

During health crisis such as the on-going COVID-19 Pandemic, the public has the right to receive reliable and up-to-date information, to make informed decisions and choices for both individual and family welfare. A government such as that of Cameroon is therefore, expected to effectively communicate with the right frames to their different publics on issues concerning COVID-19. This study examines how government performed this crucial function in obliging its citizens to effectively respect preventive and curative measures in its fight against the global pandemic. This study questioned the types of frames used by the Cameroon government to communicate its crisis response messages on COVID-19 pandemic in Cameroon, it also sought to find out if there were any contrasting frames as well as the differences and similarities of the frames used by the Cameroon government to those of other countries. In other to attain these objectives, this study applied a qualitative approach; collecting secondary data (other journal articles) and primary data through thematic analysis of 81 press releases published by the government from January 2020 to September 2021. The findings reveal that the government used multiple categories of frames such as responsibility attributive frame, war frame, economic frame, amongst others to pass across its message. It also used contrasting frames such as gain versus loss frames, social versus natural frames and hope versus fear frames. Given that not all the press releases were in English, interpreting the aspect of frames was challenging. This study therefore recommends the adaptation of crisis response messages to suit the language and culture of the population in order for the right frames to be understood.

Keywords: Government, appropriation, crisis communication, frames, health pandemics, COVID-19, Cameroon

Introduction

Numerous pandemics have been recorded in human history, including smallpox, cholera, plague, dengue, AIDS, influenza, SARS, West Nile disease and tuberculosis. Influenza pandemics are unpredictable but recurring events that can have severe consequences on societies worldwide. Influenza pandemics have struck about three times every century since the 1500s, or roughly every 10-50 years. In the 20th century, there were 3 influenza pandemics which were named "Spanish flu" in 1918-1919, "Asian flu" in 1957-1958, and "Hong Kong flu" in 1968-1969. Recent years have seen at least six large-scale outbreaks with potential to become pandemics—Hantavirus Pulmonary Syndrome, SARS, H5N1 influenza, H1N1 influenza, Middle East respiratory syndrome and Ebola virus disease.[1]

Quite apart from other pandemics which have plagued the world mentioned above, the COVID-19 pandemic is one that has hit the world to its core since after the 9/11 attack in the USA. In less than three months, COVID-19 turned from a local outbreak in mainland China to a global pandemic. While the Chinese government reported the outbreak to the WHO in mid-January 2020, government reports suggest that the first cases of the disease can be traced back to the Chinese city of Wuhan as early as November 2019.[2]

The context of the crises in Cameroon is a complex one. It is one comprising of challenges ranging from natural disasters such as the landslides in Limbe (early 2000s) and Bafoussam (2019), terrorists' attacks of Boko Haram and the Anglophone crisis (with devastating on the nation since 2014 and 2016 respectively), as well as health pandemics including cholera and AIDS prevail. Cameroon has experienced recurrent cholera epidemics with high mortality rates. In September 2009 for example, epidemic cholera was detected in the Far North region of

---

[1] Gostin, L. O., Tomori, O., Wibulpolprasert, S., Jha, A. K., Frenk, J., Moon, S., Dzau, V. J. (2016). *Toward a Common Secure Future: Four Global Commissions in the Wake of Ebola. PLoS Med, 13*(5), e1002042.

[2] South China Morning Post (2020). *Coronavirus: China's first confirmed COVID-19 case traced back to November 17.*

Cameroon and the reported case-fatality rate was 12%.[3] As if this was not enough, the COVID-19 pandemic has recorded 21,203 infected cases with 423 deaths between the months of March to September 2020.[4]

Cameroon has been the most affected country in the central African region.[5] Since the first case was declared on 6th March 2020, many measures have been taken by Cameroonian government which have been amended thrice; (17th March 2020, 4th March 2020 and 30th April 2020) with the aim of reducing the transmission rate of this virus.[6] A few days after the start of COVID-19 in Cameroon, the Prime Minister Head of Government gave a press conference to announce the virus as well as government's measures to fight it. Following statistics of 12 August 2020 by the World Health Organisation, Cameroon had: 18 389 confirmed cases, 401 deaths with (2.2%), 16 459 (89, 5%) cured, 141/190 (74, 2%) health districts affected, 67 cases hospitalised with 04 on oxygen as well as 159 192 tests carried out in total (TDR+PCR).[7]

Pandemics it should be noted present large risk not only to human health, but also have the ability to cause significant political, economic and social disruptions on aspects such as tourism, travel and trade.[8] In Cameroon for instance, several authors[9] attest to the fact that the pandemic has left grave socio-economic effects on both the citizens and the country as a whole. This accounts for the validation of a budget to the tune of 21, 973, 799,873 FCFA by the Cameroon Government to manage the COVID-19 crisis in 2020.[10]

The devastating effects of public health emergencies such as pandemic outbreaks (involving risks and uncertainties as the incidents

---

[3]Salma Daoudi (2020). *The War on COVID-19: The 9/11 of Health Security? Policy paper*, Policy Center for the New South, www.policycenter.ma

[4]World Health Organization (2020). WHO discontinues hydroxyl-chloroquine and lopinavir/ritonavir treatment arms for COVID-19.

[5]Sopponntouba, R. (2020). *COVID-19 in Cameroon: What effect on economy? Independent scholar*, Munich Personal RePEc Archive

[6] Ibid

[7] Ibid

[8] World Health Organization (2020). WHO discontinues hydroxyl-chloroquine and lopinavir/ritonavir treatment arms for COVID-19.

[9] Sopponntouba (2020) Op.cit; Fuein V. & Kouam, H. (2020*) Socio-economic implications of COVID-19 in Cameroon and proposals to reduce the economic fallout*, Nkafu Policy Institute, http://www.nkafu.org/coronavirus

[10] Minsante Press Release, 2020

unfold) have created a niche for crisis communication in the course of these pandemics.[11] Crisis communication is a useful tool which prioritises stakeholders' views, perceptions of risk, enhancement of collaboration, and the development of appropriate responses to the crisis requiring extensive information sharing and collaboration among all stakeholder organizations.[12]

The Redevelopment site[13] in an article on Crisis Communication in the section titled: *"Crisis communication from A-Z"* demonstrates the importance of government crisis communication by presenting dos and don'ts such as: Always prepare for a variety of crisis situations; Communicate with empathy, compassion and care; Develop a communications plan for your team and train them; Enlist the help of others—internally and externally; Form an inclusive communications team; Help the media as much as you can; Incorporate Internet strategies into your plan; Open the door to two-way communications; Look before you leap and anticipate trouble; Respect the media and respond to media inquiries quickly and professionally (Rehearse your statements); Your reputation depends on how you handle the media and Zero tolerance of media distortion, inaccuracy and bad press.

While trying to communicate in crisis, the government also has the responsibility to apply suitable frames which will appeal to the minds its citizens and cause them to adopt preventive mechanisms towards the crisis. This paper therefore seeks to answer the following questions:

- What types of frames has the Cameroon Government used to communicate its COVID-19 crisis messages?
- In what ways have the frames used by the Cameroon Government to communicate its COVID-19 crisis messages contrasted?
- To what extend are the frames used by the Cameroon Government to communicate its COVID-19 crisis messages similar to that of other countries?

With pertinence on the COVID-19 pandemic crisis, the above research questions shall be analysed following two key theories as well as

[11] WHO, 2020, Op.cit

[12] Sopponntouba (2020), Opcit and Fuein & Kouam (2020) Op.cit

[13] Redevelopment (2010) *Crisis Communication from A-Z*, pp. 64-66, https://redevelopment,net >uploads>2010/10,

the qualitative research approach. It will also draw inferences from secondary data through the review of the works of other authors.

Theoretical Framework

This study makes use of two theories: the Framing theory and the Situational Crisis Communication Theory (SCCT). In the face of the COVID-19 pandemic, the Cameroon government's framing of the messages on the pandemic stands a greater chance to either convince the public towards preventive positive action or negative conflicting action. Because no previous study has investigated the role of government communication of a health crisis through gain and loss framed messages our work is going to be carrying qualitative content analysis to evaluate if the government frames its communication messages on COVID-19 from a gain or loss frame approach. This study therefore assumes that the government has framed its messages on the COVID-19 pandemic by using the gain frame, loss frame as well as the other 9 categories of frames (economic consequences, human interest, conflict, morality, attribution of responsibility, politicization, ethnicisation, hope and fear) mentioned by Semetko and Valkenburg; Ogbodo in Chabanga[14] in the messages communicated by the government. The Situational Crisis Communication Theory (SCCT) by Coombs outlines three major aspects of a crisis: the crisis situation, crisis response strategies, and a system for matching the crisis situation with the crisis response strategies. The goal of this theory in this study is to show how the government uses frames as a crisis response strategy to match the crisis situation.

Methodology

This study made use of the qualitative approach for data collection and data analysis. For data collection, the study applied the purposive sampling technique to analyse the content of all government press releases (81) published on the Ministry of Public Health official website from January 2020 to September 2020. This website was chosen because it was the main site used by the government within the period of the study. It also sampled all SMS sent by the Government within the same period as well as two official speeches of the Head of State in 2020 which addressed key issues on the COVID-19 pandemic.

---

[14]Chabanga, E., (2021). *Mass Communication Theories*, Handout, University of Buea, Cameroon

The thematic analysis technique was used to group content according to the different categories of frames identified from the works of several authors (loss, gain, social, natural' economic consequences, human interest, conflict, morality, attribution of responsibility, politicization, ethnicisation, hope and fear).[15] The finding gotten from these categories of frames were used to analyse the first two research questions while the works of other authors were reviewed to obtain data to analyse the third research question.[16] Reliability and validity of this study are ensured through the presentation of evidence to prove that these samples manifested the different types of frames. This article is structured following the three research questions, conclusion and recommendations.

Categories of frames used in government messaging during the COVID-19 pandemic in 2020

To respond to the different categories of frames used by the Cameroon government, the findings of the study revealed the following categories of frames:

Human Interest frame:

The human interest frame is that frame which shows an aspect of concern and empathy in a situation. Within the context of this study, it questions the government's ability to present its COVID-19 message with a human face and emotion for the population and stakeholders. The government paid attention to this frame in several different dimensions. First, it showed great concern and sympathy to victims:

> I would now avail myself of this opportunity to extend my sympathy to the families that have lost loved ones to this terrible disease. I extend my heartfelt encouragement to patients admitted to our hospitals and wish them a speedy recovery. I also call on those who have tested positive to strictly adhere to the rules of confinement.[17]

Beside the heavy heart towards the pains of victims, the government also paid great attention to the medical core. It consistently appreciated the bravery of medical practitioners and personnels:

---

[15]Ibid.

[16]Brandt & Wörlein (2020). *Government crisis communications during the pandemic*, Sciences Po Centre for the Sociology of Organisations.

[17] President Paul Biya's Speech, May 19, 2020

I take this opportunity to pay homage to the valiant health workers whose efforts and professionalism made it possible to give birth to the first baby girl weighing 2.015 grams in this case, born to a COVID-19 positive teenager, about 48 hours ago, at the Yaoundé Central Hospital.
This is an opportunity for me to recognize the bravery, sacrifice and unwavering determination of these health care workers who are on the front line of this fight against COVID-19. It is therefore important for us to remember that tomorrow is World Health Day, under theme "Support Nurses and Midwives", and we must support them without restraint.[18]
I also wish to hail the courage of Cameroonian health professionals and those assisting them. With the resources available to us, they are doing the utmost to treat those infected with the disease. Indeed, they are not giving up in the face of the gravity of COVID-19 infection. The Nation, through me, congratulates and urges them to keep it up.[19]

Consequence frame:

Consequences can be wide ranging that is through the pursuing of a policy which is unwise in terms of unity in action or in terms of the status of a nation globally. An example of such frame through the Cameroon government's crisis response messages can be seen below:

> Unfortunately, the onset of the COVID-19 pandemic brought about a deterioration of the macroeconomic and fiscal balances. The trends in our foreign exchange reserves have declined. Our regional integration has had insufficient knock-on effects on intra-community trade. The weak structural diversification of our economies and the extraversion of our development models have limited our capacity to react. CEMAC
> Despite our efforts, COVID-19 plunged many families into mourning and seriously hampered the functioning of our economy and society. NEW YEAR
> Today, we are facing new challenges resulting from the collapse of stock markets, falling commodity prices and an unexpected sharp decline in trade. The coronavirus pandemic will therefore have a negative impact on the global economy as well as our economy.[20]

Morality frame:

This frame is pertinent in revealing the moral values of key actors in relation to the crisis at hand. It addresses the indiscretions of political actors; or alternative, policies considered to be morally questionable. In the context of the COVID-19 pandemic in 2020, the President in one of

[18] Press Declaration of the Minister of Public Health, Yaoundé 06 April 2020, pp. 3 and 4
[19] President Paul Biya's Speech, May 19, 2020
[20] President Paul Biya's Speech, 19 May 2020

its official speeches on 19 May 2020, appealed to the moral conscience of political actors:

> Most of you have understood that it is necessary to put aside political squabbles and adopt a common front in the face of the insidious danger posed by COVID-19. Some political leaders who do not belong to the ruling majority shared this view. I thank them for that.[21]

Responsibility frame:

This frame has to do with the attribution of responsibility, either for a cause or a solution. Examples found in the Cameroon government's messages include:

> In the current situation, everyone is facing their responsibilities. In order to overcome this crisis, we must make significant sacrifices. Each individual positive action can allow us win the fight against COVID-19. Above all, we must think of public interest. It is not only a matter of protecting ourselves individually, but also of protecting the greatest number.
>
> So, let us all remain mobilized, committed to the fight against COVID-19 and continue to comply with barrier measures put in place by the Government, namely:
>
> - Washing hands with clean running water and soap or using an alcohol-based solution;
> - covering your nose and mouth with a disposable tissue when coughing, sneezing or using a bent elbow;
> - Above all, stay at home as much as possible. Go out only when necessary. And wear a face mask when going out.
>
> For any information related to COVID-19, the toll-free number **1510** is available.
>
> Let us protect ourselves! Let us protect others![22]
>
> I know I can once again count on your patriotic spirit, your sense of responsibility and your courage to enable us to collectively overcome this scourge that is affecting the entire planet. In this connection, we should avoid stigmatizing those suffering from the disease. Everyone must feel concerned and contribute their quota to the fight against the spread of the virus. We should bear in mind that negligence by a single individual can seriously harm the entire community. We should therefore not be complacent.[23]
>
> I strongly urge all political, religious and opinion leaders, all officials of associations, all traditional rulers and all dignitaries to fully participate in the fight against COVID-19. Of course, this should be done within the framework defined by the Government and in compliance with the laws and regulations of the Republic.[24]

---

[21] Ibid

[22] President Paul Biya's Speech, 19 May 2020

[23]Daily Press Briefing by the Minister of Public Health COVID-19 Pandemic Management Public Health Emergency Operations Center, Yaoundé 29 June 2020, p. 2)

[24] President Paul Biya's 19 May 2020 speech

I therefore call on Cameroonians to have trust in public authorities. The Government is fully aware of the gravity of the situation and is prepared to take all necessary measures. I can already state that:
- As soon as a treatment is found, steps will be taken to put it at the disposal of our fellow citizens; before that,
- The wearing of face masks in public places will be mandatory until further notice.
To that end, the local industry should continue to engage in the manufacture of face masks and alcohol-based solutions in strict compliance with Government and WHO prescribed standards.[25]

Military Frame

This frame painted the virus as an enemy which needs to be fought and conquered. In the messages the medical core was also constantly referred to as soldiers with the white coat or jacket:

> You have certainly understood that we need to make a lot of efforts to fight COVID-19 that may pose a threat to the stability of our states…. I therefore appeal for a kind of "united front" of all the vital forces of the Nation against the coronavirus pandemic. In that connection, I commend, once again, the attitude of virtually all political leaders and religious authorities who have accepted to join in this national struggle. I also encourage all efforts geared towards developing an endogenous cure for COVID-19. Let us channel all our energies towards fighting this common enemy.[26]
> Despite these efforts, the number of infected persons keeps increasing daily, thus indicating that the fight against this pandemic is complex and difficult. I therefore call on each and every one of you to get involved. Each of us must comply with the measures that have been taken. This is one of the conditions for us to achieve the desired victory against the virus.[27]
> The strict compliance to barrier measures is our main prevention weapon.[28]

The demonstration of contrasting frames used by the Cameroon Government

Results from the data analysed with regards to the frames used by the government reveals the following contrasting frames:

Gain versus Loss frame

Health-promoting messages can be framed in terms of the gains associated with healthy behaviours that serve to prevent an illness such

[25] President Paul Biya's 19 May 2020 speech
[26]President Paul Biya's 19 May 2020 speech
[27] Ibid
[28] Daily Press Briefing by the Minister of Public Health COVID-19 Pandemic Management Public Health Emergency Operations Center, Yaoundé 23 May 2020, p. 3

as COVID-19, while loss frames on their part are associated with unhealthy behaviours and actions which serve to detect an illness such as skin self-examination and testing. Analysis of the press releases published by the government, shows that the government used both gain and loss frame in the management of its crisis communication messages on COVID-19. Examples of these frames used by Government include the following:

Gain frame (presentation of barrier measures and vaccination campaign)

> The Minister of Public Health invites the populations to be more vigilant and respect basic hygiene rules;
> -Wash your hands regularly with clean water and soap or use a hydro alcoholic solution
> -Cover your nose and mouth with a tissue when coughing or sneeze in the crease of your elbow
> -Avoid close contact with anyone with flu-like symptoms or with wild and farm animals
> -Properly cook beef and eggs before consuming them.
> In addition, any person who has travelled out of Cameroon or who has been in contact with a sick traveller, and who presents the aforementioned symptoms in the last 14 days preceding the onset of the disease, should immediately call 1510, for proper care. Health personnel should also strengthen preventive measures and report any suspected cases according to the directives in force. For further information, the toll-free number 1510 is open to everyone and operates from 8 a.m. to 4 p.m.[29]

In all 81 press releases studied, the government mentioned the need for barrier measures as a preventive mechanism to fight COVID-19 in Cameroon. The Head of State, President Paul Biya in his 31 December 2020 address to the nation, also used the opportunity to decry the non-respect of the measures and he therefore encouraged the population towards the adoption and persistent respect of the barrier measures:

> In any case, we should not rest on our laurels. I have personally observed that most of our fellow citizens no longer comply with the protective measures prescribed by the Government.
> At a time when, everywhere else, there is a second wave of the epidemic, coupled with the appearance of a new and more contagious strain of the virus, I urge you once again to put on your face masks, to wash your hands regularly and to consult a physician or any other health personnel if you notice any symptoms. This is the only way to save lives and to curb the spread of the virus.[30]

---

[29] Press Release, Ministry of Public Health, January 28, 2020
[30] President Paul Biya's 31 December 2020 speech, para.7

Beyond the government presentation of barrier measures, it has also adopted a community communication strategy to encourage citizens to get vaccinated as a mechanism to control the manifestation of the virus:

> However, we must remain vigilant and mobilized, for this rapidly changing health crisis is still around. Together, we must resolutely continue the crucial phase of the fight against this virus through vaccination. Africa needs broad and equitable access to the vaccine. Indeed, how can we achieve herd immunity with less than 5% of our citizens currently vaccinated?[31]

The Ministry of Public Health has also been sending several messages to citizens on the vaccination campaign:

> Campaign to intensify Vaccination against COVID-19, from 07 to 11 July 2021 in all 10 regions of the country. For a COVID-19 free Cameroon, let's get vaccinated[32]
> The Ministry of Public Health is organizing a national vaccination campaign against COVID-19, from 17 to 21 November 2021 for everyone aged 18years and above.[33]
> Are you aged 18+? Kindly go to the nearest vaccination centre in your locality to get vaccinated![34]

Though each one of these messages were communicated and repeated on a later date for emphasis and for a more productive result of the frame, there were still some lapses of the gain frame.

Loss frame (Track, Test and Treat)

Within these lapses of the prevention of the COVID-19 pandemic, the government also used the loss frame messages geared towards mass testing to identity infected cases of the virus. Examples of such messages include:

> As regards the situation in our country, the result to date indicates sixty (60) new cases bringing up the total number to three hundred and six (306) COVID-19 confirmed cases. It should be noted that the detection of these cases is increasing due to the reliability of our tracing system and the active search for cases within our communities.... With regard to patient management and case follow-up, the resettlement of COVID-19 cases at the Olembe site is effective. Concerning the awareness and testing campaign announced during our previous

[31] President Paul Biya's 18 August 2021 speech, para.6
[32] SMS by MINSANTE, 5 and 9 July 2021
[33] SMS by MINSANTE, 7 November 2021
[34] SMS by MINSANTE, 14 and 18 November 2021

press briefings, it will be carried out in the next few days in the Littoral region, in collaboration with all stakeholders.[35]

In the same light, the Minister of Public Health announced several active search campaigns for COVID-19 cases in Douala as well as the outcomes of these searches:

I would therefore like to point out that the active search for cases, particularly through the massive testing launched in Douala, has indeed begun and is producing satisfactory results in terms of identifying cases and isolating them in order to protect everyone. As far as Yaoundé is concerned, our action has first of all made it possible to quickly identify positive cases among people quarantined in hotels when they returned home from foreign countries, the vast majority of whom are in a real epidemic situation.
Furthermore, it is important to capitalize on the encouraging results already achieved so far by our system of tracing and actively searching for cases in our communities and to consider strengthening the teams and their means of action. This will help, in particular, to ensure an early and efficient management for all infected persons. The latter will require better medical regulation of dedicated health facilities.[36]

Still using the loss frame, the Minister presented Government 3 T strategy against Corona virus in Cameroon to media practitioners in a press briefing:

Ladies and Gentlemen
As you already know, on the high instructions of the Prime Minister and Head of Government, our strategy is articulated around the "3Ts"; Track, Test and Treat. Permit me this evening to reemphasis on the first T- "Track" reminding you that it refers to the active search of cases; identifying them and their contacts as well. Permit me this evening to insist on the key elements of this T: "follow-up of contacts". This follow-up comprises of three fundamental elements:

- Listing of the contacts of those close to the case on daily basis
- Identification of this contacts physically
- Follow-up of this contacts within a period of two weeks within which the contacts are at high risks are placed on quarantine at home, geolocalised and follow-up by our equip through telephone at home in order to detect the appearance of symptoms compatible to COVID-

[35] Daily Press Briefing by the Minister of Public Health COVID-19 Pandemic Management Public Health Emergency Operations Center, Yaoundé 02 April 2020.
[36]COVID-19 Pandemic Control, Press Declaration of the Minister of Public Health, Yaoundé, 06 April 2020

19. Those who manifest one sign of COVID-19 during this period of follow-up are taken care of by our team for testing and treatment.[37]

After looking at the gain and loss frames, frame analysis further looked at two other comparative set of frames that is natural versus social frames and hope versus fear frames:

Natural versus Social frame

These frames tie with the interpretation given to primary frameworks prescribed by Goffman[38] on how people interpret what is going on around the world. The natural frame used by the Cameroon government presents Coronavirus as a natural virus caused by natural symptoms and transmitted through natural channels like many other diseases. It identifies the events around this pandemic as physical occurrences taking natural processes and not attributing any social forces to the causation of the events.

> Since December 31st, 2019, an epidemic caused by a new type of Coronavirus is prevailing in China with worldwide spread in countries such as Thailand, Japan, South Korea, the United States and France). The disease is characterized by symptoms of a respiratory tract condition such as cough, sore throat, runny nose and / breathing difficulties, sometimes accompanied by fever, and can lead to death. The virus is mainly transmitted from animal to humans, but humans – to-human transmission is also possible.[39]

On the other hand, there have been controversies about the occurrences of the virus. It has also been viewed from the perspective of human manipulations. The President used the social frame on two instances to express man's role in the inciting and combatting of the virus.

> Should man take the blame because of his wanton exploitation of the planet's natural resources and his constant engagement in conflicts leading to massacres and diseases, as well as experiments to develop new weapons? I believe the question needs to be asked. Whatever the answer, our era should take credit for clearly posing the problem of the relationship between man and his natural environment.[40]

---

[37]Daily Press Briefing by the Minister of Public Health COVID-19 Pandemic Management Public Health Emergency Operations Center, Yaoundé 23 June 2020 - Translated from French).

[38]Goffman, 1974 in Chabanga, E., (2021), Op. cit.

[39] Press release by the Secretary General of Ministry of Health; Shiro Sinata in Cameroon January 28, 2020, para.1 and 2

[40] President Paul Biya's Speech, 31 December 2020

> I take this opportunity to congratulate our fellow citizens who have already made contributions. I call on those who can, to do same. National solidarity so requires. In our current struggle, the Government will go to great lengths to combat any manipulation or exploitation of this tragedy for political, economic or social ends.[41]

Hope versus Fear frames

The COVID-19 virus has left many unknowns in the minds of medical practitioners. Worst ill is the number of deaths this pandemic has left across many countries and continents of the world. This government through its communication strategy has put in a lot of effort to show case hope than fear frame. This in no way cancels the fact that it has been open with statistics of infected and death cases, but it has also given special attention to hopeful information such as recoveries and acquisition of vaccines to curb the impact rate of the pandemic.

---

[41] President Paul Biya's Speech, 19 May 2020

Table 1: Fear versus Hope frame

Fear Frame	Hope frame
On the 15 February 2020, the technical services of the Ministry of Public Health investigated two cases of the novel coronavirus disease currently named COVID-19 by the World Health Organisation.[42] The Minister of Public Health announces the confirmation of a COVID-19 case in Cameroonian territory. It is a French citizen aged 58 who arrived Cameroon on the 24 February, 2020.[44]	Both cases were safely transported to the isolation rooms of the Yaoundé Central Hospital, specimens were collected and analysed at the Centre Pasteur of Cameroon. Fortunately, the results were negative for COVID-19. The clinical status of the suspect patients is satisfactory…[43] The Minister of Public Health thus wishes to reassure Cameroonians that a tracking system of all travellers, namely from China, has been set up...[45]
The Minister of Public Health hereby announces the confirmation of a second case of COVID-19 in Cameroon involving a (30-year-old) Cameroonian who has been in close contact with the first confirmed case.[46]	The Minister of Public Health hereby informs the public that after 14 days of treatment, the first two COVID-19 cases in Cameroon were retested and declared negative. The patients left their isolation facility this Thursday 19 March, 2020 to return home where they will remain under observation for a few days.[47]
The epidemiological situation to date reports 24 deaths, one confirmed case in Ngaoundere and two hundred and sixty 260 recoveries. However, the confirmation of COVID-19 positive case in the Adamawa Region calls on everybody to be more vigilant.[48]	It is important to note that based on the different indicators of epidemiological follow-up we note that more and more, Cameroon has a satisfactory mastery of the pandemic. It involves the recovery rate of 91%, death rate of 2, 1%, severity rate of less than 0,5% as well as bed occupation rate fluctuating between 4% to 6%.[49] I take this opportunity to pay homage to the valiant health workers whose efforts and professionalism made it possible to give birth to the first baby girl weighing **2.015 grams** in this case, born to a COVID-19 positive teenager, about 48 hours ago, at the Yaoundé Central Hospital.[50]

Source: Field data, 2021

[42] MINSANTE Press Release, 19 February 2020
[43] Ibid
[44] MINSANTE Press Release, 06, March 2020
[45] MINSANTE Press Release, 19 February 2020
[46] MINSANTE Press Release, 06, March 2020
[47] MINSANTE Press Release, 06, March 2020
[48] Daily Press Briefing by the Minister of Public Health COVID-19 Pandemic Management Public Health Emergency Operations Center, Yaoundé April 18, 2020
[49] Press Release, 24th August 2020
[50] Press Declaration of the Minister of Public Health, Yaoundé 06 April 2020, pp. 3 and 4

The table above presents examples of fear versus hope frames. While the hope frame gave Cameroonians a reason to believe there will be a solution for the pandemic, the fear frame constantly reminded them of the devastating characteristics of the virus.

A comparative analysis of the frames used by the Cameroon government with that of other countries

Developing appropriate preparedness and response to a public health emergency requires extensive information sharing and collaboration among a variety of loosely coupled stakeholder organizations.[51] "Communicate … has always been an important cornerstone in crisis management planning. Its importance has increased tenfold in a crisis where physical distancing is integral to the crisis coming to an end."[52] Effective data and information collection and quick communication of information, which is an essential resource that translates into supplies, logistics and cooperation, are keys to success.[53] Interventions to communicate health risks and promote disease control measures depend upon increasing coordination among governments and different professional sectors as well as community leaders. It also relies on development and dissemination of formal guidance and resources by multi-lateral international organisations and other relevant stakeholders.[54] Given that non-aligned frames during crises can have demobilising effects on governments and recipients, comparing this aspect in the government crisis communication of different countries is very pertinent.

To start with, Brandt and Wörlein[55] carried out a comparative study on the government crisis communication strategies of France, Germany

---

[51]Rewar, S., Mirdha, D., & Rewar, P. (2015). Treatment and Prevention of Pandemic H1N1 Influenza. *Annals of Global Health*, 81(5), 645-653. doi: http://dx.doi.org/10.1016/j.aogh.2015.08.014

[52] Todd Burke, 2020's article on "Crisis Management during the COVID-19 Pandemic", Gowling WLG, Ottawa.

[52] Zhong N, Zheng B, Li Y, Poon L, Xie Z, Chan K., et al (2003). Epidemiology and cause of severe acute respiratory syndrome (SARS) in Guangdong People's Republic of China, in February. *The Lancet.* 2003; pp.362:1353-8.

[53] Ibid

[54] Schiavo, R., May Leung, M., & Brown, M. (2014). Communicating risk and promoting disease mitigation measures in epidemics and emerging disease settings. Pathogens and global health, 108 (2), 76-94.

[55] Brandt and Wörlein, 2020, Op.cit

and the United Kingdom. *Following their study, they* argued that analysing crisis communication by governments during the COVID-19 crisis has been particularly feasible and relevant. Using a qualitative approach, they analysed the different frames used by the presidents or their representatives in the countries understudy. Given that all three governments fulfilled the above criteria, they were therefore particularly relevant for the analysis of crisis communication as they all communicated with the general public through three spokespersons: the Head of State, the Prime Minister and ministers.

In the case of France, Brandt and Wörlein[56] revealed that the President Emmanuel Macron in his first address consistently developed a "war" framework, designating the virus as an "enemy." This type of framing according to Brandt and Wörlein[57] suggests that the attacking force originated outside society. Reasons for which the next messages of communication of the President dwelled on "general mobilisation" on March 12, definition of the crisis management as a war effort on March 16, and further refined this line of argument in his March 20 address, which is entirely structured around war metaphors: 'deceased nurses "falling" during the crisis, a response organised around "lines [of defence]", "the children of the nation" "fighting" against the virus."[58] The second frame detected from President Macron's speeches by Brandt and Wörlein[59] was directed towards a militarised frame.

In Germany, Brandt and Wörlein[60] noted that Angela Merkel, the German Chancellor initially delegated the crisis communication to her minister of health but as the severity of the crisis became clearer; she took up the crisis communication batten of command while her ministers presented other practical details. As regards her tone and frame, Brandt and Wörlein[61] state that Merkel has been using a calm and caring- but also analytical- tone in her responses to the crisis with more of a humane frame.

> She regularly discusses technical issues, such as the importance of correct behaviour amid an absence of medical treatments and vaccines, the introduction

---

[56]Brandt and Wörlein, 2020, Op.cit

[57] Ibid

[58] Brandt and Wörlein, 2020, para. 6

[59]Ibid

[60]Ibid

[61] Ibid

of short-term allowances for affected workers, and, more recently, the supply of protective gear from Asia and new production in Germany.[62]

On his part Brandt and Wörlein[63] analysed the UK Prime Minister Boris Johnson to have adopted a proactive and pragmatic framing of the crisis until his own hospitalisation. "He took the time to explain the importance of hand-washing".[64]

The frames used by the leaders of France, Germany and the UK are similar to that of Cameroon to some extent. For instance, the President of France used the war frame describing the virus as enemy just like Cameroon's President in his state address where he referred to medical doctors as "brave soldiers in white jacket… the strict compliance to barrier measures is our main prevention weapon… let us channel all our energies towards fighting this common enemy."[65] The Cameroon government was also humane in its frame approach like the German Chancellor: President Paul Biya in his humane frame, wrote:

> I would now avail myself of this opportunity to extend my sympathy to the families that have lost loved ones to this terrible disease. I extend my heartfelt encouragement to patients admitted to our hospitals and wish them a speedy recovery. I also call on those who have tested positive to strictly adhere to the rules of confinement.[66]

Lastly, the Cameroon government's frame was also similar to that of the UK with the application of the gain frame; a style used by the British Prime Minister to emphasise on the barrier measures. This aspect was evident in all the 81 press releases issued by the government on the subject.

Conclusions and Recommendations

The purpose of this study has been to explore the Cameroon Government's use of frames in its crisis communication of COVID-19 pandemic in Cameroon. It also intended to find out if there were some categories of frames which manifested contrast at national. Given that COVID-19 is a global virus, the study also had as objective to find out if

---

[62] Ibid para.8
[63] Ibid para.8
[64] Ibid para.9
[65]Daily Press Briefing by the Minister of Public Health COVID-19 Pandemic Management Public Health Emergency Operations Center, Yaoundé 23 May 2020, p. 3
[66] President Paul Biya's Speech, May 19, 2020.

the findings of this study are in anyway similar to those of other countries. The results of the study revealed that the government framed its messages on the COVID-19 pandemic with diverse frames as the 81 press releases, SMS and the 2 Presidential speeches analysed, and all had traces of different categories of frames used. In terms of conflicting frames, the findings were also able to identify and contrast elements messages of loss versus gain frames, natural versus social frame and hope versus fear frame.

In line with the third objective which was to find out the similarities of the frames used by the Cameroon government in line with that of other countries, results reveal that the government was similar to French government in using the war/military frame by constantly referring to the virus as an *"enemy"*. The results also conformed to that of Germany as the Chancellor took a humane position likewise the President of Cameroon in his speeches as well as other Cameroonian spokespersons. Lastly like the UK, Cameroon applied the gain frame style of the British Prime Minister of emphasising on the barrier measures; which was evident in all the 81 government press releases on the subject. Frome the above findings, one can therefore conclude that the research questions were all responded to and objectives met.

Even though this study was limited in that it did not measure which frame was more used than the other, the study recommends that Governments in developing frames should be more proactive and work more on gain frames which are appropriate for crisis prevention than the loss frames which serve for crisis control. This will help them win public trust for future purposes. Secondly the study had some lapses in terms of data collection because some press releases were available only in French language. This therefore leads to a preceding recommendation which calls for the adaptation of government crisis communication messages to the language, sociology and culture of the public in order to guarantee the interpretation of the right frames.

UB Law and Political Studies Quarterly (ULPSQ)

EDITOR'S NOTE

ULPSQ is a quarterly peer-reviewed Journal involving discussions on contemporary issues cutting across the fields of law, international relations, peace and conflict trends, human rights and humanitarian law, comparative politics etc. It is a publication of the Faculty of Laws and Political Science of the University of Buea, Cameroon.

Contributions in the form of articles, commentaries and book reviews in the above-mentioned and related fields are welcome. Contributions should be in 12 Times New Romans font and 1 ½ line spacing. Articles should not exceed 8000 words for articles (footnotes inclusive), 3000 words for commentaries and 1500 words for book reviews. Continuous footnotes should be used, and in-text references are not allowed.

All contributions submitted within stated deadlines for any issue, shall be immediately sent out for peer review and, if accepted, forwarded to the contributor for immediate corrections and adjustments, if at all.

Structures éditoriales du groupe L'Harmattan

L'Harmattan Italie
Via degli Artisti, 15
10124 Torino
harmattan.italia@gmail.com

L'Harmattan Hongrie
Kossuth l. u. 14-16.
1053 Budapest
harmattan@harmattan.hu

L'Harmattan Sénégal
10 VDN en face Mermoz
BP 45034 Dakar-Fann
senharmattan@gmail.com

L'Harmattan Cameroun
TSINGA/FECAFOOT
BP 11486 Yaoundé
inkoukam@gmail.com

L'Harmattan Burkina Faso
Achille Somé – tengnule@hotmail.fr

L'Harmattan Guinée
Almamya, rue KA 028 OKB Agency
BP 3470 Conakry
harmattanguinee@yahoo.fr

L'Harmattan RDC
185, avenue Nyangwe
Commune de Lingwala – Kinshasa
matangilamusadila@yahoo.fr

L'Harmattan Congo
219, avenue Nelson Mandela
BP 2874 Brazzaville
harmattan.congo@yahoo.fr

L'Harmattan Mali
ACI 2000 - Immeuble Mgr Jean Marie Cisse
Bureau 10
BP 145 Bamako-Mali
mali@harmattan.fr

L'Harmattan Togo
Djidjole – Lomé
Maison Amela
face EPP BATOME
ddamela@aol.com

L'Harmattan Côte d'Ivoire
Résidence Karl – Cité des Arts
Abidjan-Cocody
03 BP 1588 Abidjan
espace_harmattan.ci@hotmail.fr

Nos librairies en France

Librairie internationale
16, rue des Écoles
75005 Paris
librairie.internationale@harmattan.fr
01 40 46 79 11
www.librairieharmattan.com

Librairie des savoirs
21, rue des Écoles
75005 Paris
librairie.sh@harmattan.fr
01 46 34 13 71
www.librairieharmattansh.com

Librairie Le Lucernaire
53, rue Notre-Dame-des-Champs
75006 Paris
librairie@lucernaire.fr
01 42 22 67 13

www.ingramcontent.com/pod-product-compliance
Lightning Source LLC
LaVergne TN
LVHW010921061026
849535LV00007B/2164
* 9 7 8 2 1 4 0 3 1 4 0 6 3 *